SEMEIA 48

READER PERSPECTIVES ON THE NEW TESTAMENT

Guest Editor:
Edgar V. McKnight

©1989
by the Society of Biblical Literature

SEMEIA 48

Copyright © 1989 by the Society of Biblical Literature

All rights reserved. No part of this work may be reproduced or transmitted in any form or by any means, electronic or mechanical, including photocopying and recording, or by means of any information storage or retrieval system, except as may be expressly permitted by the 1976 Copyright Act or in writing from the publisher. Requests for permission should be addressed in writing to the Rights and Permissions Office, Society of Biblical Literature, 825 Houston Mill Road, Atlanta, GA 30329, USA.

ISSN 0095-571X
ISBN 978-1-58983-594-8

Printed in the United States of America
on acid-free paper

CONTENTS

Contributors to this Issue v

Preface
   Edgar V. McKnight vii

INTRODUCTION

Coming to Grips with the Reader in Biblical Literature
   Bernard C. Lategan 3

I. THEORY

The Reader in the Text: Narrative Material
   Willem S. Vorster 21

Is There an Encoded Reader Fallacy?
   Wilhelm Wuellner 41

The Roles of the Readers or the Myth of The Reader
   Wolfgang Schenk 55

II. ANALYSIS

Mark

The Reader of Mark as Operator of a System of Connotations
   B.M.F. van Iersel 83

The Rhetoric of Direction and Indirection in the Gospel of Mark
   Robert M. Fowler 115

Philippians

Response to W. Schenk, *Die Philipperbriefe des Paulus*
   H. J. Bernard Combrink 135

The Implicit and Explicit Readers and the Genre of Philippians 3:2-4:3, 8-9: Response to the Commentary of Wolfgang Schenk
   Detlev Dormeyer 147

Some Things Old, Some Things New: A Response to Wolfgang Schenk, *Die Philipperbriefe des Paulus*
   James W. Voelz 161

Galatians

Levels of Reader Instructions in the Text of Galatians
   Bernard C. Lategan 171

III. Evaluation

Reading In/to Mark
   Temma F. Berg 187

CONTRIBUTORS TO THIS ISSUE

Temma F. Berg
　Department of English
　Gettysburg College
　Gettysburg, Pennsylvania

H.J. Bernard Combrink
　University of Stellenbosch
　Stellenbosch, South Africa

Detlev Dormeyer
　University of Münster
　Münster, West Germany

Robert M. Fowler
　Baldwin-Wallace College
　Berea, Ohio

Edgar V. McKnight
　Furman University
　Greenville, S.C.

Bernard C. Lategan
　University of Stellenbosch
　Stellenbosch, South Africa

Wolfgang Schenk
　Eppstein, West Germany

B.M.F. van Iersel
　Catholic University of Nijmegen
　The Netherlands

James W. Voelz
  Concordia Theological Seminary
  St. Louis, Missouri

Willem S. Vorster
  University of South Africa
  Pretoria, South Africa

Wilhelm Wuellner
  Pacific School of Religion
  Berkeley, California

PREFACE

The essays in this volume grow out of activities of participants in a series of seminars of the Society for New Testament Studies. In a five-year seminar on "Linguistics and Exegesis," which met first at Duke University in August of 1974, texts were analyzed with the help of textual theories developed in French structuralism. That early seminar was transformed in 1979 into a seminar on "Symbols, Metaphors, and Models in the New Testament." Literary studies in the structural-semiotic tradition had progressed from structural linguistics through text linguistics into general semantics and pragmatics; and our new seminar attempted to relate these studies to analysis of New Testament texts.

In 1985, the seminar choose the theme "The Role of the Reader in the Interpretation of the New Testament." The reader oriented emphasis, as the earlier transformation of the seminar, did not mean that the goal of empirical and logically consistent analysis and interpretation was abandoned. The progressive enlargement and extension of earlier models, in fact, is important for understanding the essays. Also important is the multi-national membership of the seminar and the fact that the different waves or stages of influence from Europe and America (formalism, new criticism, structuralism, poststructuralism, and so on) have swept upon the authors in different ways. Also, the different authors have their own "sets" from which they have "naturalized" those influences.

The volume is made more challenging and interesting by the fact that the essays in the volume represent second and third stages of a continuing dialogue among the diverse seminar participants. The first stage was the essays as they were originally mailed to members of the seminar months before the meeting. Most frequently, responses were prepared and distributed prior to the actual meeting. In the sessions of the seminar, then, the forms of the essays which were given orally had been revised in light of the reactions of respondants. The present forms of the essays represent yet a new revision and benefit from the several stages of dialogue.

As a result of the various stages, genuine differences have not been toned down, they have become sharper. In part, at least, misunderstandings have been perceived and corrected. Perceptive readers will recognize not only that later essays must be read in light of earlier essays, but that early essays must be understood in light of later essays. Statements in the essays are not only developments of theses but are defenses against counter arguments and counter theses to be found in other essays.

In order to make it easier for readers, there is a logical ordering of the essays in the volume. Bernard Lategan, the chairman of the current seminar, introduces the entire series with an essay on "Coming to Grips with the Reader in Biblical Literature." In Part One, three theoretical papers are offered. They deal with the role of the reader in narrative and argumentative material and with the multiple roles of the reader in general terms. The essays in Part Two analyze or evaluate the analysis of three New Testament texts: Mark, Philippians, and Galatians. The final section is an evaluation of the essays from the perspective of a literary critic, Professor Temma F. Berg of Gettysburg College.

The essays on Philippians require a special note. They were originally given in a session of the seminar devoted to a discussion of Wolfgang Schenk's *Die Philipperbriefe des Paulus* (Kohlhammer, 1984). Schenk's commentary was based on textlinguistic principles set forward in a 1973 essay in *ThLZ* ("Die Aufgaben der Exegese und die Mittel der Linguistik") and in a 1980 essay in *NTS* ("Textlinguistik als Kommentierungsprinzip [Hebr 4:14–16]"). The seminar (and the essays in this volume) concentrated upon one of the three letters discerned by Schenk in Philippians, the Letter of Admonition ("Warnbrief") of Philippians 3:2–4:3,8–9. Since the theoretical essay by Schenk is an example of the simultaneous setting forth of theses and countering of objections, that essay must be read as the background for the critical essays on his commentary which follow and as a response to those essays. Authors of the individual essays provide sufficient detail of the work of Schenk for understanding their discussions.

Edgar V. McKnight

Introduction

INTRODUCTION
COMING TO GRIPS WITH THE READER

Bernard C. Lategan
University of Stellenbosch

ABSTRACT

In order to provide a backdrop for the essays collected in this volume, some basic aspects of reader-oriented research are discussed. Although exegetes have always been sensitive to the role of the audience or reader in the interpretation of biblical texts, it is only with the upsurge of reader studies in general literary theory that this aspect has become the focus of special attention. The concept of the reader in the text is explained with reference to the distinction between theoretical and empirical research, the different levels of reading, and the dynamic nature of the reading process.

1. Introduction

1.1 In a certain sense, it was inevitable that the reader should become a focal point in the interpretation of biblical texts. These texts themselves are very "reader-" or rather "audience-conscious." Often, for example in the prophetic books or in the letters, the intended recipients are identified by name. In other cases, like the historical books or some of the Gospels, they are only assumed. Frequent use of the technique of retelling and recontextualization causes shifts in the audience: Matthew's retelling of the story of Jesus' retelling of the story of David is accompanied by a shift from the priests to the Pharisees to the Matthean community as audience (Matt. 12:3–4). But on a much more basic level, the kerygmatic intention of these texts ("Hear, oh Israel," "Listen, then, if you have ears!"), makes it essential to include the audience in the theoretical reflection on and in the practical application of exegetical methods.

1.2   It is therefore not surprising that long before the rise of reception theory in literary studies, the reader did feature in various hermeneutical frameworks developed for the interpretation of biblical texts. For example, the creative role of the early communities in the shaping of the Jesus tradition was recognized from the outset by the History of Religions school. The *Sitz-im-Leben*, the famous concept developed by form criticism, presupposes a reconstruction of the audience and of the situation of reception (cf. Kümmel:419–423). The existential hermeneutics of Bultmann takes as its point of departure the present-day reader who wants to make sense of an ancient text. The question of *existentialia*, which forms an integral part of this exegetical technique, presupposes a link with the self-understanding of the reader. In the New Hermeneutic, the concept of a *Sprachereignis* or a "language event" is indicative of the involvement of the reader in the process of understanding (cf. Ebeling:197: "Die Sprache versammelt Redenden und Horenden am selben Ort").

1.3   Despite this long-standing (if diffuse) interest in the reader, the latest surge in reader-oriented work in biblical exegesis has been stimulated by developments from outside the discipline. The rise of reception theory in general literary studies and the proliferation of reader response analyses have not only highlighted a neglected area in biblical hermeneutics, but also demonstrated the possibilities of this approach. *Semeia* 31 (1985), under the title *Reader Response Approaches to Biblical and Secular Texts*, was one of the first attempts to explore these possibilities. By offering a theoretical orientation and examples of reader response criticism applied to both biblical and non-biblical material, the volume provided a valuable introduction to the potential and limitations of this approach. It also took the discussion a decisive step further and prepared the way for further ventures in this field. At the same time, as Robert Detweiler warns the reader in the preface, "reader response criticism is by no means a unified interpretative method but rather an aggregate of approaches that interact with each other." It is indeed a diverse and complex field of research. If could therefore be expected of a subsequent volume of *Semeia* on this topic to be clear about its focus and purpose.

1.4   The essays collected here evolved from a seminar initiated by Edgar V. McKnight in 1984 on "The Role of the Reader in the Interpretation of the New Testament" in the context of the *Studiorum Novi Testamenti Societas*. The main purpose was to test the usefulness of a reader-oriented approach for the interpretation of New Testament texts. Theoretical reflection was complemented by the actual analysis of texts. It soon became clear that both the intratextual and the extratextual aspects of the reading process required special attention. The first two years were devoted to "text-internal" problems, the following two to the interaction between text and context. Material prepared for the first phase of the project has been reworked for this volume, with the focus on the reader "in" the text. What exactly is meant by this concept and what is its importance for the understanding of biblical texts?

1.5   To answer this question, it is certainly not the intention to provide once again a comprehensive exposition of the theoretical basis of a reader-oriented approach. This is available elsewhere, both with regard to general literary theory (cf. Iser; Eco; Tompkins; Suleiman & Crosman; Holub) and to its implications for biblical material (cf. Detweiler; Fowler; Petersen; McKnight). As the theoretical aspects of the concept "the reader *in* the text" are discussed extensively in the contributions of Vorster and Schenk, we can restrict ourselves to a preliminary working definition at this stage. With the "reader in the text" is meant the "encoded" or "textually defined" reader. It does not refer to a real reader, but to the anticipated role a potential reader is expected to play in order to actualize the text. In order to provide a background for the essays collected in this volume, the rest of this introduction will be devoted to a brief sketch of the wider context in which the quest for the reader in the text takes place. We shall do this by examining three closely related aspects: the distinction between empirical and theoretical reader research, the different levels and types of reading and, thirdly, the dynamics of the reading process itself.

2. *Theoretical and empirical reader research*

2.1   In the field of reader-oriented studies, the most basic distinction is that between theoretical and empirical reader research (cf. Schmidt; Verschuren; Segers). This goes back to the difference between *Wirkung* and *Rezeption* as understood by Jauß—a distinction which is not unproblematic, but which basically understands *Wirkung* as referring to the aspects determined by the text and *Rezeption* to those determined by the reader. This distinction is linked to the idea that the text only offers a *potential* reading, which a real reader has to actualize.

2.2   Obviously, a study of actual reception is only possible where a *record* of such a reading or readings exists. Records of all kinds present themselves, both from the past and the present. This has led to a further distinction between historical and contemporary empirical research (cf. Van Gorp, Ghesquiere & Segers). An example of the former is the well-known project of Jauß to write a history of literature in terms of a history of reception (cf. Jauß; 1975). Contemporary reception research based on actual responses to texts has enjoyed great popularity in some circles (cf. Holub; Steinberg; Schmidt) and was accompanied by extensive theoretical reflection (cf. Groeben; Schmidt). This type of research makes use of either responses documented by readers themselves in the form of reviews and the like, or self-initiated surveys by means of questionnaires. The latter is only possible where respondents are available and accessible, but has the advantage that a wide spectrum of aspects can be covered, with the possibility of follow-up surveys.

2.3   As far as biblical material is concerned, the first obvious field for historical empirical research would be different translations of the Bible or of sections of text, as each of these represent a specific reading. Commentaries are also a record of actual readings. In this case we are dealing with a more specialized kind of reader, depending on what level of the text is read (cf. the next section). Luke's reading of Mark is the record of a specific reception (cf. Fowler, 1986). The use of textual traditions and citations in the Bible, the use of the Old Testament in the New, can be studied from a reception point of view. The formation of the canon represents a reception process. Writing a history of theology or of dogma in terms of a history of reception would indeed by an interesting counterpart to Jauß's undertaking.

2.4   At this stage, the contemporary empirical research of biblical material is still virtually unexplored territory, although many opportunities present themselves. Some projects are under way which will provide a good test for the usefulness of this approach (cf. Lategan and Rousseau).

2.5   Empirical research therefore presupposes real readers, or rather: evidence of their reading in some form or another. An example would be the *first readers* of biblical texts, that is, their historical recipients, who often form part of the history of the text itself (the Matthean church, the Johannine community, the historical Philemon, etc.). The problem is that very little *evidence* of these readings exists. Other examples are the *past readers* of the text, whose successive readings constitute the reception history of the text. By far the most accessible are *contemporary readers* of the Bible, who offer examples of a wide variety of readings—"Western" and "non-Western," "black" and "white," academic and liturgical, visual (film and television) and non-visual.

2.6   The distinction between real and implied readers is closely linked to what has become known as the "inside" and "outside" of the text. In almost all conceptualizations of the reading process, this demarcation line is clearly drawn. In the case of Petersen (39) it is in the form of a box which separates the implied author/reader from the actual author/reader. Link (25) distinguishes carefully between an extratextual level and several "texinterne" levels. In the very complex diagram which Chatman (267) uses to explain the reading process, the real author and the real audience are pushed out to the very edges on either side.

2.7   The studies in this volume concentrate on the "inside" of the text. The concern is therefore not with real readers of flesh and blood, but with how readers are *anticipated* by and in the text. It is interested in all that can be gleaned from the text in the form of instructions given to, and presuppositions shared by the potential reader of the text. Hence, the focus on the *role* of the reader. From all the information gathered in this way, an image of the intended reader can be reconstructed or envisaged—the *implied reader* in Iser's terms. The text creates a "structured mold" ("strukturierte Hohlform"—Iser 61), that is, a textual space to be occupied, a role to be assumed by a real reader during the reading process. Eco goes further by stating that the text not only gives instructions to its potential reader, but also builds up the competence needed to read a specific text. He prefers to talk of a model reader, which is "a textually established set of felicity conditions...to be met in order to have a macro-speech act (such as a text is) fully actualized" (11). Only the text can tell us what kind of reader it postulates. In fact, the text is nothing but the semantic-pragmatic production of its own model reader (10). By selecting specific codes, style, and indices, the text opts for a specific reader and at the same time, creates the competence of this model reader (7).

2.8   In order to make quite clear that the "reader in the text" is a literary construct and not a real reader, Schenk in his contribution to this volume proposes that we avoid any talk of a "reader" and replace it with "addressee" when dealing with the "inside" of the text. He therefore also prefers the threefold distinction of "author—addressee—reader," where "addressee" refers to the *textimmanent* reader as the anticipation of the future (real) reader. This may sound like a drastic proposal, but Schenk is correct that reading does not consist of a direct interchange between author and reader, and we shall return to this aspect in the final section of the paper.

3.   Levels of reading

3.1   Once the field is narrowed to the (potential) reader in the text in contrast to real readers, further distinctions can be made. One of the most important is the level on which the instructions of the text are actualized. The variation in the level of actualization can be due either to limitations in competence or lack of familiarity with codes on the part of the reader, or to a conscious choice to read the text from a specific perspective or for a specific purpose.

3.2   For example, Fowler (1983) has developed Steiner's distinction between the "reader" and the "critic" and applied it to the text of Mark. The reader accepts the text at face value, is intent on a positive realization of the text and in this sense becomes a "servant" of the text. The critic reads reflectively, keeps distance and thus becomes a "judge and master" of the text (cf. Fowler, 1983:32–8 for a full discussion of this contrast). Dormeyer (1987a:120) has shown that further distinctions are possible by describing the reading attitude of a naive, understanding, and critical reader. For the naive reader, reading is a direct experience aimed at affirming his or her reading attitude. For the understanding reader, it is a reflective activity which is open to a change of reading attitude. For the critic, reading means an analytical activity which takes place on a meta-level and which aims at an objective attitude towards the text.

3.3   These different reading positions form a continuum (Fowler, 1983:35). The same individual can assume different attitudes or poses as reader. Such distinctions have no inherent superiority in relation to each other, but are very useful devices to clarify exactly what aspect of the reading process we are talking about. A text may even be read by unintended readers for unintended purposes. A literary text may be read to pinpoint a geographical site, a biblical text may be scrutinized for examples of certain grammatical constructions.

3.4   The fact that texts can be and are actualized on various levels is due not only to differences in reading attitudes—it can also be caused by factors over which the reader has little control. We are not and never will become the readers for whom the letters of Paul were originally intended. For this reason Petersen makes the important distinction between authorial and non-authorial readers. Failure to observe this difference lies behind much of the misreading of biblical texts. But, despite the particularity of every text, it also contains certain universal features which enables a later (unintended) reader to read it—the so-called "Grundbestand an Universalität" (Dormeyer, 1987b). Although the modern reader is not the original reader, he or she may share the tradition or value system expressed in the text or know enough of the code to make a reading possible (cf. also Betz:24 on the modern reader). The question of continuity and discontinuity, of particularity and universality, will therefore be a recurring theme in the following essays.

3.5   These essays have been written from the perspective of the critical reader, but then a critical reader who wants to understand how the "normal" reader will actualize the text. Van Iersel's article on Mark illustrates the point, in so far as it attempts to systematize retrospectively on a theoretical level what has emerged from the actual analysis of the text. In his commentary on Mark (10–13), he explains his choice of perspective more fully—instead of opting for the position of either the original or the present readers, he confines himself to that which is common to both positions. But this leads us to a further distinction which is relevant when talking about the reader in the text.

3.6   The instructions given to a potential reader are of two kinds. On the one hand, these appear as signals which give a wide variety of directives to the reader as to how to actualize the text. On the other hand, the implementation of these directives is dependent on some underlying and often hidden assumptions. Perelman (31) has shown how the constant interplay between speaker and audience is possible only because of shared convictions. These form a substratum to which the speaker appeals and which activates the dialogue. Some of the following studies pay special attention to these explicit and implicit instructions to the reader. But thereby we are already dealing with the dynamic aspects of the reading process.

4.   *Reading as an interactive process*

4.1   In the preceding sections, the methodological significance of a clear distinction between real and implied readers, between the inside and the outside of the text, has been emphasized. These distinctions do not, of course, deny the dynamic nature of the actual reading process—although, as theoretical abstractions, they may give a rather static impression. In exploring the concept of the reader in the text, we have to give account of the interaction which takes place during the reading process itself. The fact remains that any theoretical observation and any statement about the encoded reader is dependent on a *prior* actual reading of the text by the theorist.

4.2   If we accept that reading is a "mysterious merger of text, reader and context" (Fowler, 1983:45), how should we conceptualize the process? Todorov (67) warns us that reading appears to be a deceptively straightforward activity, until we start analyzing it. It would seem that there are some readers inside the text who want to get out, while there are others outside who cannot get in. Fowler is correct to stress that reading is both a dialogical process and a temporal experience. Iser has explicitly stated that the concept of the implied reader is a way to describe the transactional relationship between text and reader. "Das Konzept des impliziten Lesers umschreibt daher einen Übertragungsvorgang, durch den sich die Textstrukturen über die Vorstellungsakte in den Erfahrungshaushalt des Lesers übersetzen" (67). We have already seen that the implied reader is a device to engage the real reader by offering a role to be played or an attitude to be assumed. It is often suggested that the real cross-over point lies between the implied author and the implied reader. Fowler sees these two, and also the narrator and narratee, so closely linked that they actually are mirror images of each other. At the same time, a transfer of values takes place between the implied author and reader. "The diction of the narrator is refracted like a sonar wave off the outline of the posited narratee and returns to the sender to be emitted again—each reflects the presence of the other" (1983:42).

4.3   But, in the act of reading, is the contact point really the implied author and reader? I would suggest that the communicative process moves along other lines. (For a more extensive explanation, cf. Lategan & Vorster, 1985.) It is more like a dual movement starting from opposite poles. The real author, when writing, is reaching out for the implied reader (as no other reader is present at this moment). The real reader, when reading, is reaching out for the implied author (as no other author is present). Thus, instead of real author → implied author (narrator) → implied reader (narratee) → real reader, the process is more like:

Real authors can address only what they imagine or intend their readers to be; real readers can reach the real authors only via the implied authors, that is, they have to figure out what the real authors are getting at by concentrating on the clues and signals given by the encoded authors.

4.4   What has been described so far is only the initial or intuitive phase of the process. The real author is not tied to the implied reader, but can (and does) certainly consider the effectiveness of the implied author. The real reader, on the other hand, is not stuck with the implied author, but is free to move around in the text and to consider other options. Iser (115) has shown how important this wandering viewpoint is for understanding the text. As movement is made back and forth, the reader's understanding of the text increases and competence as reader grows. A later insight can lead the reader to revise an earlier position or cause the reader to reverse the procedure and make a fresh approach (cf. also Schenk's essay below).

4.5   There are, of course, numerous models to explain the interaction between author and reader. When trying to account for the diversity of readings, Todorov (1980:72–73) argues that the reader's reading does not describe the universe of the book itself, but this universe as it is transformed by the psyche of each individual author. He diagrams the process as follows:

4.6   In an intriguing proposal, Petersen has pushed further in this direction. By making use of a distinction similar to the artefact/aesthetic object contrast introduced by Mukarovsky (cf. Link:138), Petersen differentiates between the text and the reader's realization of the text. The marks on a printed page are signifiers which do not even form a series, just a display. The joining of these signifiers to signifieds according to specific codes takes place in the reader's mind, not in the text. The physical objective text must be distinguished from the mentally subjective work.

4.7   For Petersen the important point is that the imaginative character of the work produced from the text is visual, rather than conceptual. Therefore, we tend to experience texts in terms of visual images, which, for their part, can combine to form perceivable worlds. He explains the movement from language to vision, rather than to concept, and back to language, as follows (42–43):

> While the works we create from texts are subjective in the sense of being mental phenomena, and are therefore *in us*, it is also and more importantly true that while reading *we are in the worlds of our works*. In order to appreciate this seeming paradox, it is necessary to remember the temporal, processual nature of the reading experience. Precisely because reading is processual, moving from the beginning of the text to its end, we not only gradually build up a narrative world from the text we are processing, but we also progressively create that world from within it. While reading, we build up a world around us. For this reason, a text's narrative world has its primary reality as an imaginatively visual phenomenon experienced during the process of reading. Like a dream, visual images from it

can be recalled after the process has ended, and like a dream we can also linguistically conceptualize that imaginative world in order to talk about it with other people. But also like a dream, the reality of a narrative world is that of an experiential process in which we have participated. Reader response criticism must therefore take into account not only the relationship between readers and texts, but also the relationship between readers and the worlds they create from texts.

4.8   Petersen goes on to explain that the mediation between text and reader proceeds via the world created from the text. Some readers, because they are authorial readers, are in the text, other readers are not. But both authorial and non-authorial readers are in the *work*. For the non-authorial reader, the way to gain entry to the text is to enter the world of the text, which is also shared by the authorial reader. However, the non-authorial readers must be aware of their limitations. They can be present in the world of the text, but they cannot act in it, lest they change the story. On the other hand, encoded authors and readers are actors, both in the world of the text and its work. The distinctions Petersen develops here form part of a much broader attempt to get a better methodological grip on the setting and "sociological" aspects of literary texts. This will be the main focus of the second phase of the SNTS seminar's work under the theme "text and context."

4.9   Fowler (1983:49–52) is therefore correct when he emphasizes reading as a temporal experience which should not lose its dynamic character, even in our theoretical reflection on, and *post factum* plotting of the process. The problem is that we are trying to describe an event in time by means of static terminology or imagery. Or rather—the moment we attempt to describe this movement, we interrupt its flow by this very description, by this step back in order to see and understand our actions. That is the dilemma of being both a reader and a critic, as Fowler explains. Therefore the imagery of the film is useful—the temporal flow of the reading process can be stopped at a certain point to allow us to analyze the (synchronic) relations of the frozen image on the screen. We can even replay the sequence in slow motion to pinpoint significant moves or to isolate what was too quick for the eye. But, at the same time, we know that the stopping of the movement is "unnatural" and that in actual fact the process proceeds uninterruptedly.

4.10   The combination of the static and dynamic elements correspond to the reflective and participatory dimensions of the communication process which affects not only the reader and the reception, but also the author and the production of the text. A useful way of mapping these shifts in the communication process is provided by Ricoeur in his *Interpretation Theory* (1976). He distinguishes three pairs of related but contrastive concepts, namely event and meaning, sense and reference, and explanation and understanding.

4.11   The communicative *event* which forms the basis and the impetus behind the production of the text is in itself a fleeting moment in history. The *meaning* of this event is retained in the text, or rather, the event is solidified in the form of a text. The process of inscripturation has the advantage that it makes it possible for the communication event to transcend itself and reach readers who had no part in the original event. Despite the negative attitude often found in historical studies with regard to the adequacy of written documents, they have in fact remarkable communicative abilities.

4.12   The *sense* of the text is determined by the internal relations of the text which can be analyzed by a number of text-immanent techniques. But, however important the internal relations are, by force of their *referential* potential they transcend the text by reaching back to the author and the situation of origin and forward in anticipation of the actual reading process.

4.13   The *explanation* of the text in all its complexity (par excellence the task of the critic) is in the final analysis aimed at its *understanding*. The analysis of its different relations and components is to serve its effective communication by creating the necessary conditions for its understanding. The effect on the reader remains an important focal point.

4.14   Ricoeur's three pairs can be developed even further if we realize that each pair contains both a static (meaning, sense, explanation) and a dynamic (event, reference, understanding) element and these contrasts are eminently suitable for describing the interplay between the various constituents of the reading process as a temporal experience. But this requires further argumentation which cannot be developed in this brief introduction.

4.15   Against this background, the following studies employ a wide variety of techniques and approaches, but all have the reader in the text as their focal point. The authors explore both the strength and the weaknesses of a reader orientation and an attempt has been made to preserve the atmosphere of dialogue between the different participants. Both narrative and argumentative texts were analyzed and the aim was to illustrate the interplay between theoretical reflection and the actual analysis of texts.

Vorster and Wuellner start off by a theoretical discussion of the usefulness of the reader concept for narrative material and find themselves in constant interaction with one another. Schenk then provides the theoretical basis for the analysis of non-narrative texts. The wider context of his contribution is his commentary on Philippians, in which he extensively discusses the instructions given to the reader and the theoretical parameters of a reader approach.

Fowler and van Iersel illustrate two types of reader analysis applied to a narrative text, in this case the Gospel of Mark. Fowler takes the rhetorical strategy of direction and indirection as point of departure, showing how the reading experience is guided by this technique. In doing so, he expands and clarifies the possibilities of reader response criticism. Van Iersel approaches Mark from a different theoretical framework and concentrates on the role of the reader as an operator of intertextual references and connotational meanings in realizing the text. His essay forms part of a much more comprehensive study of the reader in Mark and provides a rare example of the interplay between theory and praxis.

The contributions of Combrink, Dormeyer, and Voelz were originally intended as reactions to the Philippians commentary of Schenk—a fact which might not be so clear from the present form and order of the essays. In large measure it was in response to the criticisms of these three that Schenk wrote his present contribution in which he clears up some of the uncertainties and refines his theoretical framework. Lategan applies a reader analysis to a different Pauline text, showing how reader instructions operate on different levels of Galatians.

In a final essay, an evaluation of the work of the seminar group is provided by Professor Temma F. Berg, who is neither part of the group nor a biblical exegete, but a literary theorist with extensive experience in reader response criticism.

WORKS CONSULTED

Betz, Hans Dieter
    1979   *Galatians: A Commentary on Paul's Letter to the Churches in Galatia.* Hermeneia. Philadelphia: Fortress.

Chatman, Seymour
    1978   *Story and Discourse: Narrative structure in Fiction and Film.* Ithaca: Cornell University Press.

Detweiler, R., ed.
1985   *Reader Response Approaches to Biblical and Secular Texts. Semeia* 31. Decatur, GA: Scholars Press.

Dormeyer, D.
1987a   "Das Verhältnis von 'wilder' und historischkritischer Exegese als methodologisches und didaktisches Problem." *JRP* 3:11–126.
1987b   "Anfragen zu Norman R. Peterson, 'Prolegomena to a reader-oriented Study of Paul's Letter to Rome.'" Unpublished response presented to the SNTS Seminar on The Role of the Reader in the Interpretation of the New Testament, Göttingen.

Ebeling, G.
1971   *Einführung in theologische Sprachlehre.* Tübingen: Mohr.

Eco, Umberto
1979   *The Role of the Reader: Explorations in the Semiotics of Texts.* Bloomington: Indiana University Press.

Fowler, Robert M.
1983   "Who Is 'the Reader' of Mark's Gospel?" Pp. 31–53 in *SBL 1983 Seminar Papers.* Ed. P.J. Achtemeier. Chico: Scholars Press.
1986   "Reading Matthew Reading Mark: Observing the First Steps toward Meaning-as-Reference in the Synoptic Gospels." Pp. 1–16 in *SBL Seminar Papers.* Ed. K.H. Richards. Atlanta: Scholars Press.

Groeben, N.
1977   *Rezeptionsforschung als empirische Literaturwissenschaft.* Kronberg: Athenaum.

Holub, Robert C.
1984   *Reception Theory: a Critical Introduction.* London: Methuen.

Iser, Wolfgang
1976   *Der Akt des Lesens: Theorie ästhetischer Wirkung.* München: Wilhelm Fink.

Jauss, H.R.
1970   *Literaturgeschichte als Provokation.* Frankfurt: Suhrkamp.

1975 "Der Leser als Instanz einer neuen Geschichte der Literatur." *Poetica* 7:325–44.

Kümmel, W.G.
1958 *Das Neue Testament. Geschichte der Erforschung seiner Probleme.* Freiburg: Karl Alber.

Lategan, Bernard C. and J. Rousseau
1988 "Reading Luke 12:35–48: an empirical study." *Neotestamentica* 22: 391–413.

Lategan, Bernard C. and Willem S. Vorster
1985 *Text and Reality: Aspects of Reference in Biblical Texts.* Philadelphia: Fortress.

Link, Hannelore
1976 *Rezeptionsforschung: Eine Einführung in Methoden und Probleme.* Stuttgart: Kohlhammer.

McKnight, Edgar V.
1985 *The Bible and the Reader: An Introduction to Literary Criticism.* Philadelphia: Fortress.

Perelman, C. and L. Olbrechts-Tyteca
1979 *The New Rhetoric: A Treatise on Argumentation.* Notre Dame: Notre Dame University Press.

Petersen, Norman R.
1984 "The Reader in the Gospel." *Neotestamentica* 18:38–51.

Ricoeur, P.
1976 *Interpretation Theory.* Fort Worth: Texas Christian University Press.

Schmidt, S.J.
1980 "Receptional Problems with Contemporary Narrative Texts and Some of their Reasons." *Poetics* 9:119–46.
1982 *Grundriss der empirischen Literaturwissenschaft II.* Braunschweig: Vieweg.

Segers, Rien T.
1980 *Het lezen van literatuur: Een Inleiding tot een Nieuwe Literatuurbenadering.* Baarn: Ambo.

Steinberg, H.
1983 "Socio-empirical Reading Research: A Critical Report About Some Revealing Surveys." *Poetics* 12:467-79.

Suleiman, Susan R. and Inge Crosman, eds.
1980 *The Reader in the Text: Essays in Audience and Interpretation*. Princeton: Princeton University Press.

Todorov, T.
1980 "Reading as Construction." Pp. 67-82 in *The Reader in the Text: Essays in Audience and Interpretation*. Ed. S. R. Suleiman and I. Crossman. Princeton: Princeton University Press.

Tompkins, Jane P., ed.
1980 *Reader-Response Criticism: From Formalism to Post-Structuralism*. Baltimore: Johns Hopkins University Press.

Van Gorp, H., R. Ghesquire and R.T. Segers, eds.
1981 *Receptie-onderzoek: mogelijkheden en grenzen*. Leuven: Acco.

Van Iersel, B.
1989 *Reading Mark*. Edinburgh: T&T Clark.

Verschuren, H.
1986 "Receptie-onderzoek en literatuursociologie." *Forum der Letteren* 27:42-55.

I

Theory

THE READER IN THE TEXT: NARRATIVE MATERIAL

Willem S. Vorster
University of South Africa

ABSTRACT

Because of the many ways in which the notion "reader in the text" is used by literary theorists, including New Testament scholars, it has become ambiguous and paradoxical. In this essay the following questions are addressed: Is there a reader "in" the text? Who or what is the reader in the text? And, how is the reader in the text? These questions are confronted with regard to the interpretation of New Testament narratives. In the first part of the essay the theoretical background of the notion is reviewed and different models are discussed. The second part deals with the reader in New Testament narratives. In conclusion a few possibilities and limitations of this theoretical model are discussed with regard to the interpretation of the New Testament.

0. The notion "reader in the text," however ambiguous and paradoxical, has become part of the jargon of New Testament scholars. Because of the many ways in which the concept is used by literary theorists and the variety of applications in literary and New Testament studies, it is necessary to review the theoretical background of the notion as well as its potential for analyzing and interpreting narratives in the New Testament.

0.1 The purpose of this essay is to address the following problem areas concerning narratives in general and narratives in the New Testament in particular: Is there a reader "in" the text? Who or what is the reader in the text? And, how is the reader in the text? Since every text is constructed with specific readers in mind, the question arises whether heuristic devices like the "implied," "encoded," or "model reader" can help the flesh-and-blood reader to follow the contours of the text presentation and to actualize the text? I will confront these problems theoretically and methodologically with a view to the interpretation of narratives in the New Testament. In order to achieve this, I will first pay attention to the problem of the reader in the text in literary theory. Against this background, the second major part of the essay will address the phenomenon of the reader in the text in New Testament narratives.

0.2   The theme of the essay will be treated in terms of structural semiotic literary theory, keeping in mind the rhetorical and phenomenological background out of which the notion of "reader in the text" developed. It is assumed that in the context of reception theory, the phenomenon "text" is not simply an object which has an immanent meaning, but that it is part of a communication transaction in which both the generation of meaning by the author of the text and the attribution of meaning by the consumer of the text (the reader) are significant.

1.   *A reader in the text?*

1.0   The reader is said to be "in the text" because of his/her/its presence as an *image*, created by the author, and because of his/her/its encoding in linguistic signs and textual strategies. This image has to be constructed by the real reader. What does this mean?

1.1   The idea of a reader in the text originated with Wayne Booth's concept of an implied author in 1961 and its counterpart, the so-called implied reader, which he and others later developed. According to Booth (138): "The author creates...an image of himself and another image of his reader; he makes his reader, as he makes his second self, and the most successful reading is one in which the created selves, author and reader, can find complete agreement." This view is seminal to numerous developments by Iser (1974) and others (cf. Chatman and Suleiman and Crosman). In order to come to grips with the theoretical implications of the reader in the text, it is necessary first to look at its counterpart, the implied author.

1.1.1   The first thing to notice is that the implied author is not identical with the real author, even if there may be an occasional overlap (Rimmon-Kenan:87). According to this view (cf. Booth:420–31) the implied author is the governing and organizing principle in, or implied by, the narrative text, the source of the judgments and values embodied in the text. It chooses what we read and how we read, and exerts power over our reading process. It is the implied author that chooses the detail and quality that is found in the work or implied by the work. Its function is to instruct the implied reader how to read by the signs of its presence in the text. It knows what is invented and that all the work's norms may not hold in "real life." An implied author may embody totally different views and values in a narrative than the author who created the implied author. That is why implied authors in different works of the same author need not be and often are not the same.

1.1.2   The implied author is created by the real author, but as the term says, it is implied in the text. How? According to Booth (70–71) as an image:

> As he writes, he creates not simply an ideal, impersonal "man in general" but an implied version of "himself" that is different from the implied authors we meet in other men's works.... Whether we call this implied author an "official scribe,"...it is clear that the picture the reader gets of this presence is one of the author's most important effects.

Although impersonal, the implied author's presence in the text is implied in terms of personal traits. It is an author with beliefs and values and interests. It is inscribed in the text in linguistic, literary, rhetorical, and other signs and traces from which the real reader has to infer its profile. But it is not simply a "set of implicit norms" or a mere literary construct as Rimmon-Kenan (88) would maintain. According to him it is not possible to "cast it in the role of the addresser in a communication situation." The detection of the implied author, and thus also the implied reader in the text, is directly influenced by the view of its role in communication. Because of the importance of a proper understanding of the function of the implied author, I will discuss the relation between the implied author and the narrator before we proceed to the implied reader.

1.1.3   It is common knowledge that every story has a storyteller (narrator) and somebody to whom the story is told (narratee), no matter whether it is an oral or a written story. But the real author is not identical with the narrator. Even in the case where the author tells the story (author=narrator) it is necessary to pay attention to the voice of the narrator as a narrative instance. Distinct from the real author, the narrator also differs from the implied author. Chatman (148) makes the following observation about the implied author which can help us determine the relation between the two:

> He is "implied," that is, reconstructed by the reader from the narrative. He is not the narrator, but rather the principle that invented the narrator, along with everything else in the narrative, that stacked the cards in this particular way, had these things happen to these characters, in these words

or images. Unlike the narrator, the implied author can *tell* us nothing. He, or better, *it* has no voice, no direct means of communicating. It instructs us silently, through the design of the whole, with all the voices, by all the means it has chosen to let us learn.

Chatman is correct in distinguishing between implied author and narrator, but he fails to see the place of the implied author in the communication process. His observation about the "instruction" the implied author gives has to be taken a little further.

1.1.4 Although the implied author does not *tell*, at least it *instructs* the reader how to read. When the reader is misled by an unreliable narrator, it is the implied author who enables the correction of false views. This is done, for instance, by way of the order of material, opposing perspectives, and other correctives which are encoded in the text. In the case of irony, for example, the reader is activated by the difference in "world view" between the implied author and the narrator, as Brink (148) correctly observes. The implied reader is the organizing principle, even the interpreting principle, behind the narrator, and as such serves as an important participant in the narrative communication situation (cf. Brink:149). The implied author is obviously a literary construct, as Rimmon-Kenan maintains, but this does not mean that it is a contradiction in terms to cast it in the role of a participant in narrative communication (88). It is implicitly in the text as the one who instructs the reader how to read.

1.2 Let us now turn to the implied reader. The implied author, as we have seen, has a counterpart in the implied reader. Similar to the implied author, this is also a literary construct, the profile and image of which has to be constructed by the real reader. Its presence in the text is similar to that of the implied author. It is not identical with the real reader of the text. Not even the original, first flesh-and-blood readers are to be thought of as identical with the implied readers.

1.2.1 Implied readers can be envisaged as the readers intended by the authors as readers or hearers of their narratives. Even though they "can never know their actual readers," authors cannot make artistic decisions without prior assumptions (conscious or unconscious) about their audience's beliefs, knowledge, and familiarity with conventions" (Rabinowitz:234). The "authorial audience," as Rabinowitz calls the intended actual readers, is of great importance for the reader since the text of any work is designed with this audience in mind and, as he argues (244), "we must—as we read—come to share its characteristics if we are to understand the text." This is in agreement with the view of Booth

(138–39) that the implied reader is the reader we have to be willing to become in order to bring the reading experience to its full measure.

1.2.2 In Booth's opinion (428–29), the implied reader is the kind of reader selected or implied by a given narrative whose values and beliefs must, at least temporarily, accord with the values and beliefs of that narrative. The implied reader must be a relatively credulous listener within the narrative, who accepts the narrative as it is told without questioning its values or events and existents. And furthermore he/she/it has to be capable of refusing to become the implied reader of an unreliable narrator. In this way the implied reader is enabled to interpret complex ironic structures in a narrative.

1.3 These ideas about the presence of the reader in the text were developed by Iser (1974) with regard to a textual condition and the production of meaning in the reading process and by Eco with regard to the role of the reader in narrative fiction. Both views are important for our development of the idea of the reader in New Testament narratives.

1.3.1 Iser, who approached the notion of an implied reader from a phenomenological perspective, was mainly interested in the actions involved in responding to a text in order to produce meaning. He maintains (1978:34) that the implied reader:

> embodies all those predispositions necessary for a literary work to exercise its effect—predispositions laid down, not only by an empirical outside reality, but by the text itself. Consequently, the implied reader as a concept has his roots firmly planted in the structure of the text; he is a construct and in no way to be identified with any real reader.

1.3.2 Criticism has been made of Iser for defining the implied reader in purely literary terms as almost synonymous with the structure of appeal of a literary work, thus making the "reader" a term which is "senseless, if not downright misleading" (Holub:85). If not seen in terms of its paradoxical nature as a reader who is present in the text both as an image, as Booth argues, and in terms of the directives in the reading process, the term obviously becomes misleading. The point is however, that one should take the notion of implied reader as a literary construct seriously with regard to its presence in the text—in other words, the way it is present in the text. I would agree that too much focus on the encoding could easily distract critics from the idea that they are still busy with inferring an image of the reader from all the components of the text.

1.3.3   Using the ideas of Roman Ingarden, Iser argues that in the absence of the sender of the text and with the inability of the text to react as a participant in the communication transaction, there are directives in the text which guide the reader in the reading process. These directives are defined with regard to the so-called "Leerstellen," that is "gaps" or "open places," "negation," and "negativity," three modalities of indeterminacy or "Unbestimmtheit" present in the text. These modalities operate on both the syntactic and paradigmatic levels. On the syntactic level, for instance, the breaks in a narrative between episodes or in the plot line, changes in perspective, and the clashes in presentation, offer the real reader the opportunity to fill in the gaps thus created and to return to previous interpretations in attributing meaning to the presented material. On the paradigmatic level, negation takes place when the ideas with which the real reader comes to the text are shattered, and the repertoire is changed. Negativity is involved when something in a text entices the reader to replace its direct meaning with a deeper meaning (cf. Iser, 1978:228 and Koopman-Thurlings).

1.3.4   It is not only what is in the text, but also what is not in the text, which directs the reader to make an appropriate reading of the text, according to Iser. Silence can be very effectively used by authors to direct readers in attributing meaning to a narrative, as Booth (271–301) has also convincingly shown. The ending of the Gospel of Mark is a very good example of what the author says by not saying anything (cf. Magness).

1.4   With respect to the presence of the reader in the text, Eco has made valuable observations about the production of meaning by reading the codes in the text. According to him, these syntactic, semantic, and pragmatic codes define the reader in the text, which he calls the "model reader." He maintains (7) that:

> The author has…to foresee a model of the possible reader (hereafter Model Reader) supposedly able to deal interpretatively with the expressions in the same way as the author deals generatively with them.

1.4.1   He furthermore contends that the text selects its appropriate reader (7), and also that it projects an image of such a possible model reader through the choice of: "a specific linguistic code," "a certain literary style," and "specific specialization-indices." Some texts even presuppose a specific encyclopedic competence (think of the model reader of an apocalyptic text!). These codes are often not only implicit, but also explicit, as in the case of children's literature where typographical signals and direct appeals play such an important role. In a philosophical treatise, on the other hand, the reader's intellectual profile is determined by "the sort of interpretive operations he is supposed to perform" (11). In this sense the "author" and "reader" become textual strategies according to Eco.

The model reader is also encoded in the structure and rhetoric of the text. In the case of narratives, this means being encoded in the plot and all the other aspects which form part of the narrative mode, such as point of view, characterization, time, and order.

1.4.2   Eco developed the notion of the reader in the text much further than Booth or Iser and made it an encompassing concept of what is encoded in a text with regard to and for the sake of the reader. To say it in the words of Rimmon-Kenan (119):

> the "reader" is...a construct, a "metonymic characterization of the text"..., an "it" rather than a personified "he" or "she".... Such a reader is "implied" or "encoded" in the text "in the very rhetoric through which he is required to "make sense of the content" or reconstruct it "as a world."

1.5   This is not the place to criticize the foregoing models of the reader in the text. I shall rather give a summary of what I regard as the essence of the notion of the reader in the text and the purpose for which it can be used. The summary must also serve as my opinion of what the reader in the text is.

1.5.1   The reader in the text is a literary construct, an image of a reader which is selected by the text. It is implied by the text, and in this sense it is encoded in the text by way of linguistic, literary, cultural, and other codes. It is not identical to any outside flesh-and-blood reader. It is an image that is created by the author which has to be constructed by the real reader through the reading process in order to attribute meaning to the text, that is to actualize the text. The construction of the reader in the text is central to the establishment of the meaning of a narrative according to this view (cf. Ruthrof:122).

1.5.2   The purpose of constructing the reader in the text is not to move from the text to the context of communication outside the text, that is, to the actual reader or even the actual author, but to establish a meaning of a narrative.

2. *The Reader in New Testament Narratives*

2.0   Modern narratology is not necessarily directly applicable to ancient narrative material, for there have been many and different developments in the art of storytelling of which the ancients had no idea, and modern narratology must deal with these developments and with theoretical matters concerning modern narratives. On the other hand, ancient theorists like Aristotle laid the basis for modern thought about many aspects of modern literary theory. Narration is, moreover, one of the very few ways of organizing material in a discourse. It is basic to human communication. One can, therefore, expect similarities between modern and ancient narratives. Developments during the last decade in narrative approaches to New Testament material have indicated the advantages in analyzing the narratives in the New Testament with the help of modern narratological tools. The present question is whether theory about the reader in the text reviewed above is applicable to New Testament narratives. If so, in what manner and for what purpose? Before answers are ventured, let us first make a few general statements about New Testament narratives and present some features peculiar to them.

2.1   A very substantial part of the New Testament is presented in the narrative mode. In addition to the Four Gospels of Matthew, Mark, Luke, and John, the Acts of the Apostles and the Revelation of John are narratives. Furthermore, a large number of smaller narrative units are embedded in the Gospels and Acts of the Apostles. But we also find material which is organized in narrative style in argumentative texts of the New Testament. The parables of Jesus, miracle stories, and Paul's presentation of the difference of opinion between himself and Peter in Galatians are good examples of short stories in the New Testament. These texts display characteristics which are different from those normally dealt with in narratology. Most of them are religious and were told for religious purposes, that is, for communication about religious matters. They were intended to be read aloud to audiences of hearers and not to be read silently by individual readers as we now read them (cf. among others Aune). The first to hear the stories after they had been written down consisted of both newcomers and committed followers of a new religion. Many of these narratives contain materials which were transmitted orally. This makes the phenomenon of intertextuality and the reader in the text all the more important. Their significance for the subcultures for whom they were intended also makes them different from ordinary stories, even though they still remain stories. We also have to keep in mind the fact that in the end they became part of a set of canonized books, the Christian Bible, which, as a collection, is made up of two testaments.

As Christian scriptures, they are read and used for devotional purposes, in search for meaning in life, as sources for the making of sermons, as historical sources, etc. Undoubtedly these overcodings will play a role in the reading process. But for the purpose of this essay it will not be possible to pay attention to all the implications of these sorts of overcoding in the course of history. I shall limit my discussion by bracketing out the implications of canonization.

2.1.1   The above mentioned texts are said to be narratives because they have the characteristics of narratives. One of the distinctive criteria for classifying texts and determining genre, is the type of speaker involved in a text and his/her function (cf. Bal:21; Van Luxemburg, Bal, and Weststeijn:121). In the case of one speaker, as in poetry, the text is a monologue. When one speaker allows other speakers in a text also to speak, the text is organized in the narrative mode. New Testament narratives are characterized as narratives by this feature among others.

2.1.2   Most New Testament narratives are told by omniscient narrators who allow other speakers like Jesus also to tell stories or simply to speak. That is why these texts also have various narratees. The narrator in the Gospel of Mark tells the story of Jesus to an unidentified narratee. But Jesus also speaks. Jesus tells stories to the crowd and informs his disciples secretly. He even has an inside hearer group among his disciples when, in Mark 13, he informs the four disciples about the future and about their conduct in the light of the coming future (cf. Vorster, 1987b). Thus, within the narrative world of Mark, there are different narratees as there are different narrators. The main narrator, whom we may call Mark, is not a separate voice as we often find in modern novels. He narrates the story on behalf of the author, and that is why we may call him an authorial narrator. This does not imply that he is identical with the blood-and-flesh author. The narrator is an intratextual communicant. The same can be said of narrators and narratees in the other Gospels and in Acts. The we-passages in Acts, of course, pose their own problems in terms of narrators and readers in the text (cf. Kurz, 1987:208–219); the narratee is identified as Theophilus. In the Revelation of John, the text is organized in the form of an autobiographic narrative concerning the visions of a certain John (cf. Vorster, 1988). In all these narratives, authors and readers are implied in the text. They have to be distinguished not only from the actual authors and readers, but also from the narrators and narratees. These authors and readers have to be constructed by the actual reader from the many codes which I mentioned above. The following diagram illustrates the different communicants involved in New Testament narratives.

NARRATIVE (e.g. GOSPEL)

	INTRATEXTUAL NARRATIVE WORLD		
actual author	implied author	implied reader	actual reader
	narrator	narratee	

2.2   The implied author and implied reader as well as the narrator and narratees are intratextual communicants, while the actual author and the actual readers/hearers are outside the text. Similar to communication in other stories, in New Testament narratives communication is a transaction between the text and its intratextual communicants and the actual reader. The actual author disappears behind the narrative presented. It is in this respect that the reader in the text, the author in the text, the narrator and the narratee, the presentation of the story, the emplotment, order, time, events, and other existents in the narrative world become important. Also important for the establishment of the profile of the reader in the New Testament narratives is the relationship between the presentational process, the presented world, and the implied reader or reader in the text.

2.3   Ruthrof has convincingly argued that the way in which a story is presented, the world presented in a narrative, and the reader in the text are functions of one another. There is a direct relationship between the implied author of any particular text and the implied reader in that text. The implied reader forms a complement of the implied author. Let us give a few examples taken from his book (138): In myth, where the narrator functions as an authority, the narrative world is presented as a dictate and the implied reader as a minor. In a parable, where the narrator is a preacher, the world is presented as analogue and teaching and the implied reader functions as a believer, normally with limited faculties. In prophecy, the narrator is a prophet who presents the world as divine vision and future truth to rebellious believers as implied readers. And in a narrative of ideas, the narrator is presented as an ideological visionary who presents the world as ideology to disciples. Omniscient narration normally involves a narrator who is clairvoyant. He presents the narrative world in unrestricted terms, especially as mental processes, to initiates.

2.3.1   If we now turn to New Testament narratives, it seems to me clear that Ruthrof's insights can help us further in establishing profiles of readers in the text. Let us look at a few examples in which the profile of the reader in the text is in direct relation to the presented world and to the image of the implied author.

2.3.2   The parables of Jesus are presented in the New Testament as narratives told by an authority on the Kingdom of God in which the world is disclosed in the form of "ideology" about another way of looking at reality. The parables are addressed to minors with limited intellectual faculties due to the fact that they do not have the same insight as the narrator. These "minors" are often presented as believers, or, in the case of Mark, initiates who find it difficult to grasp the riddle, but who are nevertheless informed as to how to listen and understand. Mark 4:11–12 is very interesting in this respect: "To you has been given the secret of the kingdom of God, but for those outside everything is in parables; so that they may indeed see but not perceive, and may indeed hear, but not understand; lest they should turn again, and be forgiven." To the initiates the mystery is given; they have the ability to understand. The outsiders however receive everything in parables, that is, riddles which remain riddles. The implied reader is obviously one who has to become a hearer who is able to hear (cf. however Sternberg:49). The movement from hiddenness to revelation in Mark's Gospel is one of the ways in which the implied reader is structured. It is common knowledge that the Gospel of Mark is structured by the so-called messianic secret. With a large number of subtleties the narrator encodes the riddle of how the Son of God, although a miracle worker, could die on a cross. The reader in the text is obviously a decoder of the riddle, somebody who can follow the movement from hiddenness to revelation.

2.3.3   The image of the apocalyptic visionary of the Revelation of John, presenting visions of otherworldly realities to a subculture whose members have to overcome the pressures of their society, undoubtedly implies a reader in the text who has to accept the authority of these visions. He/she has to be an insider in apocalyptic imagery and symbolism, a believer in the triumph of God in the second coming of Christ. The story of Jesus according to Matthew, on the other hand, obviously implies a totally different reader. The story is told from the perspective of how Jesus, "God with us," is present in the community of followers. The narrator is an observer in the life and works of Jesus, the Jew. The reader in the text is a follower who has to take the evidence seriously and live as a witness of the will of Jesus.

2.3.4   The implications of the relation between the presentational process, the presented world, and the reader in the text, are obvious. This relationship helps to create an image of the reader in the text which directs the actual reader. It is in this connection that peculiarities of New Testament narratives come into play. Most narratives are religious. The presentation is, therefore, also about religious communication which determines the image of the reader in the text. Beliefs and values obviously form part of the image one constructs of readers in texts. The worldview presented in the miracle stories of Jesus, for instance, influences the image of the readers. The readers in the text of the miracles of Jesus are readers who believe not only in healing practices but also in nature miracles. Actual readers are invited to accept this worldview and to share the characteristics of the stories if they are to understand the texts.

2.4   Every aspect of encoding is relevant and needs to be taken into account when the profile of the reader in any New Testament narrative is established. Although it will not be possible to go into all the detail, a few matters need our attention.

2.4.1   Since the structure of any text is designed with the reader in mind, traces of the reader in the text are to be looked for on all the levels of the structure and functions of narratives. Pro- and retrospection, gaps and indeterminacy, selection and organization, are signs of the reader, as Iser and Eco have indicated. All the narrative features such as plot, characterization, point of view, narrative commentary, order of narration, and time and space give clues to the actual reader in his or her construction of an image of the implied reader. Granted that the reader in the text is the total equipment an actual reader needs to actualize an appropriate reading of a text, every word, every group of words, every sentence or cluster of sentences become important. Every aspect of the text matters because the reader in the text is the ideal decoder of the complete text and not only of an aspect of it. As Kingsbury says, "the important thing to keep in mind is that it is the implied reader who is silently and invisibly present throughout Matthew's story to attend to every word" (1986:37). Knowledge of the basic dictionary of the text, as well as knowledge of the rhetoric of narratives, are important aids in establishing the reader in New Testament narratives, as Fowler's investigation of irony and narrative commentary in Mark clearly shows (1981:155, 157). I shall limit my discussion of these matters to two further examples to indicate the presence of the reader in New Testament narratives. The first concerns the ending of Mark.

2.4.2   The shorter ending of Mark's Gospel leaves the story open-ended. Many actual readers and critics find Mark 16:8 so abrupt that a variety of suggestions have been offered to explain or complete the ending. From a literary point of view it can, however, be argued that the refusal of our narrator to say more and to leave the response of the women unnarrated stimulates the imagination (Moule:132-33; cf. Petersen, 1980; Magness). This explanation fits well the very structure of the Gospel of Mark. I have already mentioned that the presentation of the story of Jesus in the Gospel of Mark as a riddle which was deliberately encoded as such by the narrator invites the reader to become an insider who is able to decode the mystery of the death of Jesus. The lack of understanding by the disciples, prospection of what is to come (cf. Mark 8:31, 9:31 and 10:33), and reliability of the narrator, to mention only a few things, help us build an image of the reader in the text who has to react to the unnarrated response of the women to the report of the news of the resurrection. The suspension of the end of the story is a very suggestive and powerful way to stimulate the reader. Taking into account the fact that the reader in Mark's text is somebody who has to decode the riddle, one immediately senses that he or she is a reader who is able to respond to the silence in the text by becoming, unlike the disciples who lack understanding in the greater part of the Gospel of Mark, an understanding follower of Jesus.

2.4.3   Characterization in narratives also gives valuable indications of the reader in the text, because the reader either has to identify with or reject characters. The traits given to characters are, therefore, indicative of the image of the reader in the text who is intended to reject certain characters and to identify with others. Characterization of Jesus in the Gospel of Mark, for example, in comparison with opponents of Jesus or with Peter, clearly illustrates the point. The image of Jesus as reliable in every aspect, over against the disciples, including Peter (cf. Vorster, 1987a), indicates that the image of Jesus and his point of view is to be accepted; the reader in the text is expected to reject the image of those who oppose and do not understand Jesus. Incomprehension is a trait of the disciples, but not of the reader in the text. The reader in the text is someone who understands and is willing to become a follower of Jesus the Crucified.

Both structure and characterization give insight into the image of the reader in the text, an image which the actual reader constructs from the codes in the text. In addition to the syntactic and semantic aspects, the pragmatic aspect of New Testament narratives has to be considered to help establish the image of readers in New Testament narratives.

2.5   The study of the reader in the text from the perspective of pragmatic function is especially appropriate since New Testament narratives were doubtless written to convince and persuade hearers and readers. In this respect special attention should be given to the sociolinguistic aspect of language and in particular of religious language. Language is a social interaction. That is why statements, sentences, paragraphs, etc. can have different functions in accordance with the context and participants of communication (cf. Chatman:162ff.; and Halliday, 1978:19f.). These include *expressive, exhortative, informative, social,* and *persuasive* pragmatic functions. Narrative commentary in the Gospel of Mark introduced by γάρ (cf. 1:16, 22; 2:15; 3:10, 21 and others) is normally informative, but one can make out a good case that the commands to be silent (cf. 1:44) or the lack of understanding of the disciples (cf. 4:13), on the other hand, have the function to persuade. These pragmatic functions obviously help determine our image of the reader in the text. Let us now turn to the reader in the text and intertextuality and then to a few remarks about the fact that New Testament narratives were intended to be read aloud to an audience of listeners.

2.6   The use of the Old Testament in narrative material, such as the Gospel of Matthew, points to the importance of intertextual competence of the reader in the text. In the Gospel of Matthew, the knowledge of the reader in the text concerning the Old Testament is used to bring about a new understanding of the story of Jesus and also to reinterpret the Old Testament. In this manner, an interaction takes place between the texts that are quoted and Matthew's text. The reader in the text is presented as a reader who knows about other texts and who can use his intertextual competence to interpret the story of Jesus in the light of a reinterpretation of other texts which are quoted (cf. Rabinowitz). The same happens in the other Gospels, in Acts, and also in the Revelation of John.

2.7   That New Testament narratives were not intended to be read silently but to be heard also influences the image of the reader in the text. The very structure of New Testament narratives is often determined by the fact that these narratives were intended to be read to audiences. Studies on redundancy in Matthew, like those of Burnett and Anderson, demonstrate one way that the intended reader/hearer prestructured the text of Matthew.

2.8   Rather than attempt a comprehensive treatment of readers in the text of New Testament narratives, this essay seeks to answer the question of whether and how the reader is present in these narratives and for what purpose one constructs the image of the reader in the text. It has become clear that there are many different clues in New Testament narratives from which the actual reader is able to construct an image of the reader in the text. I have indicated a few of these, but others are to be found. Culpepper, for example, has made valuable observations about the implied reader in the Gospel of John by asking what the narratee, whom he presents as the implied reader, knows and when he or she knows it. The same can obviously be done with the other narratives of the New Testament in order to establish images of readers in the text. As to the purpose of establishing the profile of the reader in the text, it has also become clear that this is related to the meaning the actual reader attributes to the text. It helps in the actualization of a specific interpretation or reading of a particular narrative.

3. In conclusion I would like to make a few remarks about the possibilities and the limitations of the theory concerning the reader in the text with regard to the interpretation of New Testament narratives.

3.1 The shift in emphasis from author to text to reader in the process of interpretation of the New Testament was a necessary and meaningful shift. It was necessary as the documents came to be interpreted as ancient documents within a theoretical framework of *communication* and not merely as artefacts to be interpreted in view of the intention of the author, their origin, or as texts without authors or readers. This has given rise to reflection about the nature of New Testament documents as textual messages between senders and receivers. Because of the focus on the text, much more attention had to be paid to the nature of texts and how they function. The rediscovery of the narrative character of a large number of New Testament writings and the application of insights of narratology, ancient and modern, and what that implies with regard to the reading of these texts, opened the possibility of rephrasing old questions and offering new answers within new theoretical frameworks. The outcome of the application of this interest in texts and readers is in many ways still open since much work still has to be done. By interpreting the New Testament from the perspective of the reader in the text, as has for instance been done in volume 31 of *Semeia*, additional possibilities and limitations will be discovered.

3.2 One of the most important limitations is the fact that there is, to my mind, no possibility of using the reader in the text to go directly through the text to the flesh-and-blood original readers. The fact that the New Testament consists of texts without their original contexts of communication need not be a problem in connection with New Testament narratives and communication or in connection with the phenomenon of the reader in the text. It is, however, remarkable how scholars attempt to use the notion of the reader in New Testament texts to move from this reader to the actual first-century readers. Petersen (1984:39–40), among others, to my mind overstresses the potential of the reader in the text by relating the implied reader to "extratextual communicants, to people who belong to the text's historical, interpretive context." In spite of Culpepper's awareness that a characterization of the narratee (as implied reader) can only be used in a debate over the actual, historical audience on the assumption that the narratee is identical to the actual reader, he (206-37) nevertheless establishes a profile of the narratee within the framework of this debate. To my mind one should avoid the temptation to infer historical information about the actual readers from the reader in the text unless it can be confirmed by other extratextual data. It is theoretically impossible to make inferences from the reader in the text about the actual readers of first-century Christian narratives except in terms of broad generalities. This is not to deny the important principle of historical criticism that a text is evidence for the time in which it was written. I only wish to stress the fact that the profile of a reader in the text is constructed in the first place to enable the reader to attribute meaning to a text, and that it is an intratextual construct. In this respect New Testament narratives are similar to other narratives.

3.3   Another limitation is the fact that the reader in the text is something which has to be constructed, an image of an imaginary reader. It is here that the interpreter comes into the picture and the role of the reader becomes a matter of either the reader controlling the text or the reader being controlled by the text. It is furthermore true that it is impossible to escape the hermeneutic circle. "I construct the images of the implied reader gradually as I read a work, and then use the images I have constructed to validate my reading" (Suleiman:11).

WORKS CONSULTED

Anderson, Janice C.
    1985   "Double and Triple Stories, The Implied Reader, and Redundancy in Matthew." *Semeia* 37:71-89.

Aune, David E.
    1979   "The Apocalypse of John and the Problem of Genre." *Semeia* 36:65-96.

Bal, Mieke, ed.
    1979   *Mensen van Papier: Over Personages in de Literatuur*. Assen: Van Gorcum.

Booth, Wayne C.
1983   *The Rhetoric of Fiction.* 2nd ed. Chicago: University of Chicago Press.

Brink, André P.
1987   *Vertelkunde: 'n Inleiding tot die Lees van Verhalende Tekste.* Pretoria: Academica.

Burnett, Fred W.
1985   "Prolegomenon to Reading Matthew's Eschatological Discourse: Redundancy and the Education of the Reader in Matthew." *Semeia* 31:91–109.

Chatman, Seymour
1978   *Story and Discourse: Narrative Structure in Fiction and Film.* Ithaca: Cornell University Press.

Culpepper, R. Alan
1983   *Anatomy of the Fourth Gospel: A Study in Literary Design.* Philadelphia: Fortress.

Eagleton, Terry T.
1983   *Literary Theory: An Introduction.* Oxford: Basil Blackwell.

Eco, Umberto
1979   *The Role of the Reader: Explorations in the Semantics of Texts.* Bloomington: Indiana University Press.

Fokkema, Douwe W. and Elrud Kunne-Ibsch
1977   *Theories of Literature in the Twentieth Century: Structuralism, Marxism, Aesthetics of Reception, Semiotics.* London: Hurst.

Fowler, Robert M.
1981   *Loaves of Fishes: The Function of the Feeding Stories in the Gospel of Mark.* SBLDS 54. Chico: Scholars Press.
1985   "Who Is 'the Reader' in Reader-Response Criticism?" *Semeia* 31:5–23.

Genette, Gerard
1980   *Narrative Discourse.* Trans. J. E. Lewin. Oxford: Basil Blackwell.

Halliday, Michael A.K.
  1978   *Language as Social Semiotic: The Social Interpretation of Language and Meaning.* Arnold.

Holub, Robert C.
  1984   *Reception Theory: A Critical Introduction.* London: Methuen.

Iser, Wolfgang
  1974   *The Implied Reader: Patterns of Communication in Prose Fiction from Bunyan to Beckett.* Baltimore: Johns Hopkins University Press.
  1978   *The Act of Reading: A Theory of Aesthetic Response.* Routledge and Kegan Paul.

Kingsbury, Jack D.
  1986   *Matthew as Story.* Philadelphia: Fortress.

Koopman-Thurlings, Marika
  1984/85   "Tekstinterpretatie en Open Plek: Over de Bruikbaarheid van Isers 'Leerstellen'". *Spektator: Tijdschrift voor Neerlandstiek* 14/6:398–411.

Kurz, William S.
  1987   "Narrative Approaches to Luke-Acts." *Biblica* 68:195–220.

Magness, J. Lee
  1986   *Sense and Absence: Structure and Suspension in the Ending of Mark's Gospel.* Atlanta: Scholars Press.

Moule, Charles F.D.
  1965   *The Gospel According to Mark.* Cambridge: Cambridge University Press.

Petersen, Norman R.
  1980   "When is the End not the End? Literary Reflections on the Ending of Mark's Narrative." *Int* 34 151–66.
  1984   "The Reader in the Gospel." *Neotestamentica* 18:38–51.

Rabinowitz, Peter J.
  1980   "What's Hecuba to Us? The Audience's Experience of Literary Borrowing." Pp. 241–63 in Susan R. Suleiman and Inge Crosman.

Riffaterre, Michael
  1983   *Text Production.* New York: Columbia University Press.

Rimmon-Kenan, Shlomith
    1983   *Narrative Fiction: Comtemporary Poetics*. London: Methuen.

Ruthrof, Horst
    1981   *The Reader's Construction of Narrative*. Routledge and Kegan Paul.

Segers, Rien T.
    1980   *Het Lezen van Literatuur: Een Inleiding tot een Nieuwe Literatuurbenadering*. Baarn: Ambo.

Sternberg, Meir
    1986   *The Poetics of Biblical Narrative: Ideological Literature and the Drama of Reading*. Bloomington: Indiana University Press.

Suleiman, Susan R.
    1980   "Introduction: Varieties of Audience-Oriented Criticism." Pp. 3–45 in Susan R. Suleiman and Inge Crosman.

Suleiman, Susan R. and Inge Crosman, eds.
    1980   *The Reader in the Text: Essays on Audience and Interpretation*. Princeton: Princeton University Press.

Van Aarde, Andries G.
    1982   "God met Ons: Die Teologiese Perspektief van die Matteusevangelie." DTh Thesis, University of Pretoria.

Van Luxemburg, Jan, Mieke Bal, and Willem Weststeijn
    1982   *Inleiding in de Literatuurwetenschap*. 2nd ed. Muiderberg: Couthino.

Vorster, Willem S.
    1984   "Der Ort der Gattung Evangelium in der Literaturgeschichte." *VuF* 29:2–25.
    1987a   "Characterisation of Peter in the Gospel of Mark." *Neotestamentica* 21:57–76.
    1987b   "Literary Reflections on Mark 13: 5–37: A Narrated Speech of Jesus." *Neotestamentica* 21:91–112.
    1988   "'Genre' and the Revelation of John: A Study in Text, Context and Intertext." *Neotestamentica* 22:103–23.

IS THERE AN ENCODED READER FALLACY?

Wilhelm Wuellner
Pacific School of Religion

ABSTRACT

Against the prevailing trend of seeing the reading experience shaped solely by indigenous textual qualities as defined by linguistic and literary theory, six issues are singled out for consideration of a more contextual approach which is more sensitive to the ideological, religious, and material factors informing both theory and practice of reading religiously.

0. *Introduction*

By the fallacy of the encoded reader I mean the misleading claims made for interpretation or reading of texts as determined by the autonomy of the text and its encoded reader. I do not dispute the encoded reader as a literary theory. I do dispute the value of the theory for reading and interpretation, especially do I challenge claims which actually denigrate reading itself.

The significances for biblical studies of literary theory in general is a matter which deserves attention. For Sternberg (1985:57), the producers and consumers of literary theory ought to be, as he thinks they will be, attracted by the Bible; but he balances the contributions, which producers and consumers of literary theory can make to the study of the Bible, by the returns they will receive in exchange.

J. Hillis Miller's claim that "reading is always theoretical" (289) sheds light on the discussion of literary theory/-ies of the encoded or implied reader as applied to biblical studies. He understands by theory "the displacement in literary studies from a focus on the meaning of texts to a focus on the way meaning is conveyed" (283). McKnight's study of *The Bible and the Reader* (1985) illustrates Miller's point. But what can account for the fact that in the United States as well as in Europe and in South Africa critical theory dominates in literary studies, hence also in religious, and specifically biblical exegetical, studies? Miller offers several reasons, but the one which interests me most is his claim that "the triumph of theory in American literary studies...reflects an evident incommensurability between the sign system and its material base." Or, more provocatively put, "the triumph of theory is the resistance to reading" (288). By this Miller means to say that "theory erases the particularity of the unique act of reading....[and that]...even the most vigilant and theoretically enlightened reading [like the encoded reader-theory guided reading] is the resistance to [the particularity of the unique act of] reading" (289).

With these considerations in mind, I propose six issues for discussion about the role of the encoded reader (=the implied reader, or the ideal reader[1]) in the interpretation of the New Testament.

1. *The Encoded Reader Theory and the Biblical Exegete*

1.1   The first issue to be raised is the claim that the encoded reader determines the interpretation of both the parts of texts and texts as a whole.

This raises, in turn, the following question: How can such a heuristic device "determine," in and of itself, the appropriate or adequate interpretation of specific texts?

In answer to this question I submit two considerations. (1) No theory of literature, least any of the formalist, structuralist variety (linguistic, sociological, or semiotic), can account for what makes an appropriate interpretation, given the particularity of the unique act of reading, or, what Fowler (18–21) calls "reading as a temporal experience." Mitchell (1–10) challenges "the general assumption [held by literary critics and biblical exegetes alike] that everyone has a theory that governs his or her practice...[hence] the only issue is whether one is self-conscious about that theory." Along with others advocating "the new pragmatism" in literary studies, Mitchell pleads for replacing the priority of theory by some interaction of theory and practice. This point we will explore further below.

(2) Too much and one-sided energy continues to be expended on the theory of general language and text communication. There is a difference between a theory of the encoded reader/audience in language and literature generally, and a theory of the encoded reader in the New Testament, whether of New Testament documents individually, or of "texts as a whole" in terms of the canon. What the "shades of difference" are has been spelled out in several essays devoted to "the theological text" or "religion as texture."[2] Sternberg (1985: 48–56) even claims to dis-

cern a difference in the encoded reader between the Old and the New Testament.

1.2   The second issue to be raised is that, while there is an encoded reader in every text, real readers, as critical interpreters or as theorists of reading, have different and varying perceptions of this heuristic device of the encoded reader and its functions.

The question arises: Why does the one heuristic device invite, or make possible, indeed necessitate "different semantic functions"? Or, in Sternberg's words, why does a biblical narrative or strategy seldom proceed "along the theoretically expected grooves" (1985:57), which, I presume, includes the groove of the encoded reader?

With reference to Chatman's and Halliday's works on "language [as] a social interaction," Vorster offers three important answers to this question. One answer is said to be found in "the context," another in the "participants of communication," and a third in "the effect of language in use." I would like to elaborate and qualify these answers with reference to Mikhail Bakhtin's work which is currently attracting renewed attention in scholarly circles devoted to theories of reading. In what follows I am paraphrasing Terry Eagleton (117–18).

All signs, whether linguistically, literarily, or semiotically defined, should be viewed less as a fixed unit (like a signal) than as an active component of speech, or text, or sign, modified and transformed in meaning by the variable social tones, valuations, and connotations it condenses within itself in specific social conditions.

Since such valuations and connotations are constantly shifting, and since the "linguistic community," even or especially as religious community, is in fact a *heterogeneous* society composed of conflicting interests of various kinds, the sign and its encoded reader/audience/viewer is for Bakhtin less a neutral element in a given structure than a focus of struggle and contradiction. It is not simply a matter of asking "what the sign means" or what its encoded reader is, but of investigating its varied history. Conflicting social groups, classes, individuals, and discourses (in the case of the Bible we also have the ideologically charged exegetes and commentators) have sought to appropriate the literature with its encoded reader and imbue it with their own meanings. A good current example is the feminist appropriation.[3]

Language, for Bakhtin, is a field of ideological contention (even more so when it comes to *religious* language), and not a monolithic system, whether linguistic or semantic; indeed, signs, or what Miller (289) calls the material base or materiality of texts ("the whole region of what presumably exists outside language"), are the very material medium of ideology, since without them no values or ideas could exist, except as they exist (so Eagleton) in the minds of those devoted to traditional metaphysics and modern idealism.

Bakhtin did respect what might be called the "relative autonomy" of language or literature. He acknowledged the fact that neither language nor literature can be reduced to a mere reflex of social interests. (And I may add that neither can rhetoric be conceived simply as a branch of the social sciences.) Bakhtin insisted, nevertheless, that there was no language, no text, not even or particularly a religious text, which was not caught up in definite social relationships, and that these social relationships were in turn part of broader political, ideological, and economic systems (Eagleton: 118).[4]

What is said here of the reading and interpretation of texts is equally applicable to the reading and interpretation of texts about texts, or texts of literary theory. Bakhtin's judgment that most existing literary theory (of his day) could be shown to be utterly inadequate in its application to a new literary genre, the novel, applies to the inadequacy of contemporary literary theory in its application to the Bible as inspired, which is to say as ideological literature (Sternberg, 1985:84–128, 482–515). We will return to this point in the last of the six issues under discussion.

1.3   The third issue to be raised is the claim that the application of insights of narratology, and of theories of argumentation and of persuasion, is said to open up new possibilities for reading/interpreting texts in general, and the Bible in particular. McKnight's book on *The Bible and the Reader* further illustrates this point.

But the question arises: Why is the outcome of this application "in many ways still open"? Vorster offers two reasons, to which I want to add the following two considerations, followed by a third point.

(1) Vorster's first reason, "much work still has to be done," is, of course, true in one sense. For there is always much more to be done, but the question is: What more is to be done—more theory, more elaborate "beautiful" theories (Bruss)? To account for *"every* (emphasis mine) aspect of encoding" by which the reader becomes apparent is a scientist's utopian goal in setting about to discover "the perfect embodiment of meaning in the formal qualities of texts" (Mitchell:5). On the "utopian perspective" of theory in the interpretation of texts, Mitchell (7) notes:

> Theory is monotheistic, in love with simplicity, scope, and coherence. It aspires to explain the many in terms of the one, and the greater the gap between the unitary simplicity of theory and the infinite multiplicity of things in its domain, the more powerful the theory. Theory is thus to thought what power is to politics….But theory is also the critique of ideol-

ogy, the expression of intellectual alienation, self-criticism, and reflection on the origins of theory.

While there are no "foolproof methods to ascertaining meaning" in the reading of texts, least of all in reading religious texts, we need not swing to the other extreme of advocating "rescue from the illegitimate sovereignty of theory." While distinctions, such as those between intra-, inter-, and extra-textual readers, arise not from theory, but "arise in practice, in ordinary usage, and are developed into theories," yet such theories about reading and readers, like all theories, "are doomed to 'fail' at one point or another—'fail' in the sense of not achieving the goal of complete mastery..." (Mitchell:9).

(2) Vorster's second reason for the openness "in many ways" of narratology's application to New Testament interpretation is the ongoing controversies among narratologists. Take the example of the narrative genre which is "very important" for Vorster for the encoded reader in New Testament texts.

On the level of narrative characters and the narrator, Chatman argues for a clear distinction to be drawn between the character in the *story*, with *its* encoded reader, and the narrator in the *discourse*, with *its* encoded reader. Chatman sees mounting confusion in our interpretation and reading, if we ignore this distinction. How the encoded reader functions in the presentation of the story, which is to say how it functions on the diegetic level, should be distinguished, Chatman says, from the encoded reader's function on the authorial level, in the narrator's presentation of the discourse. The narrator's "judgmental commentary...should not be confused with the characters' seeing, thinking and judging events and existents in the story-world from an observational post within that world."

The function of the encoded reader in the narrator's focalization, especially in "omniscient narration" (Sternberg, 1985:84–128) which is so all important in biblical literature, is of particular interest to biblical exegetes, especially when it comes to the seemingly "non-focalizing" narrator with the power of the "God's-eye" view.

Chatman proposes different terms to communicate the "point of view" of the *character*, for which Chatman proposes the term "filter" for views *in*ternal to the story, as opposed to the "point of view" of the *narrator*, for which Chatman proposes the term "slant" for views *ex*ternal to the story. The *in*ternal views are "sights" for the encoded reader, with access to the mind of any character; the *ex*ternal "views" are not "sights" but offer "knowledge" for the encoded reader, with access to information which no character has.

(3) A third consideration for the applicability of the encoded reader theory to New Testament interpretation is the theory's extension beyond narrative argumentation to include also the large area of didactic discourse which we find in the epistolary literature of the New Testament. While progress has been made in more sophisticated analysis and interpretation of didactic discourse (Patte:85–129; Melançon), the encoded reader issue has been treated only in terms of the typology of readers (for 1 Corinthians, see Wuellner:54–60).

1.4   The fourth issue is contained in the claim that the encoded reader has *to be* constructed by the real reader, by the interpreter.

The leading question is: Why must the extratextual reader inevitably come into the picture? Why is it impossible to discuss, even theoretically, the encoded reader without the extratextual reader/interpreter having to construct "an image of an imaginary reader"? Why the belated concern for "the limitations of the theory concerning the reader in the text" which Vorster mentions?

One answer can be found in Bruner's observation (37) that, no matter how great the literary power of a given text, including its encoded reader, "the actual text needs the subjectivity that makes it possible [indeed necessary] for a reader to create a world of his [or her!] own...the writer's greatest gift to a reader is to help him [or her!] to become a writer."

The alternative is misleading in Vorster's sentence which says "either the reader [is] controlling the text or the reader [is] being controlled by the text." It is not an Either/Or, but a Both/And at best, or a Neither/Nor at worst.

1.5   In the fifth issue I want to return to a point raised earlier. The theory of the encoded reader, or "the reader in the text," raises the question: What text? Even if we focus our discussion only on the New Testament, rather than on the canon of Old and New Testaments, there is a difference in the perception of the encoded reader, and even in the conception of the theory of the encoded reader, if we approach the text, or if the text is presented to us (by such "interpretive communities" as the religious community, or the academic guild, or the cultural artistic community, etc.) in one of the following "materialities":

(1) The whole Bible, or the whole New Testament, as "sacred" canon. The authority which generated and maintains a canon also and thereby created and maintains an encoded reader in the canon as a whole. Neusner (147–59) has analyzed the difference between (a) those who use the notion of intertextuality in support of the claim that in a canon, as "a community of texts," all texts possess intrinsic traits of

order, cogency, and unity; and (b) those who, while acknowledging the relative autonomy of texts, see the unity of the canon generated and maintained by what Neusner calls the "textual community." The encoded reader in the canon is inevitably defined by the religious community/ies using the canon (Sanders).

(2) The Bible as a collection of individual books, with each book constituting an allegedly autonomous text. Here the encoded reader is determined by historical and literary scholarship's perceptions of the nature and purpose of each document. Doctrinal or historical criteria are cited by members of the academic guild of biblical scholars in their identification of the encoded reader, rather than what Frye calls "imaginative criteria." The latter alone can bring "this huge, sprawling, tactless book" into a unit determined by the common denominator of an encoded reader which is Frye's "central thesis of the role of the reader" (xviii and xxii).

(3) The Bible as manuscript and in print. The textual encoded reader, whether as canon or as individual text encoded reader, is seen linked with the text's "materiality," whether that of the producers' text or the consumers' text. These materialities range from the earliest manuscripts, to the later printed texts. Producing and consuming those material texts (what Bruner calls "the actual text") gets further textually encoded by interpretive devices ranging from punctuation and paragraphing to iconographic "illustrations," let alone various annotations, whether of the *lectio divina*-tradition, or of the academic school tradition of grammar, logic, and rhetoric (Evans, 1980, 1984).

(4) The Bible in cassette and disk. Finally, what happens to the encoded reader in texts of what Ong calls the "secondary orality type" produced by "technologizing the Word" in terms of audio cassettes and video cassettes, computer and compact disks? Neither the interpreter of the encoded reader, nor the theorist about the encoded reader and its function, can afford to ignore the materialities of the text under consideration.

The importance of the "materiality" of the text, literary or oral, for the theory of the encoded reader and its application, has only recently been recognized (Ong; Engler; Winquist). Miller (287) even sees "a frontier topic in literary studies today" in the concern for "the relation between material base and ideological superstructure."

1.6   A final issue for consideration is raised by the question: What difference does it make, if any, when "belief" or "systems of conviction" are taken into account in the theory of the encoded reader and its application? Two aspects of this question call for elaboration.

(1) Is the distinction between secular and religious reader, between secular and religious belief, justifiable when it comes to the interpretation of literature, both narrative and didactic?

Some part of me wants to say that such distinction is not justifiable, and I am even prepared to argue against such a distinction. But when all is said and done (see also the following point), I must say that it is justifiable. But aren't all values, truths, convictions, and ideologies categorically the same? Yes and no, as for instance the collected essays on *Midrash and Literature* show (Hartman and Budick). All literature (narrative, didactic, poetic, or any other), "viewed as the art of communicating with readers" (in the Bible it is the art of imposing religious worlds), does two things simultaneously: "depend on and impose what I called 'beliefs' and 'norms,' what modern jargon calls 'values,' what Bakhtin and other continental critics call 'ideology'" (Booth:417–19; cf. Bogdan).

Closely related to belief, norm, value, and ideology in the producing and consuming of texts are two areas of increasing importance to the literary critic, as well as the theorist of literature. One is the area of narrative or argumentative *modality*: the modals of obligation and necessity, of ability and possibility, of epistemic possibility and contingency, of volition and prediction (Coates; Fleischman; Palmer; White). The other area is that of indexical expressions, or *deixis*, as one of the means by which the construction and reconstruction of the encoded reader are achieved (Rauh; Sternberg, 1983; Bates; Lyons, 1984).

(2) Absent from Vorster's theoretical considerations on the encoded reader is the distinction, so important to biblical literature, between literal and figurative, carnal and spiritual, plain and plenary. In the background of such distinctions lurks the notorious patristic and medieval distinction between four or more senses of Scripture, and with them four or more encoded readers. Jameson (31) found that "the system of the four levels or senses is particularly suggestive in the solution it provides for an interpretive dilemma which in a privatized world we must live far more intensely than did its Alexandrian and medieval recipients: namely [the] incommensurability...between the private and the public, the psychological and the social, the poetic and the political."

The encoded reader in the Bible as religious literature is as varied, and hierarchically varied, as is the divine Torah, or the Christ Logos, in all parts, ranging from Israel and Christianity, to humanity at large, and finally to all parts of the cosmos (Burke:194–333).

2. Conclusion

Vorster sees mostly promising possibilities and few limitations in the study of the encoded reader and the application of this and related theories to the interpretation of the New Testament. By contrast, I see growing liability in this orientation and approach. Indeed, I see it as at least potential fallacy.

I see greatly reduced and modified possibilities for the study of the intratextual reader, especially if continued in isolation from other and new theories of reading. I am thinking here of what Miller sees as "the future of literary studies [which] depends on maintaining and developing that rhetorical reading which today is most commonly called 'deconstruction'" (289). I am also thinking of theories developed by Genette's (1982) explorations beyond intertextuality into transtextuality (understood as the relationship of a text to other texts) and especially into hypertextuality (understood as one text grafted on another, e.g. as the New Testament is grafted on the Old, or some of the Gospels grafted on others).

I also see greatly increased limitations, especially if (1) the different materialities of actual texts, and (2) the special character of biblical texts as "inspired" or "ideological" remain excluded from theoretical considerations. Such exclusion may be due to an exclusive alliance with theories and methods appropriate to general language communication and to modern fictional literature. All kinds of exchanges between "Athens" and "Jerusalem" are to be encouraged, because of "the great code." But the theologically engaged and engaging exegesis is more than just an extension of currently acceptable practices of literary criticism and their related literary theories. As exegetes of the Scriptures we are also the stewards of the mystery of the divine word to the "insiders," that is our religious communities, but also, and no less so, to the "outsiders," that is our society and culture.

The very theories we (in the First World, or members of a patriarchal culture) promote about textually encoded readers as heuristic devices for the interpretation of normative texts can consciously or unconsciously perpetuate the cultural and sexual imperialism which, at best, we readily disavow, or, at worst, readily disregard. If "the triumph of theory" in recent literary and exegetical studies makes us aware of, and face these limitations and liabilities, then its assets are also apparent, but not otherwise.

NOTES

[1] For definitions of these terms of recent literary theory, see Fowler:5–23.

[2] See in Winquist (5–64) the essays by Robert P. Scharlemann, Mark C. Taylor, Carl Raschke, and David Miller. Out of a methodologically more coherent frame a similar plea is being made by a group of South African scholars, Johan Visagie, Christo Saayman, Johan Oosthuizen, Andries Snyman, in their collaborative work entitled *The Beginning of the Word: Aspects of a Theory of Archaeological Discourse*. Bloemfontein: University of the Orange Free State, 1987 (unpublished)

[3] Mieke Bal, *Lethal Love: Feminist Literary Readings of Biblical Love Stories* (Bloomington: Indiana University Press, 1987); Adela Yarbro Collins (ed), *Feminist Perspectives on Biblical Scholarship* (Decatur: Scholars Press, 1985); Jean C. Lambert, "An 'F Factor'? The New Testament in some white, feminist Christian theological construction," *Journal of Feminist Studies in Religion* 1 (1985) 93–113. For an appreciation of Bakhtin's position relative to feminist criticism, see Wayne Booth, "Freedom of Interpretation: Bakhtin and the Challenge of Feminist Criticism." *Critical Inquiry* 9 (1982) 45–76; see also Booth's "Introduction" to Bakhtin's *Problems of Dostoevsky's Poetics* THL 8 (Minneapolis: University of Minnesota Press, 1984) xiii–xxvii.

[4] See also Ricoeur (xix–xx) on his notion of ideology as the symbolic structure of action and the symbolic mediation which is constitutive of social existence. Ideology is "the rhetoric of basic communication"; it is an expression of "the social imagination." Bruner (34–35) speaks of "the strategy and repertoire which *readers* bring to bear" (emphasis mine). It is, of course, a common-place in linguistics to recognize "the context" as that which makes language and reading behavior "a culture-dependent activity" (Lyons, 1981:217–19) which is related to Grice's notion of language-behavior as cooperative interaction, which Searle (viii) extends when he speaks of "the fact that language is essentially a social phenomenon and that the forms of Intentionality underlying language are social forms." See also Meyer (105–140, ET:85–135).

WORKS CONSULTED

Adams, Hazard and Leroy Searle, eds.
    1986   *Critical Theory Since 1965*. Gainesville: Florida State University Press.

Bates, E.
    1976   *Language and Context: The Acquisition of Pragmatics*. New York: Academy Press.

Bogdan, Radu J., ed.
   1986   *Belief, Form, Content, and Function.* Oxford University Press.

Booth, Wayne
   1983   *The Rhetoric of Fiction.* 2nd rev. ed. Chicago: University of Chicago Press.

Bruner, Jerome
   1986   *Actual Minds, Possible Worlds.* Cambridge, MA: Harvard University Press.

Bruss, E.
   1982   *Beautiful Theories. The Spectacle of Discourse in Contemporary Criticism.* Baltimore: Johns Hopkins University Press.

Burke, Kenneth
   1950   *A Rhetoric of Motives.* Berkeley: University of California Press.

Chatman, Seymour
   1986   "Characters and Narrators: Filter, Center, Slant, and Interest-Focus," *Poetics Today* 7:189–204.

Coates, Jennifer
   1983   *The Semantics of the Modal Auxiliaries.* Bechenham: Croom Helm.

Detweiler, Robert, ed.
   1985   *Reader Response Approaches to Biblical and Secular Texts.* Semeia 31. Decatur, GA: Scholars Press.

Eagleton, Terry
   1983   *Literary Theory. An Introduction.* Minneapolis: University of Minnesota Press.

Engler, B.
   1982   *Reading and Listening.* Bern: Francke.

Evans, G.R.
   1980   *Old Arts and New Theology. The Beginnings of Theology as an Academic Discipline.* Oxford: Clarendon.
   1984   *The Language and Logic of the Bible: The Earlier Middle Ages.* London/New York: Cambridge University Press.

Fleischman, Suzanne
    1982   *The Future in Thought and Language*. New York: Cambridge University Press.

Fowler, Robert M.
    1985   "Who Is 'The Reader' in Reader Response Criticism," *Semeia* 31:5–23.

Frye, Northrop
    1981   *The Great Code. The Bible and Literature*. New York/London: Harcourt Brace Jovanovich.

Genette, Gerard
    1982   *Palimpsestes*. Paris: Seuil.

Hartman, Geoffrey H. and Sanford Budick, eds.
    1986   *Midrash and Literature*. New Haven/London: Yale University Press.

Jameson, Fredric
    1981   *The Political Unconscious. Narrative as a Socially Symbolic Act*. Ithaca, N.Y.: Cornell University Press.

Knapp, Steven and Walter B. Michaels
    1985   "Against Theory," Pp. 11–30 in Mitchell.

Lyons, John
    1981   *Language, Meaning and Context*. Bungay: Chaucer.
    1984   "Deixis and subjectivity: loquor, ergo sum?" In *Place and Action*. Ed. R. J. Jarvella and W. Kelin. New York: Wiley.

McKnight, Edgar V.
    1985   *The Bible and the Reader. An Introduction to Literary Criticism*. Philadelphia: Fortress.

Melançon, Joseph
    1983   *The Semantics of Didactic Discourse*. Toronto Semiotic Circle Monograph 2. Toronto, Canada.

Meyer, Michel
    1982   *Logique, langage et argumentation*. Paris: Hachette. ET: *From Logic to Rhetoric* (1986).

Miller, J. Hillis
    1987   "The Triumph of Theory, the Resistance to Reading, and the Question of the Material Base," *PMLA* 103:281–91, (MLA Presidential Address 1986).

Mitchell, W. J. T., ed.
    1985   *Against Theory. Literary Studies and the New Pragmatism.* Chicago: University of Chicago Press.

Neusner, Jacob
    1987   *Canon and Connection: Intertextuality in Judaism.* University of America Press.

Ong, Walter J.
    1982   *Orality and Literacy.* London: Methuen.

Palmer, F. R.
    1986   *Mood and Modality.* Cambridge Textbooks in Linguistics. Cambridge University Press.

Patte, Daniel
    1983   "Method for a Structural Exegesis of Didactic Discourses. Analysis of 1 Thessalonians," *Semeia* 26. Chico, CA: Scholars Press.

Rauh, Gisa, ed.
    1983   *Essays on Deixis.* Tübingen: Narr.

Ricoeur, Paul
    1986   *Lectures on Ideology and Utopia.* Ed. George H. Taylor. New York: Columbia University Press.

Sanders, James A.
    1987   *From Sacred Story to Sacred Text. Canon as Paradigm.* Philadelphia: Fortress.

Searle, John R.
    1983   *Intentionality.* Cambridge University Press.

Sternberg, Meir
    1983   "Deictic Sequence: World, Language and Convention." Pp. 277–316 in Rauh.
    1985   *The Poetics of Biblical Narrative. Ideological Literature and the Drama of Reading.* Bloomington: Indiana University Press.

White, Alan R.
1975   *Modal Thinking*. Oxford: Blackwell.

Winquist, Charles E., ed.
1987   *Text and Textuality*. Semeia 40. Decatur, GA: Scholars Press.

Wuellner, Wilhelm
1986   "Paul as Pastor. The Function of Rhetorical Questions in first Corinthians." Pp. 49–77 in *L'Apôtre Paul. Personalité, Style et Conception du Ministère*. Ed. A. Vanhoye. BETL 73. Leuven University Press, 1986.

THE ROLES OF THE READERS
OR THE MYTH OF *THE* READER

Wolfgang Schenk
Eppstein, West Germany

ABSTRACT

Contemporary reception theory is used to make distinctions between the addressee and reader, on the one hand, and the research-scholar and reader, on the other hand. Caution is also directed against the confusion of production-aesthetics and reception-aesthetics in the field of New Testament scholarship. Implications are drawn for: a strict categorization of the canon of the New Testament as a phenomenon of reception, criticism of the categories of effect-/influence-history (*Wirkungsgeschichte*), and an aesthetics-of-reception critique of the inadequate generalizations of tradition-history.*

A. *The Confusion between Formulation of the Question and Method*

The interpretation of texts suffers from confusion between the concepts of formulation of the question (*Fragstellung*) and method. The alternatives "text-oriented" and "reader-oriented," for example, are attempts to find out different things by alternative formulations of the question; therefore, they do not stand in opposition or rivalry nor is there any possibility or necessity of mediation.[1] The warning still remains valid:

> The use of the notion "method" is unacceptably confused today; the human sciences are inclined to distinguish all and everything with this term and to speak of different "methods" where only different "formulations of the question" is meant. If it is the case that one literary critic claims that the "style" of a work must be examined, while a second requires a sociological analysis of the work, and yet a third insists on the study of the literary-historical connections, then, obviously, it is a matter of deviate hy-

potheses concerning the relevance of different "formulations of the questions." It would be an evident misuse of language to speak of different "methods," because "method" means "procedure," whereas the preference for different "formulations of the question" says nothing about a procedure. Only within the same "formulation of the question" is an argument over the best "method" of solving a problem meaningful; indeed, different "formulations of the question" may involve the same basic "method." (Titzmann:381)[2]

B.   *Different Names: Addressee vs. Reader*

1.   The extra- (better: trans-)textual (real/actual) author/sender has encoded himself or herself in the text.

1.1   If the category "encoded" is used for the sender as well as for the addressee in a generalizing and unifying way, then we encounter the danger that the essential difference between the two will not become clear and that a non-existing equivalence will be imagined. For the addressee also encoded by the sender corresponds only to the self-encoding sender. The same precision is necessary with the oppositions "implied/abstract sender" vs. "addressee," because even they are not homogeneous and equivalent but are defined in an aesthetics-of-production fashion.

2.   Insofar as the difference of level within the text, the question arises whether the differentiation "encoded" (= explicit) vs. implicit (= abstract) is adequate for purposes of descriptive. The question arises since the author encodes both the explicit (if occasion arises) as well as the implicit. The "code" is the more comprehensive idea, and "explicit" and/or "implicit" are sub-categories of the encoding only. The difference lies only in the way by which this encoding is accomplished.

2.1.   The explicitly-self-encoding sender is obviously present in the explicitly used morphemes of the first person. The addressee, even from the explicitly encoded sender, is obviously present in the explicitly used morphemes in the second person of the address (singular and/or plural), the verb, and/or names as in corresponding renominalizations and pronominalizations.

2.2.   The addressee (not explicit but implicit reader), implicitly encoded by the sender, also corresponds to the implicitly self encoding sender (not the explicit but the implicit "I"); any definition of the "implied" as "not-encoded" is unacceptable because it is misleading. The textsignals in question are difficult to determine because they consist mostly of connotations and slots in empty positions.

2.2.1. In order to avoid confusion, the proposed triadic differentiation of "author-addressee-reader" seems to be helpful (Naumann, 1971; 1973). The "addressee," as textinternal reader, is defined as an "anticipation of the future reader" in the work itself and corresponds to the "implied reader" of Iser (cf. Grimm:41, 275f. n.109).

2.2.2. A "narrator," implicitly self-encoding, does not constitute a third level but is a subcategory of the second subcategory. In the light of this sub-category of a second order, the suspicion arises whether—under the pressure of system only—the complementary function of an implicit addressee of narrative as a specific category could or would be related formally to such an implicitly encoded sender as narrator.

2.2.3. In addition to the signals noted to this point, the function of the addressee can be present in the narrative by narrated figures, "if they serve the function of a mouthpiece, thus being bearer of meanings with which the author identifies himself" and to which identification the author wants to lead his addressees (Grimm:40). Such is the case in the Gospels (with the pretension to see and to speak from the perspective of God and not men; Mark 1:22–27; 8:33; 11:30).

2.2.4. With New Testament writings, we are not concerned with "aesthetic" or "fictional" texts, because within these texts "polyvalency" or "indeterminacy," "scope of interpretation," or "ambiguity" are not clear factors. The empiricist is able to make these factors clear as "criteria for distinction between aesthetic (especially fictional) and tendentiously disambiguous, expository texts (Grimm:45; cf. 34 with Gröben, 1972). "Fictional texts" are constituted by a "pseudo-referential use of language" (Stierle, 1975:362; 1977; Gumbrecht, in agreement with Grimm:280f. n. 149). New Testament texts must be "ascribed disambiguously to the category of non-fictional texts" (Fischer:258). If today (in developments following the Enlightenment) for many readers "they seem to be fictive texts" or are "declared as such" (Fischer:269), then this is not the result of the nature of these texts and their claims (especially in the Gospels the scheme of "fulfillment" of "prediction" makes an expositional claim), but only the result of the active role of reading recipients who take the role of fictional communicators towards these texts, thus "valuing" them in this way (but not just "interpreting" them), thereby establishing a "fictionalization" and by this making a special "judgment" (Gumbrecht:198). This is obviously a procedure of the aesthetics of reception.

3. The use of the category "reader" for text-internal as well as text-external factors is a source of further confusion, especially if we speak in the singular of "the" role of "the" reader.

3.1. Since reading is an action, it is appropriate to limit the use of the term to the text-external reception. This involves decoding procedures, following encoding procedures, and such procedures are correctly defined as re-active processes. This understanding excludes such attractive but misleading formulations as "the reader creates/makes the sense" (Fish, 1970; 1976; Suleiman and Crosman); it is only possible to say "re-creates" (cf. Iser's, 1976:55–60 criticism of Fish's 1971 concept of the "informed reader" and the uselessness of textreceptional processes), and this only with the possession of a given code competence. This means: "The 'ideal receiver' is a reader who is governed by the same code in which the work is constituted and who reconstructs this code. To this extent the reader is nothing other than the author who is transformed into the role of his own hearer" (Grimm:37).

3.1.1. In terms of anthropological ontology this means: The "objectived mind" within the text is the product of a "personal/subjective mind" (sender) for another "subjective mind" (addressee) on the basis of the "objective mind" (code-system).[3] The failure to bear in mind that the "code" is the decisive factor leads to oversimplified generalizations concerning relationships which become false conclusions, an example being the assertion of a convergence between "text" and "reception."

3.2. If the "intended reader" is defined as an extra-textual receiver, then the encoded addressee-signals are indeed reader-oriented and should not be described with terms like "encoded explicit" or "implicit" reader, but only with terms like "explicit" and/or "implicit encoded addressee" to mark the differences between encoding and decoding, on the one hand, and text-external and text-internal, on the other hand. Only in this way will the danger of overemphasis and confusion be overcome.

3.3. Furthermore, it must be affirmed that "reading" as action does not consist of a single act but of a process with a starting point, a course, and an ending point. A distinction is also necessary because the elements encoded in view of the reader are not oriented in a static fashion toward the totality of the reading-process. In that case, the elements would have to be structured in a static fashion from a more comprehensive perspective than that of communication.

3.4. Since the "reader" (=the processor) is an active worker in the strict sense of the word, the reader is a factor in reception-theory, not in the explication of the text itself (an exception would be in the case of a reception-text which stands in relation to an earlier text, Matthew and Luke as readers of Mark, for example). "The more that reading occurs individually, the more it is an active process.... The simple stimulus-response-model has to be given up in favor of more complicated models of sender, distribution, and reception" (in New Testament analysis above all in the form of "tradition" and "redaction"/"interpretation," or "continuity" and "contradiction," or simply "transformation"). As an act of appropriation, the reading-process (much more than just a "reading-act") can be distinguished essentially from the practical text concept "in reference to the sense-dominants, selection, and combination" (Grimm:18f; therefore Schenk, 1980:310 insisted on a strict categorial distinction between "Bibel-Auslegung/-Interpretation," "-Anwendung" and, "-Verwendung"; cf. Maier 11–13, 57–59 for a helpful typology of forms of reception in early Judaism).

3.5. Aesthetics-of-reception analysis is only possible where a reception-text stands in relation to an earlier text. (The reception text is seen as a total reorganization, with parts assuming resemblances or form-remodeling of conventional schemata). This is true since reception-aesthetics "derives its judgments from the facticity of work-reception" (Grimm:24): "The reception-result ('concretization') documents the fact that a communication-act has taken place" (Grimm:31; cf. Ingarden's 1965 category of "concretization" as "condition of possibility." Cf. also Detweiler:32–35; Schenk, 1980:308f.; 1981:85f.).

4. The extra-textual reader can obviously be defined as the reader "intended" by the author, in so far as the reader is a competent code-participator (the explicit intention for the competent reader accompanies an unconscious intention evidenced by the potential hints of the historical code—the determination of which remains difficult) (Grimm:33).

4.1. In contrast to a primary extra-textual reader is the category of a secondary reader intended by the author and a yet undefined remainder-category (defined purely negatively as "non-authorial"). These categories as such allow no positive definitions and conclusions. The reception of such kinds of readers can also involve decoding, but it can also involve "transcoding: "If they have missed this, they become guilty of faulty decoding [better: "trans-coding"] and/or an illegitimate substitution of their interpretative contexts for that of the text; Reader-Response-Criticism warns actual readers to be wary of such a seduction by an undercoded text" (Petersen:41).

4.2   In this connection the distinction between researcher and reader remains important (Groeben:137, 168f.; Schenk, 1980:307–13; 1984:27f.). The code-analysis is the decisive point: "Non-Authorial-Readers who know the codes in which the text is encoded may conceivably be able to understand the text as well as the authorial readers"[4] For this procedure the explicit and/or implicit code-elements given in the text itself are helpful (especially the text-imminent meta-linguistic and meta-communicative elements like definitions, clarifications, and contrasts).

4.3.   In addition, we can perceive further reading-helps in the composition of a text, which facilitate a prospective way of observation and means the "stretching of perception-time" so that the transition from a dangerous "spontaneous-synthetic perspective" to a more adequate "successive-analytic way of perception" becomes possible (Köller:380f.). This work we are not always forced to do anew, if we have communicative-equivalent translations. With respect to biblical scriptures the problem is more complicated, since the present-day reader starts with translations, which do not satisfy the conditions of communicative equivalence; thus the reader is occupied with transcodings by incompetent translations and congregational traditions: "A reader of the Luther Bible truely hears the biblical message only in the homiletic retelling and translation of Luther" (Käsemann:280). "In most cases pious outrage is the only alternative to scientific methodology" (Käsemann:276). The so-called simple reader is no "tabula rasa" but is the product of congregational codes, which "historically and theologically remain anchored in the eighteenth century."[5]

C.   *"Reception" vs. "Interpretation" in light of the roles of the readers*

1.   "The problem of the necessary distinction between reception and interpretation" is the result of a more precise understanding of the category of reception: "For the reception-act there remains to be stated: The expectation of the reader defines the object of reception; in distinction to 'interpretation,' in the case of 'reception' the real intention of an author is not the criterion, but the intention of the author as supposed by the recipient" (Grimm:44; cf. Hirsch, 1972:15–42, 263ff.).

1.1.   "The only true criterion for distinguishing between reception/concretization and interpretation is the postulate of work-adequacy" for which the "inter-subjectivity of any apprehension of a text is decisive" (Grimm:51). Since the communicative and functional translation is the target and result of "interpretation," the postulate of work-adequacy is also vital in this connection.

1.2   The confusion which arises from a lack of distinction is documented by a discussion of the last decade: While Iser expansively absolutized his reception-aesthetic starting-point in the direction of an assertion concerning the constitution of meaning as such ("meanings of literary texts are not generated until the reading-event as such") (so Iser, 1970:7 = 1975:229), he was strongly criticized by the Slavist Link. We can follow neither the universalization of Iser (with which "interpretation" is totally integrated into "reception" and loses its special identity) nor the contrary way of Link who defined "reception-aesthetics" in such a way that it means the same as "interpretation" in a strict sense (cf. the clarification in Grimm:49–54): "Insistence on the necessity of the decoding of the author's intention for 'adequate interpretation' is the starting point" which can and must be acknowledged for the task "but not as an exclusive fundamental maxim of a reception-history analysis" (Grimm, 1977:52). We must keep in mind whether we are concerned with clarifying a problem of the text or a problem of its reception. Even here different "formulations of the question" must not be confused (moreover we have to bear in mind that in this debate both Iser and Link had only specific "fictional texts" in mind—this fact is usually overlooked by their theological adapters).

1.3.   Now we have to work with the more precise definition: "The reception of a text is principally subject-oriented, for the subject tries to make the text understandable for himself or herself with no means other than his or her own prior knowledge. This is finally the same as a privately conditioned actualization" (Grimm:54). In most cases therefore the use of biblical quotations is not strictly "interpretation" but a reception which is always subjectively dominated by ones own "set" (moreover, quotations are from a translation, which is really a secondary meta-text) which has come into play without a code-analysis and without giving inter-subjective account of it.

2.   The typology of receptions given by Link (Link, 1976:23–42, list on p. 25) is interesting because the problems are typical and occur elsewhere too.

2.1.   She starts with a faulty concept of "reception": "Her procedure is one oriented toward the author within the text. It measures 'reception' by adequacy of author-intention and sees adequate reception as the central problem of reception-aesthetics. This stance results from the premise that reception-aesthetics is interested in the 'implicit reader'" (Link, 1976:43); "the real reader (understanding a text according to the author-intention) seeks an identification with the 'implicit reader'. Such a reception-aesthetics is based" on the unacceptable premise that "reception is the communication between author and reader and the reader is obliged to understand the intention of the author. But the premise that author-intention is the instance for judgment of the recipient belongs to the area of production-aesthetics."[6]

2.2   Link's reader-oriented phenomenology reduces the intratextually-defined category of the implicit reader (as introduced by Iser) to a complement of the "abstract author": "What Iser on the text-internal level unites as 'implicit reader,' is divided in Link into 'fictive reader-figure' and 'implicit reader-role.' The 'fictive reader-figure' is not necessarily contained within the text, but the 'implicit reader-role' is immanent in each text" (cf. Link, 1976:26). "Iser's 'implicit reader-figure' becomes an 'explicit fictive reader' in Link's terminology, while Iser's 'implicit reader-appeal-structure' could be paralleled with Link's 'implicit reader'" (Grimm:270 n. 83). "From Link's presentation, it is not quite clear whether she understands the 'implicit reader' as an object of narration (like Iser) or as an object of the work. Because it corresponds to the 'abstract author' of her model, which is defined as the subject of the creating-acts (generating the single work) as well as the bearer of the intention (determining the whole work), Link's implicit reader must be seen as the object of the whole work as well as the object of the narration itself" (Link, 1976:40). "The equation of the abstract level with the implicit level obliterates the possible divergences between the total-appeal of a text and the individual appeal-structure" (Grimm:273f., n. 97).

2.3   The main difference (considering the terminological confusion caused thereby) consists in the fact that Iser explicitly wants to show a dynamic "historical" development.[7] Link however wants to supply a static-phenomenological model of general value with an epoch-specific foundation. "The model of Link (with its difference between a fictive and implicit reader) fits best when analyzing texts from the eighteenth and nineteenth centuries with an explicitly 'fictive' reader-figure" (Link using texts of E. T. A. Hoffmann and H. Heine). If the "fictive reader" is the main expression of the whole signal-construct, there could be (in Iser's terminology) a "congruence" of the fictive and the implicit reader—when the main function of both (the leading gesture and the offer of identification) coincide (Grimm:36).

3.   The application of Iser in a generalizing and misunderstood manner: In the history of research we again and again have pseudo-application of methods which are developed and relevant for other "formulations of the question." This may be tolerable if used consciously

and heuristically as "zero-hypotheses" to prove and modify hypotheses. But they are not tolerable when such methodological reflections are absent.

3.1   The belief that Iser has delivered a workable, fully elaborated reception-theory (cf. Lategan:10–12; McKnight:78–82) is based on misunderstanding. This contradicts the clear statement of purpose by Iser himself, that "this book is to be regarded as a theory of aesthetic response [or effect] and not as a reception-theory" (Iser, 1976:8). He becomes more specific (even in the sub-title) in his declaration that he is only concerned with the "aesthetic response/effect" (cf. Iser, 1976:37–86, "Voruberlegungen zu einer *wirkungsästhetischen* Theorie"). This is obvious from the imposed aesthetic practice, that in his quest of a "theory of aesthetic response/effect" the text is "not understood as a documentary record of something that exists or has existed, but as a reformulation of an already existing reality, which brings into the world something that did not exist before.... A theory of reception, on the other hand, always deals with existing readers, whose reactions testify to certain historically conditioned experiences of literature" (Iser, 1976:8).

3.2   The term "literary text," therefore, is always used synonymously with "fictional text" (Iser 1976:66f.), which is defined from the special perspective of "formation of literary illusion" (Lobsien:42–74, upon whom Iser 1976:55 explicitly depends): "The sense of 'literary texts' is only imaginable because it is not explicitly given and therefore only represented in the imaginative ability of the receiver" (Iser, 1976:63). Those who make application in biblical exegesis do not bear in mind that our distinction between "literary" and "non-literary" is determined in a totally different way in time and by the fact that after the invention of book-printing a new form of multiplication became possible. Therefore the form of publication gives no clear basis for decisions concerning the the concept "literary."[8]

3.3   But Iser's concept is still more restricted; he is concerned with the reading of modern fictional texts: "The 'literary' text is a fictive entity" (Iser, 1976:87); "in its verbal structure fictional speech—especially literary prose—resembles the use of practical language" (Iser, 1976:102). Fictional texts (as products of literary art with which Iser is specifically concerned) are constituted by a double negativity: "The 'fictional text' can be restricted neither to an interpretation of empirical entities nor to the values and expectations of its possible readers" (Iser, 1976:115). Expressed in a positive way: "Novel and drama formulated possibilities, which as such did not exist under the pressure of the dominating system of society and therefore could be brought into this real world by fiction only" (Iser, 1976:122). The special "act of reading" analyzed in Iser's book is directed strictly to "the specificity of comprehension of the 'aesthetic' essence of 'fictional texts" (Iser, 1976:178).

3.4 Specially developed categories cannot be applied to the New Testament through an "incoherent generalization" of an abstract "reading act/-process." The authentic Pauline letters are produced in a practical-linguistic way, not just as "expository" texts but also as "actual speech for particular use" (Lausberg:§ 11–13). Even in their narrative elements, texts produced as "speech for further use" (Lausberg:§ 14–19) (like pseudo-Pauline and pseudo-Petrine writings, and the Jesus-biographies) do not constitute "literary"/"fictional" texts in the sense of Iser.

3.4.1. The narratives of the Jesus-biographies are also non-fictional in the sense that they are not exhausted in the denotation of empirically given objects, for what may seem to be other-worldly for a contemporary reader (devil, demons, spirit, parousia of the Son of Men), belongs completely to their world according to their code system.

3.4.2. Since the Gospel of Mark, the so-called Gospels claim to be "non-epic" works of history and practical texts as well since they fulfill the two basic-conditions in their self-understanding:

(a) "The affirmation (declaration-object) is placed in the field of empiricism and experience of the subject of the declaration (i.e. in his personal or historic past);

(b) but it exists in a real and independent way, independent of the subject and act of declaration" (Vogt, 1978:228; cf. Fischer; Gumbrecht). As "non-fictional" texts ("*Jesus has done, has said*"—*even: "predicted"* what really has happened) the represented state of affairs claims to correspond to realities. Only a later scientific comprehension can overcome an uncritical, affirmative reception, i.e., a reception not corresponding to the reception-goal of the author which is seen as partly unfounded and unentitled. But such valuation of the relevance always depends on the results of the analyzing interpretation, which recovers the self-understanding of the texts (cf. Schenk, 1985 with Hirsch).

3.4.3. Against an expanding use of the category "narrativity," we also have to bear in mind that the Jesus-biographies represent more a mere "series of episodes" than real connected linkings of actions (the latter only in the artificial schemata of prediction/fulfillment, collection /teaching/separation-phases of the disciples, provocation/rejection

/rehabilitation of the righteous) and in this way the Gospels belong more to the category of "descriptions" than "narratives" (Kelber:38).

D. *New Testament Texts in Relation to a New Testament Canon*

1. Since they are integral units according to the definition of text-theory, the individual texts have their own specific connections of origin and use/employment (i.e. communication-situations). This is not only the case with the letters; Mark and his successors are also written for the whole of their present world (Mark 8:35; 13:10; 14:9 and parallels) but (according to Mark 13:29 and parallels) not for a later generation or for posterity.

2. The anti-marcionitic "canon of the bishops" of the third century is the phenomenon of a special *reception*. It must be considered a canon of third order due to the fact that Mark (and his successors) declared themselves as canonical. Their canonicity is secondary historically and materially. But the letters of Paul point back to the resurrection-news as the prior "Gospel" and canon of first order (Campenhausen:126–53). The classification as "third order" as well as "canon of bishops" (in relation to but subordinate to a "ministry" which is understood in legal fashion like the Roman system and which has the power of sanction) emphasizes the definition of the so called "canon" as a phenomenon of reception.

2.1 This third reception, for example, uses the Pauline letters as texts which have validity as juridical authorities, while those letters themselves originally derived and claimed their value from the primary canon (temporally and factually) of the "gospel" of Easter, having their value only in their logical and demonstrable plausibility in relation to this primary canon. The problem, therefore, is not to be defined as a "canon within the canon" (as suggested by the positivists of the tertiary-episcopal-canon); their value is clearly defined and restricted through correspondence to their prior canon of the Easter-gospel and in relation to their own derived suggestions for solution of problems (1 Cor 15:1–11 : 12ff.).

2.2 The use of the term "gospel" for the Jesus-biographies; all seven occurrences of the term "gospel" in Mark are considered redactional; Matthew took them over and canonized them with his redactional closing word Matthew 28:18ff.; while Luke deletes all occurrences of the term in his first volume but claims a canonical value by his prologue Luke 1:1–4—as does John 20:30f.; 21:24 with his closing words.

3. A reinterpretation of texts which were fixed by the written form of exposition was not at all "historically necessary" (as meant by a

"deterministic concept of history"). Reinterpretation must be seen primarily as an act of reception, "as texts originating from a different context of origin and use than that for which they are destinated by this new canonization" (Fischer:262).

4. As a phenomenon of reception the so called New Testament canon is not a unified totality (i.e. not a "text" in the strict sense of the word) but a collection of several "texts." Since it is not a phenomenon of a sender, it is methodically incorrect to use expressions like: "The New Testament says...." The new insights we have on the basis of translation into contemporary target-languages (inaugurated by Humanism and the Reformation) as well as on the basis of text-analysis (inaugurated by the Enlightenment) require an evaluation of the "tertiary canon of the bishops" as a new mode of reception.

4.1. "The problem of a criticism of the canon (if it only consists of a non-canonical confrontation of 'old interpretations' by means of ideologically- critical analysis) lies in the fact that the object of canonization silently takes charge." On the ground of reception-theory, the task must be more far-reaching:

> Criticism of the canon cannot exhaust itself in the criticism of interpretations but has to question the legitimation of the object of canonization in the present day. The objects sanctified by tradition especially resist the criticism asking for their legitimation on some basis other than their "own power," but this resistance is enforced by the bearer of polished screens of reception and valuation. Processes of canonization have a social function; criticism of the canon leads finally to the question whether the canonized objects still have the old function today, or a new function, or no function at all" (Fischer:262).

4.2 Decisions concerning reception must be made under conditions which prevail today; they are not necessarily dependent and conditioned on former reception-aesthetic decisions like episcopal canonization or preferences of denominations (for example the preferences of Lutherans for John and Romans and the preference of Roman Catholics for Matthew and Ephesians).

> It cannot be questioned that the recipient is obliged to accept the author-intention. It is his individual decision to read the New Testament as "salvation-truth," "fairy-book," or "historical document." If he wants to match the authorial intention he should perceive it exclusively as a "message of God." But it is precisely the enlightened reader who will not

follow the supposed authorial intention on this point. So, the question arises whether the "ideal" reader is that one who, when subjected to the same conditions of understanding as the author, adopts those intentions without independent judgment, or whether the "ideal reader" is in truth that one who has a higher level of knowledge than the author. The latter would be a reader who does not deny the original sense, but mediates it in terms of his own horizon of understanding as the first step of a historical process of understanding. For the "active reader" the historical sense of the text does not function as an obliging authority, which is always to be accepted in an uncritical way, but it functions as a corrective of his own ideologically oriented (but not blindly restricted) text-reception. In any case the prior definition constrains the receptional point of view of the reader and his way of reworking the text (Grimm:21f.).

E. *Reception-History vs. Effect-History and Tradition-History*

1. Although the apprehension of literature in terms of aesthetics of effect was "lively from antiquity until the eighteenth century" (Grimm:12), the category "effect-history" is not clear terminologically or methodologically. By this ambiguous term such different things are understood as: "judgment-history, influence-history, history of fame, exposition of the sociology of the audience, continued life of forms, genres, contents, and so on" (Mandelkow:71; cf. Grimm:29). The least confusion arises when the term "effect" is used to denote a causal relationship. As denotation of a causal relation which sees the text as the cause for processes in the reader as effect, "effect" will essentially belong to the production-aesthetics and "effect" will thus essentially mean "influence."

1.1. But "the optimal-effect described by effect-aesthetics is only possible in case the recipient allows himself or herself to be directed by effect.... Without reception, no effect—this sentence is not reversible" (Kinder-Weber:254; cf. 234; cf. Mandelkow:83; Grimm:26). Therefore, not only is an identification of reception-history with effect-history to be refused, but "the assumption of a convergent perspective of reception-history and effect-history is also questionable. If the presuppositions of communication-research regarding the reception-act are accepted, then the usual model of 'history of influence' is as unjustified as that of 'judgment-history' in which the judged work has the decisive part in interaction or dominates it" (Grimm:29 with Mandelkow:83). This very mistake is made when the Deutero-Pauline letters are classified as a so-called Pauline School (the same mistake is made with the "Johannine" and "Matthean" schools, and so on) as well as when "Synoptic" is used in relation to a "tradition" in a generalizing way. The confusion of "reception" and "influence" has contrariwise had the negative consequence that a reception of Pauline texts in Mark and/or Luke as well as a reception of the Synoptics in John seems to be settled because of the statement that we can find no "influence." But a missing "influence" of conceptual "Paulinism" can never be an argument against a "use of Paul" because the "optimal-effect" is only one ideal-case among many possible receptions.

1.2.   Reception-research is principally concerned with reception-acts and reception-processes on the basis of reception-results ("condensations"): "The result of reception ('concretization') documents the fact that a communication-act has taken place. Since it normally consists of a statement that is more essential for understanding the subject of reception than for understanding the object received, this 'concretization' is of more interest for an analysis of the recipient as a social subject than for the study of the literary structures of the text received and it is also more productive for analysis of interpretations than of texts" (Grimm:31). What is called "redactor" in New Testament research (with less "descriptive adequacy") means strictly speaking the "recipient." "Pretexts" affirmed without proof as "traditions" are also less solid. "Traditions" especially are "flying saucers." "Consequently a whole 'reception-history' does not simply mean the history of a differently received text (how often is this claimed), but more especially it means the history of the receiving subjects. In this sense, reception-history is definitely nearer to reader-research than to the older effect-history" (Grimm:30).

1.3   As Grimm has said: "The older effect-research starts from the perspective of the text, investigating its 'effect' or 'influence,' while reception-research takes the perspective of the receiving subject" (91f.). The aesthetics-of-effect model is always object-perspectival, its procedure might be subject-oriented ("How many texts did a recipient read and how did he read them?") or object-oriented ("How many readers received a text and how did they receive it?"). The following diagram shows the distinctions (T=Text; R=Reader; C=Condensation or Concretization):

Object-perspectival + subject-oriented:	Subject-perspectival + object-oriented:
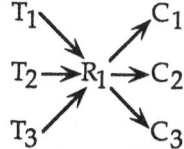	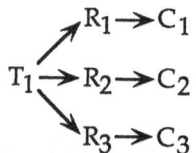

In this matter the following insight is most important: from the standpoint of the sociology of knowledge, the object-perspectivic model of "effect-history" is essentially inclined towards the actually dominating ideologies (and the "status quo" of self-justifying denominations). As Grimm has argued:

> The older history of effect conception presupposes identity between artifact and aesthetic object, whereby the latter is not thought of as the object but as the semantic substance with the quality of a subject. Therefore 'effect' represents itself as an intersubjective action with an initiation-effect from the side of the subject of the work. The 'history of effect' model describes the effect arising from the object in its perspective: the text which is the true object becomes the subject of history. Behind the thought concerning a substantial unchangeable artifact lies the conviction that a qualitatively once for all definable and recognizable essence evolves in the course of time according to a social-Darwinian mechanism.
>
> The effect-historian seeks to discover the effect of works which have effect even in the present and which have declared their value in this fashion. Here we have a conclusion concerning the value of the text from its longtime effect which finally legitimates the inquiry. This is after all a circular conclusion: Historical texts are worthy texts because they are read even today; these historical texts are read because they are worthy texts. Only those texts are worthy of inquiry, finally, which have succeeded" (28).

The present cycle of "effect-history" (against the background of a triumphalism of the Western "Corpus Christianum") is evident in idioms like "the tradition of the church" and "The Bible says." The whole is climaxed by the definition that "tradition" consists in the developing of "revelation," which means that not only effect-history but tradition-history as well is styled nobly as an explication of of "revelation." The term "God" degenerates to a mere instrument of emphasis.

2. The cycle of the principle of "effect history" shows how strongly presuppositions of the philosophy of identity are at work. This is seen in terms of a "theology of revelation" in which "tradition" is always

"revelation" of a hidden "mystery." Within the super-churchly philosophy of subject only a logic of identity differentiation is possible (which is deterministically claimed to be "historically necessary"[9]) but this does not mean real otherness.

2.1. As Grimm has explained: A special swing upwards is given to the history of effect "formulation of the question" by the "principle of the history of effect" developed by Gadamer (Gadamer:284–90; cf. Hilberath:148–83). Now the "history of effect" was no longer a mere superficial appendix to the work itself, something which was able to contribute nothing to its perception.

2.11. On the contrary, it relativized the horizon of understanding of the interpreter who is seen as conditioned by a tradition of understanding, in which he stands unreflective for the most part.

2.12. The perception of the relativity of the point of view of the interpretation was supplemented by the discernment that one's interpretation is not to be set above an earlier one in the sense of linear progression.

2.13. When the historically and socially distinctive interpretations retained their own worth, then the analysis of these different interpretations brought to light again such ideas and views which seem to be lost in the present.

In this way effect-history ascended to the unfolding of "sense-potentials" which are deposited in a work. Instead of being despised as mere appendix of an essence which was untouched by the accidental receptions, effect-history now ascended to the position of the bearer of the essence itself, which revealed itself in their different locations. (12f.).

2.2. Such effect-history, as a consequence of "fusion of horizons," has altered the status of tradition. This took place at a time when the human sciences seemed to have lost their object, with "tradition" no longer counting as an "object" and no "it" being allowed. In the sense of the object-constitution of "hermeneutic philosophy," "tradition" itself was declared to be the subject (being an "I" and a "You") (Gadamer:340; Hilberath:116–23, 176–81; cf. the criticism of Stobbe:110f., 139). But the alleged "dialogic relation" (asserted as fundamental and incorrectly justified by the communication-theoretical model of author/work/reader) "cannot deceive itself by overlooking the fact that the reading-act is by no means a true dialogue between author and reader, but a pseudo-dialogue. On the basis of the text, the reader may read the presumed statement of the author, but he can also read the text without any regard for the authorial meaning; on the other hand the author himself has no instrument to prevent a reception contrary to his intention" (Grimm:29, see also 263 n.52, 271; cf. Stobbe:65–70).

2.3. With Gadamer the ontological notion of "effect-history" was considered as a transcendental-philosophical description of the "conditions of possibilities" (and therefore just not as a "method"). But in the hasty and inadequate adoptions by literary-critics and biblical exegetes it became a "method" and even a challenge "to give (for theological reasons) attention to the traditions of the church by which we are sustained" (cf. Stuhlmacher, 1979:197–201, 208, 217, 221). "The hermeneutical demand to develop a consciousness of history-of-effect collapses into the very opposite, if it is used as a demand for a new branch of research in the human sciences with the task of comprehending the reception-history and effect-history of texts in an objective methodical way" (Stobbe:118; cf. Gadamer:285, 287).

3. In this case demand for a "history of effect consciousness" (in a way that is understood as well as misunderstood) becomes a continuation of the philosophy of subjectivity. If "tradition" appears as positive evolution of "revelation," we do get not a new "formulation of the question" but we get the continuation of the anti-historical way of D.F. Strauss, who claimed that is not the mode of the spirit (the idea, the myth), "to realize itself simply by the way it pours out its abundance on one single token or individual" (cf. especially Slenczka:46–61, 58). In Gospel-research of the early nineteenth century, such a "history of ideas" favored the model of oral collection in the "fragments-" and "traditions-hypotheses" (in opposition to the "basic-Gospel" model which ultimately led to the two-source-model of the Synoptics) (cf. Slenczka:62–84). Interest was less in the origin than in the process of the forming of traditions. From this starting point "history" as such is irrelevant for this mythical "belief." To this extent, the Synoptic form criticism of the present century (more accurately classified as "tradition-history") is the real continuation of the Synoptic "tradition-hypothesis" of the nineteenth century and not of the preceding "literary-criticism."

But even a "tradition" must be definable as a reconstructable, coherent text before anything can be said about it: "The current 'form-historical' 'formulation of the question' proves to be totally inadequate" to deal with the material of Mark; with this insight "the earlier 'tradition-hypothesis' collapsed in its attempt to derive the three synoptic Gospels from a single oral basic-gospel or from individual narratives. The arguments against the 'tradition-hypothesis' (set forth by C. H. Weise in his work founding the two-document-theory) have not lost their force against 'form-history,' which only was the renewal of the 'tradition-hypothesis' in its own fashion."[10]

4. Thus the "consciousness of the history of effect" is by no means the overcoming of "historism" (as claimed) but a retrogression into the old idealistic philosophy of subjectivity. A better effort would be to solve overdrawn codes by way of reception-theory.

Present tendencies have more the character of symptoms than of solutions. As Grimm argued:

> Kinder and Weber give a plausible explanation for the vigorous attempts to connect effect-intention and the reality of reception and thereby to legitimate a text-interpretation which emphasizes reader-signals: It is the vexation with plurality and historic inconstancy of interpretations that discourages the contemporary interpreter from challenging the interpretation of so many precursors and induces him rather to make the problem of reception itself the object of his research. In order to escape his self produced skepticism, he tries to submit the text (defining it as pre-text of reception) to a theory with the help of which he hopes to succeed in showing conventions connecting pre-text of reception to the multiplicity or even simplicity of its reception(Grimm:25).[11]

In opposition to this procedure we have to bear in mind more strongly that each meta-text expressing a result of reception gives us information about the receiver but not about the pre-text. Analysis of production and analysis of reception cannot be united nor can one be excluded by the other. To speak of a single "dialectic process of production and reception" (Combrink:30; against this opinion see Grimm:24) does not do sufficient justice to existing relationships and differences and presents no contribution for the solution of either of the "formulation of the question."

NOTES

*Reworked English translation of the German version in *Linguistica Biblica* 60 (1988):61–84. Edgar McKnight is to be thanked for help in polishing my English version.

[1] So, for example, Lategan 1984:12 with Fish, 1980 and Holub, 1984:101;151f.

[2] Titzmann, 1977:381f. The manuals on New Testament methodology are plagued specially by this erroneous practice of speaking rashly of text-/literary-critical, form-/redaction-historical "methods" (cf. the titles of the paragraphs in Zimmermann-Kliesch or the undefined use of "formulation of the question"

and/or "method" in Conzelmann-Lindemann:1-118; Haacker:56-72; but Lührmann:27 separates himself expressively from this misuse of "formulation of the question"; Schenk, 1986a:49f. The same is to be said against the generalization of "critics" [Hirsch, 1972:179-84]).

3 Cf. the categorial specification of ontological level categories in Hartmann:45-100. As a cognitive theorist he emphasizes the process of cognition as well as Hirsch, 1975:310f with the Piaget-Model of "corrigible schemata": "The model of 'corrigible schemata' is...a more useful and accurate model than that of the so-called 'hermeneutic circle'" (contradicted sharply by Stegmüller); "Unlike one's alterable and inescapable preunderstanding in Heidegger's account of the 'hermeneutical circle', a schema can be radically altered and corrected. A schema sets up a range of predictions or expectations which, if fulfilled, confirms the schema but, if not fulfilled, causes us to revise it.... The universality of making-matching process and of 'corrigible schemata' in all domains of language and thought...the private process of verbal understanding have the same character....For that which we are understanding is itself a hypothesis constructed by ourselves, a schema, or genre, or type which provokes expectations that are confirmed by our linguistic experience or, when they are not confirmed, cause us to adjust our hypothesis or schema."

4 Petersen:40. Petersen (with Ricoeur) emphasizes the fact of "omnitemporality of meaning" and (with Hirsch, 1967:52-66) adheres to the distinction between "meaning" and "relevance" against confusion and the danger of naive, uncontrolled, substitution of codes (opposing "psychologism" as well as "historism"); Schenk, 1985:81-3.

5 Käsemann:281; cf. Koch:336ff.; cf. discussion of "translation" as result and aim of text-exegesis, Schenk, 1976; 1980a; 1985:79-81; Haacker, 1981:23-31;and for the methodical conditions of "communicative and functional equivalence" see Nida-Taber; Jäger:87ff; Reiss.

6 Grimm:270 n. 83; see p. 21 for argument against such a premise for *reception-aesthetical* exercises and investigations; Grimm uses "aesthetics" always as expression of action, meaning phases of perception and apperception, avoiding on purpose a use which is related to objects and thus the distinction between aesthetic and non-aesthetic texts.

7 Iser, 1972:8-11; eighteenth century: direction of an explicit role by a reader-figure pre-drawn in the text; nineteenth century: reduction of this direction of role in favor of a role having to be discovered by the reader himself; novels of twentieth century: the same, with zero-positions for inducing the reader to establish connections of perception and reflection by himself.

8 Already asserted by Wendland:278f. against the anachronistic distinction between "private letter" and "literary epistle" followed by contemporary epistolography; cf. Thraede:1,5.

9 Cf. supplement to the fundamental analysis of Castoriadis.

10 Schmithals:170–6; cf. Güttgemanns:69ff.; also Haacker:48–63. Earlier Stammler:281 n.57 had pointed out this methodological opposition, but he formulated it somewhat erroneously, distinguishing insufficiently between "Literarkritik" and "Formgeschichte":

> Da beweist man 'literar-[no: form-] kritisch,' daß es sich nicht um Berichte, sondern um Zeugnisse handelt, und folgert daraus, daß es nicht auf (längst vergangene) Tatsachen ankomme. Die anderen sagen, weil es auf die Heilstatsachen zu Jesu Lebzeiten so ankommt, deshalb ist die Literarkritik verwerflich.—Eigentlich müßten die ersten auf die Literarkritik verzichten und die zweiten sie betreiben. Das scheint mir ein Zeichen, daß sich beide Parteien noch nicht ganz klar über ihre Voraussetzungen sind."

11 Grimm:25 with Kinder and Weber:231 especially with view to the beginnings of Jauss, Iser, and others, but even with view to the false generalizing mis-adaption of such beginnings. The self-encouraging overestimation, that here we already have a "change of paradigm" (Lategan:3f.; Combrink:26f. with Phillips:415f.) should be put aside (Link 1973) until it can be made obvious that here we do not have a mere return to the idealistic (even under color of "materialistic;" cf. Schenk, 1985a in disagreement with Lategan, 1984:13f.). If we further define the categories "exegesis" as well as "hermeneutics" in such a generalizing manner avoidable misunderstandings and erroneous solutions will block our progress (Schenk, 1986).

WORKS CITED

Campenhausen, H.F. von
    1968   *Die Entstehung der christlichen Bibel*. Tübingen: Mohr.

Castoriadis, C.
    1984   Gesellschaft als imaginäre Institution. Frankfurt: Suhrkamp.

Combrink, H.J.B.
    1984   "Multiple meaning and/or multiple interpretation of a text." *Neotestamentica* 18:26–37.

Conzelmann, H. and A. Lindemann
    1979   *Arbeitsbuch zum Neuen Testament*, 4th ed. Tübingen: Mohr.

Detweiler, R.
    1978   *Story, Sign and Self: Phenomenology and Structuralism as Literary-critical Methods*. Philadelphia: Fortress.

Fischer, L.
1977 "Auslegung der Bibel." Pp. 258–70 in *Funk-Kolleg Literatur*, Vol. 1. Ed. H. Brackert and E. Lämmert. Frankfurt: Fischer Tashenbuch.

Fish, S.
1975 "Literatur im Leser: Affektive Stilistik." Pp. 196–227 in *Rezeptionsästhetik als literaturwissenschafliche Pragmatik. Theorie und Praxis*. Ed. R. Warning. München: W. Fink.
1980 "Interpreting the 'Variorum.'" Pp. 164–84 in *Reader Response Criticism: From Formalism to Post-Structuralism*. Ed. J. P. Tompkins. Baltimore: Johns Hopkins University Press.

Gadamer H.G.
1975 *Wahrheit und Methode*, 4th ed. Tübingen: Mohr.

Grimm, G.
1977 *Rezeptionsgeschichte: Grundlegung einer Theorie*. München: W. Fink.

Groeben, N.
1972 *Literaturpsychologie*. Stuttgart: W. Kohlhammer.

Güttgemanns, E.
1971 *Offene Fragen zur Formgeschichte des Evangeliums*, 2nd ed. München: C. Kaiser.

Gumbrecht, H.U.
1977 "Fiktion und Nichtfiktion." Pp. 188–209 in *Funk-Kolleg Literatur*. Vol. 1. Ed. H. Brackert and E. Lämbert. Frankfurt: Fischer Taschenbuch Verlag.

Haacker, K.
1981 *Neutestamentliche Wissenschaft*. Wuppertal: B. Brockhaus.

Hartmann, N.
1949 *Das Problem des geistigen Seins*, 2nd ed. Berlin: W. de Gruyter.

Heidegger, K.
1927 *Sein und Zeit*. Tübingen: M. Niemeyer. (11th edition, 1977)

Hilberath, B.J.
1978   *Theologie zwischen Tradition und Kritik: Die philosophische Hermeneutik H.-G. Gadamers als Herausforderung des theologischen Selbstverständnisses.* Düsseldorf: Patmos Verlag.

Hirsch, E.D.
1972   *Prinzipien der Interpretation.* München: W. Fink. (= *Validity in Interpretation.* New Haven: Yale University Press, 1967)
1975   "Current Issues in Theory of Interpretation." *JR* 55:298–312.

Holub, Robert C.
1984   *Reception Theory A Critical Introduction.* London: Methuen.

Ingarden, R.
1965   *Das literarische Kunstwerk*, 3rd ed. Tübingen: Niemeyer.

Iser, W.
1970   *Die Appellstruktur der Texte.* Konstanz: Universitätsverlag.
1972   *Der implizite Leser: Kommunikationsformen des Romans von Bunyan bis Beckett.* München: W. Fink.
1976   *Der Akt des Lesens: Theorie ästhetischer Wirkung.* München: W. Fink.

Jäger, G.
1975   *Translation und Translationslinguistik.* Halle: M. Niemeyer.

Jauss, H.R.
1970   *Literaturgeschichte als Provokation.* Frankfurt: Suhrkamp.

Käsemann, E.
1970   *Exegetische Versuche und Besinnungen*, Vol. 2, 6th ed. Göttingen: Vandenhoeck & Ruprecht.

Kelber, W.
1979   "Markus und die mündliche Tradition." *Linguistica Biblica* 45:55–58.

Kinder, H. and H.D. Weber
1975   "Handlungsorientierte Rezeptionsforschung in der Literaturwissenschaft." Pp 223–58 in *Methodische Praxis in der Literaturwissenschaft.* Ed. D. Kimpel and B. Pinkerneil. Kronberg: Scriptor.

Koch, K.
1974   *Was ist Formgeschichte.* 3rd ed. Neukirchen: Neukirchner Verlag.

Köller, W.
1986   "Dimensionen des Metaphernproblems." *Zeitschrift für Semiotik* 8:379–410.

Lategan, Bernard C.
1984   "Current issues in the hermeneutical debate." *Neotestamentica* 18:1–17.

Lausberg, H.
1976   *Elemente der literarischen Rhetorik,* 5th ed. München: Hueber.

Link, Hannelore
1973   "Die Appellstruktur der Texte und ein 'Paradigmenwechsel in der Literaturwissenschaft'?" *Jahrbuch der deutschen Schillergesellschaft* 17:532–83.
1976   *Rezeptionsforschung: Eine Einfuhrung in Methoden und Probleme.* Stuttgart: Kohlhammer.

Lobsien, E.
1975   *Theorie literarischer Illusionsbildung.* Stuttgart: Metzler.

Lührmann, D.
1984   *Auslegung des Neuen Testaments.* Zürich: Theologischer Verlag.

McKnight, E.
1985   *The Bible and the Reader: An Introduction to Literary Criticism.* Philadelphia: Fortress.

Maier, J.
1973   "Kontinuität und Neuanfang." Pp. 1–18 in *Literatur und Religion des Frühjudentums.* Ed. J. Schreiner and J. Maier. Würzbuch/Gütersloh: Echter Verlag.

Mandelkow, K.R.
1970   "Probleme der Wirkungsgeschichte." *Jahrbuch für International Germanistik* 2 :71–84.

Naumann, M.
1971 "Autor-Adressat-Leser." *Weimarer Beiträge* 17. Heft 11:163–9
1973 "Autor und Adressat." Pp. 52–78 in *Gesellschaft-Literatur-Leser*. Ed. M. Naumann. Berlin/Weimar: Aufbau Verlag.

Nida, E.A. and C. Taber
1969 *Theory and Practice of Translation*. Leiden: Brill.

Petersen, Norman R.
1984 "The Reader in the Gospel." *Neotestamentica* 18:38–51.

Phillips, G.A.
1983 "History and Text: The Reader in Context in Matthew's Parable Discourse." Pp. 415–37 in *Society of Biblical Literature Seminar Papers*. Ed. K.H. Richards. Chico: Scholars Press.

Reiss, K.
1982 *Möglichkeiten und Grenzen der Übersetzungskritik*, 4th ed. München: M. Hueber.

Ricoeur, P.
1976 *Interpretation Theory*. Fort Worth: Texas Christian University Press.

Schenk, W.
1976 "Bibelübersetzung auf dem Wege: Von der Kunst der Übersetzung zur Wissenschaft der Translation." *Die Zeichen der Zeit*.30:344–50
1980 "Textverarbeitung in Frühjudentum, Frakirche und Gnosis." Pp 299–313 in *Altes Testament-Frühjudentum-Gnosis*. Ed. K. W. Troger. Berlin.
1980a "Was ist ein Kommentar?" *BZ* 24:1–20.
1981 "Review of *Story, Sign and Self* by R. Detweiler." *ThLZ* 106:85–6.
1984 *Die Philipperbriefe des Paulus. Kommentar*. Stuttgart: Kohlhammer.
1985 "Die Paränese Hebr 13,16 im Kontext des Hebäerbriefes: Eine Fallstudie semiotisch orientierter Textinterpretation und Sachkritik." *StTh* 39:73–106.
1985a "Wird Markus auf der Couch materialistisch? Oder: Wie idealistisch ist die 'materialistische Exegese'?" *Linguistica Biblica* 57:95–106

1986 "Hermeneutik III (NT)," Theologische Realenzyklopädie 15:144–50.
1986a "Review of *Auslegung des Neuen Testaments* by D. Lührmann." *EK* 19:49–50.

Schmithals, W.
1980 "Kritik der Formkritik." *ZTK* 77:149–85.

Slenczka, R.
1967 *Geschichtlichkeit und Personsein Jesu: Studien zur christologischen Problematik der historischen Jesusfrage*. Göttingen: Vandenhoeck & Ruprecht.

Stammler, G.
1969 *Erkenntnis und Evangelium. Grundzüge der Erkenntnistheorie als Lehr vom Sachgehalt*. Göttingen: Vandenhoeck & Ruprecht.

Stegmüller, W.
1975 "Das Problem der Induktion: Humes Herausforderung und moderne Antworten;" "Der sogenannte Zirkel des Verstehens." Darmstadt: Wissenschaftliche Buchgesellschaft.

Stierle, K.
1975a "Was heißt Rezeption bei fiktionalen Texten." *Poetica* 7:345–87.
1977 "Die Struktur narrativer Texte." *Poetica* 7:210–33.

Stobbe, H.G.
1981 *Hermeneutik—ein ökumenisches Problem. Eine Kritik der katholischen Gadamer-Rezeption*. Zürich/Gütersloh: Benziger.

Strauss, D.F.
1938/9 *Das Leben Jesu kritisch bearbeitet*, 2nd ed. Tübingen: Osiander.

Stuhlmacher, P.
1979 *Vom Verstehen des NT. Eine Hermeneutik*. Göttingen: Vandenhoeck & Ruprecht.

Suleiman, Susan R. and Inge Crosman, eds.
1980 *The Reader in the Text: Essays in Audience and Interpretation*. Princeton University Press.

Tompkins, Jane P., ed.
1980   *Reader Response Criticism: From Formalism to Post-Structuralism*. Baltimore: Johns Hopkins University Press.

Titzmann, M.
1977   *Strukturale Textanalyse*. Uni Taschenbücher 423. München: W. Fink.

Thraede, K.
1970   Grundzüge griechisch-römischer Brieftopik. München: Beck.

Vogt, J.
1978   "Bauelemente erzählender Texte." Pp. 227–42 in *Grundzüge der Literatur und Sprach-wissenschaft*. 5th ed. Vol. 1. *Literaturwissenschaft*. Ed. H. L. Arnold and V. Sinemus. München: Deutscher Taschenbuch.

Wendland, P.
1912   *Die urchristlichen Literaturformen*, 3rd ed. Tübingen: Mohr. (4th edition, 1972)

Zimmermann, H. and K. Kliesch
1982   *Neutestamentliche Methodenlehre*, 7th ed. Stuttgart: Katholisches Bibelwerk.

II

*Analysis
Mark, Philippians, Galatians*

THE READER OF MARK
AS OPERATOR OF A SYSTEM OF CONNOTATIONS

B.M.F. van Iersel
Catholic University of Nijmegen

ABSTRACT

This essay analyzes and illustrates how the reader when reading a text produces a coherent system of connotative meanings.

1. The analysis makes use of a model designed by Roland Barthes. It regards the connotation as a second meaning which supposes the first or denotative meaning. To this model are added a number of steps that can be distinguished as the decisive elements of a secondary decoding process.

2. In illustration of the decoding process the classic question of the (messianic) secret in Mark is discussed. The secret here is considered to be a central element of a connotative layer of meaning which for an important part is found in the text and the context of the parables of the seed and the vineyard and of the two stories of feeding. The words of Jesus in the story of the last supper offer the key with which to decode this system of connotative meanings.

3. The validity and usefulness of the theory developed in part one are tested in part three which represents the reader realizing the interpretation given in part two of this connotative layer of meaning in Mark.

A written text is like a musical score; just as a musical score becomes music only when it is performed, a written text produces meaning only when it is read (cf. Barthes, 1970:35–37). As a result, not a single part of the total textual meaning is significant on its own. A reader of flesh and blood is always indispensable to give meaning to a written text. This does not necessarily imply that the reader is equally involved in each part of the reading process. It appears, however, that the reader plays a particularly important part in operations which concern intertextual references and connotational meanings. This essay will be concerned only with the connotative system as found by the reader in Mark. This system has already been analyzed in the context of a study of the function of the messianic secret in Mark (van Iersel, 1985:144–59, 1986:245–48, 1987:23–25).

In this essay the connotative system will be placed in a theoretical context and, as far as possible, will be presented in terms of that context. In the first section the theoretical context will be discussed; in the second section an analysis of Mark will be given; and in the third section theory and analysis will be compared. Although the material is presented in this order, the theoretical context discussed did not to any notable extent precede the actual analysis. In fact, the theoretical aspects are attempts to systematize afterwards what is done in the analysis.

1. Connotative Meanings

1.1 Even if one does not attribute equally great importance to literary and non-literary texts (as do Roland Barthes, 1964:131, and Daniel and Aline Patte, 1–10) one has to grant that the system of connotations, which has been given considerable attention in the study of mass communications, especially of advertising, also merits attention in texts of a literary nature (Greimas-Courtés:63).

1.2 The term *connotation* was first used by the philosopher J.S. Mill in 1843 as a counterpart of *denotation*. The fact rightly observed by John Lyons (175–76) that philosophers have not been consistent in their use of these terms and consequently have caused considerable confusion, a confusion later on aggravated by linguists as a result of other inaccuracies, does not mean that these terms should be discarded. But it is absolutely necessary to define and distinguish the terms most carefully and to pay attention to the larger theoretical framework as well.

After a first attempt by L. Hjemslev it was mainly R. Barthes who clarified the question of connotation (1964:130–32). Apart from one or two objections (cf. Molino:24–30), Barthes' analysis has been generally accepted, and will therefore serve as our point of departure here. To begin with, he made a distinction between the system of primary meanings, that of the *denotation*, and the system of secondary meanings. In a first—more algebraically inspired—notation he demonstrates how a *content* (C) and an *expression* (E) are connected or *related* (R) in the process of producing meaning at the level of the *denotation*. The process is represented by the formula ERC. On the basis of this formula, depending on whether the first system (ERC) forms the basis of a second *content* or a second *expression*, he arrives at two options for a secondary meaning, represented by two formulas, (ERC)RC and ER(ERC), and by two models based on identical symbols:

Figure 1: The first model of R. Barthes

level 2	E	R	C	E	R	C
level 1	E R C				E R C	

The totality of the relationship between expression *(signifier)* and content *(signified)* on the first level is transformed into one of the elements of the system of signification on the secondary level. It becomes either the second expression *(signifier)* or the second content *(signified)*. The connection of the *signifier* with a second or subsequent *signified*, brought about at the level of the *denotation*, results in *connotation*. The connection of the *signified* with a second or subsequent *signifier*, produced at the level of the *denotation*, leads to *metalanguage*. Barthes expresses the same in two geometrical and therefore more visual models, which have since found fairly universal acceptance (Eco:55; Kloepfer:89; Schulte-Werner:99; Titzmann:65–85).

Figure 2: The second model of R. Barthes

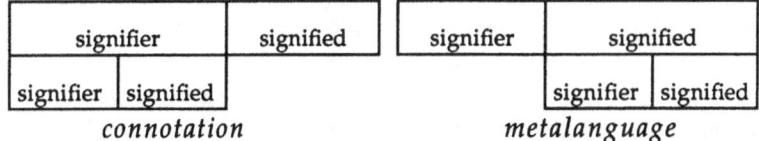

connotation · metalanguage

This essay leaves the *metalanguage* out of consideration and confines itself to the *connotation*. The model itself makes it clear that what Kloepfer (91) says with reference to a few examples has general validity: the production of the *connotative signification* demands that the reader perform a very specific operation after the connection of *signifier* and *signified* at the *denotative* level. The reader has to make a second connection at the level of the *connotation*. The connections of a *signifier* with a subsequent *signified* on the second level are diverse in character and the result is not always a *connotation*. It is necessary, therefore, to determine the limits of the *connotation* by means of a further distinction.

1.3   This new distinction relates to the *connotation* on the one hand and the *association* on the other. R. Barthes does not mention this distinction in the first instance (1964), but puts it forward with special emphasis in the second (1975:8). He words the distinction between *connotation* and *association* quite sharply as follows: "The latter refers to the system of a subject; connotation is a correlation immanent in the text, in the texts." In other words: in the *connotation* the textual dependence dominates, while in the *association* it is the subject dependence that is dominant. If we leave aside the final two words of the quotation—which classify the phenomenon of the *intertextuality* as an aspect of the *connotation*, whereas it actually makes quite different, specific demands on the reader—, Barthes' distinction between subject and text is very much to the point.

In light of the subject/text distinction, the similarities and the differences between the two could be expressed by speaking of text-dependent and subject-dependent *connotations*. On further consideration it seems more accurate to retain the term *association* for the latter where the meanings are not so much produced on the basis of textual notation as on that of extratextual data, such as personal experiences and the like. Grossklaus (174–179), who adopts Barthes' basic scheme, has a different understanding of the distinction between *connotation* and *association*. He believes that *connotation* and *association* are both somehow dependent on their extratextual context and he therefore calls them a contextual phenomenon. As to the distinction between the two, he considers it of overriding importance whether this particular connection with the extratextual reality is exclusively produced either by one, or a limited number of individual subjects—in which case he speaks of *association*—, or by the majority in a language community—in which case he calls that second meaning *connotation*. This view seems to a large extent to be related to the fact that (although he is analyzing a literary text) Grossklaus is not dealing with connotation in literature but with connotation in mass communication and in particular with the ideological aspects of mass communication. For this reason one could give preference to Barthes' description.

We return to the field of literature with Titzmann who contrasts *connotation* as well as *association* with *denotation* (81). He believes the *association* to be arbitrary and to derive from an arbitrary group or an individual *receiver*. The *connotation* may be based on a text-external cultural code or on a text-internal contextual code, and when the former can be satisfactorily reconstructed or the latter adequately analyzed he calls it an *objective connotation*. But it is only natural that the text-dependent second significations, for which Barthes reserves the term *connotation*, should have a certain degree of objectivity, so that the addition of the adjective is really superfluous.

As this article confines itself to the *connotations* there is no need to pay attention to a further distinction between various kinds of *associations*, such as a more conventional vs. a more individual association (cf. Kloepfer:91 and Schulte-Werner:99).

1.4   An important question is whether the connection made by the reader between the level of the *denotative* and *connotative* meaning is capable of further definition. On this the following three remarks may be made.

1.4.1.   First, in the case of narrative texts at any rate—things may be different with poetry (Schulte-Werner:100)—, the *connotative* meaning not only leaves the underlying *denotative* meaning intact but also requires it. This requirement is so absolute that the *connotative* meaning can only be produced on the basis of a *denotative* meaning. Although this may be gathered from Barthes' model, it nevertheless deserves specific mention because, as will appear later, it has important relevance to the question if a reader may give up a *connotation* and confine himself or herself to a meaning at the *denotative* level.

Titzmann (84–85) says that literary creations may not rightfully be read as non-literary as well; it is a misconception to think that the *connotative* meaning is so close to the *denotative* meaning that a reader could confine himself to the latter. But this is true only in a limited sense. It may actually hold for an overall secondary meaning which depends upon the connotative level. As an example of such a broad *connotative* effect Titzmann mentions the way in which a reader recognizes the literary character of a written text. With regard to our subject we could consider as an analogue the recognition of the proclamatory character of Mark. This may be seen as a *connotative* effect, which contributes to the meaning the book has for the reader and which cannot be given up without misunderstanding the book. But it seems quite clear that such a *connotation*—partly because of its global character—is nevertheless of a different kind than a specific connotative system. That is why in a case like the latter one can say that two different ways of reading are really possible and legitimate, as Titzmann's first sentence on this problem seems to confirm: "Im Falle des Systems 'Literatur' bedient sich ein Text dieser 'Sprache' immer auch der Normalsprache und tut dies in der Regel so, dass der Text bis zu einem variablen Grad mittels dieser befriedigend gelesen werden kann" (Titzmann:84). The first way of reading confines itself to the denotative level, the second explicitly uses a second, connotative level to arrive at the meaning.

1.4.2.   The textual elements of the denotative level, with which the reader can make the connection between the denotative and connotative levels of meaning, are at least of two kinds. The first kind consists of the proper *signifiers* of the *signifieds* at the *connotative* level. The second kind consists of the *signifiers* that do not refer to a certain connotative meaning but in a global manner signal the presence of meanings at a *connotative* level.

1.4.2.1. Following R. Barthes (1964:131) authors have termed the proper *signifiers* of the connotative meanings *connotators*. They are the *sememes* (particular meanings) of the *denotative* level made up of a *signifier* and a *signified* and refer in their turn to a second *signified* (see Barthes' model in 1.2., Fig. 2). Only in case the reader in any way submits to this connotating function of a connotator can or must he follow a reference to a meaning at the second level.

There is no direct connection between the number of *connotators* and the number of connotative meanings. Only incidentally, as for example in the case of an allegory where as a rule all the elements acquire a second meaning, is there a quantitative proportionality between the two systems of meaning (Barthes, 1964:131). But the presence of this proportionality is by no means a rule. Thus one single textual element, for example, may have a connotative significance for an entire text. One might think of Mark 13:14, "Let the reader understand," which has as *connotation* that the story of Mark is put explicitly within the communication between author and reader or reader and listeners, and thereby effects that a statement like, "He who has ears to hear, let him hear" (4:9; cf. 4:3; 4:23), in addition to being a denotative exhortation addressed to the disciples, in the second instance also becomes a *connotative* exhortation meant for the readers. On the other hand, it is also possible that an element of frequent occurrence has as connotation only one connotative significative effect. An example in point is "immediately" in Mark, which partly because of its high frequency lends an air of restlessness and hurry, not only at the *denotative* level to the action of Jesus, but also at the *connotative* level to the reading process of the reader. A third possibility is that a number of *signifiers* distributed over a text evoke a connotative system of a number of related elements. This will be discussed in greater detail in 1.5.

1.4.2.2. The *signifiers*, which draw the reader's attention to the presence of a second level of meaning without acting themselves as immediate *connotators*, can function in various ways. Without aiming to give an exhaustive enumeration one can point to two kinds of signalling.

The first consists in such a remarkable frequency of a textual element that it attracts the special attention of the reader. A case in point is the frequency of the sememe /way/ and its synonym /path/ in Mark 1:2-3, both of which belong to the same paradigm. They prepare the reader for the central part of the book which deals with /the way/ of Jesus and his disciples. There too the sememe /the way/ recurs frequently, especially in the syntagm "on the way" (8:27; 9:33-34; 10:32,46). The *denotative* meaning of /way/ is here undoubtedly the /route/ between Galilee and Jerusalem or the /paved road/ on which Jesus with his disciples is said to be travelling; but it seems obvious that the lexeme has the *connotative* meaning of /way of life/ and as such also characterizes the theme of the central part (van Iersel, 1982:125,135-137, 1983:50).

The second kind of signalling consists in textual elements intended to make the reader pay special attention. An example of this is the summons "Listen!" in 4:3, which in a more generalizing and stronger version is repeated in 4:9. In another way this is also the function of passages which declare that there is something to be understood that goes beyond the *denotative* level, as Jesus' conversation with the disciples about the loaves and the broken pieces left over in 8:17-21, which will be discussed below.

1.5   The foregoing justifies the question whether the summary model of R. Barthes does not increase in value and particularly whether one does not gain a clearer insight into the steps the reader has to take in decoding and organizing the *connotative* level if the model is extended. Several larger models have been tried (Eco:84-96; Patte:15,17,31,60) or proposed (Stierle:139-145) but they are unfit to illustrate the type of *connotative* meaning that we have in mind. For that reason another model is proposed here, which builds on and extends that of Barthes (Fig. 3). This new model can make no claims to being applicable to all possible kinds of connotations because as yet these have neither been listed nor classified according to structure, despite the work done by Rössler (64-104).

So the model has only a limited validity and function. It is only valid in cases in which one or several series of *connotators* refer to a coherent paradigmatic system at a connotative level. It is composed in this way because it is meant to visualize the steps that the reader must take in order to arrive at the recognition of such a connotative system and in order to understand the meaning of the system. Other kinds of *connotation* may require other models, in which the parts that are an extension of the model of Barthes will have to acquire either another form or another content, or both.

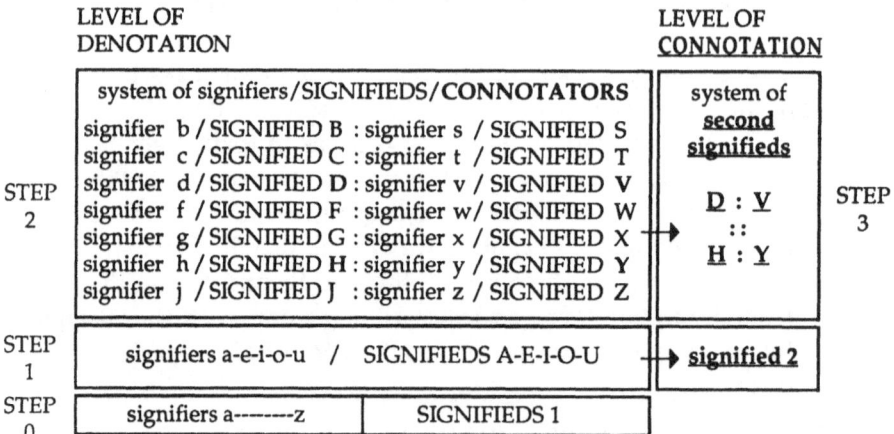

Figure 3: The steps in which a system of connotations is produced by the reader

Step 0 corresponds with level 1 of Barthes' model, but relates to the entire text of the book. The model visualizes how the reader of a written text connects a *signified*—mostly a complex signified—with the total number of *signifiers* (a-z) of the text, and thus produces a coherent total meaning at the level of the *denotation (signified 1)*. At first sight step 1 seems to relate to level 2 in Barthes' model, where it is the level of the *connotation*, but it does not, in fact. Step 1 is rather a first divergence from Barthes' level 2, while steps 2 and 3 of the model can be seen as further divergences. In step 1, the first that is specific to the *connotation*, the model shows how one or more *signifiers* (a-e-i-o-u)—which on the level of the *denotation* make their usual contribution to the meaning at that level *(SIGNIFIEDS A-E-I-O-U)*—have the function (designated by →) to point out to the reader the presence of a second layer of meaning. This is done for instance through the remarkable frequency of a lexeme or the presence of *signifiers* which make a reader realize that the text cannot be adequately or even grasped at all at the *denotative* level. In step 2 the model shows how in one or more syntagmatic series of *signifiers* (b-j and s-z) distributed over larger or smaller parts of the text the reader recognizes the actual *connotators*. On the basis of their meaning at the *denotative* level (B-J and S-Z) these *connotators* constitute for the reader a paradigmatic series which transcends the contexts in which the parts of the series occur so that this series can function as *signifier* for a *signified* still unknown but at the *connotative* level contained in the text of the book (*signifiers* a-z). In step 3 the model shows how the reader, on the basis of the text, connects four central elements of the series of *signifiers* which between themselves constitute the equivalence series $D : V :: H : Y$, with a new *signified*, which can be designated by the equivalence series D : V :: H : Y and which reveals the connotative meaning of the series D : V :: H : Y, as will be explained in the second part of this article.

With this we have distinguished three steps taken by the reader when producing the *connotative* system in question. They could be subdivided further, but for the moment it is better to leave it at this because they make it sufficiently clear that the reader has to perform a number of different operations in order to produce the second meaning at the *connotative* level.

2. *The Secret in Mark, with Reference to a Connotative System*

2.0 *The messianic secret in Mark*

Ever since William Wrede (1901) the messianic secret has remained the central theme in the study of Mark. The importance of this theme may be gathered from the fact that the series "Issues in Religion and Theology" started with this subject (Tuckett, 1983). In 1973 and 1976 H. Räisänen argued forcibly against the lumping together of the messianic secret and the enigmatic character of the parables. But his arguments rely on a diachronic research model and are based on irregularities and contradictions in the text. However, these arguments lose much of their force in a synchronic approach in which the enigmatic quality of the parables, the secret of Jesus' identity, and the lack of understanding on the part of the disciples are regarded as interrelated data acting together as a *connotator* for a *connotative* level of meaning.

2.1 *Signals referring to the presence of a second meaning*

The reader of Mark is able to read the first three chapters as a story about Jesus—and is able to remain confined to the *denotative* level of meaning. With chapter 4 the reader comes across a cluster of *signifiers* which indicates that certain passages in this chapter have meanings that cannot be grasped at first.

2.1.1. It is not with the first but with the strongest signal that the reader becomes aware of the presence of a potential meaning which at that moment he is still unable to produce. This is found in 4:11, and reads as follows: "To you has been given the secret of the kingdom of God, but for those outside everything is in parables." In this statement, put into Jesus' mouth by the narrator, "the secret of the kingdom of God" is set in contrast with "in parables." Even if "parables" refers to incomprehensible riddles (Pesch:239, and Gnilka:162–63), it does not necessarily follow that the "secret of the kingdom" refers to a secret that has been revealed (Pesch:239). This view is inconsistent with the fact that the verb on which "the secret" is dependent as an object (δίδωμι) differs from the verbs normally used to indicate the revelation of a secret: ἀποκαλύπτω (LXX: Sir 3:18; 27:16,17,21; Theod: Dan 2:19,28,29,30,47,49; cf. ἀποκάλυψις in Rom 16:25 and Eph 13:3), ἀνακαλύπτω (LXX: Dan 2:28,29; Theod: Dan 2:29), ἐκφαίνω (LXX: Dan 2:19,30,47), δηλόω (LXX: 2:29,47), γνωρίζω (Eph 1:9; 3:3; 6:19; Col 1:27), καταγγέλλω (1 Cor 2:1), λαλέω (Col 4:3) and λέγω (1 Cor 15:51). Only in one place, viz. 1 Cor 14:2, is λαλέω used to indicate the utterance of secret language which is not understood. The syntagm δίδωμι τὸ μυστήριον does not occur once in the OT or the NT, and only in one comparable case in which there is mention of the giving of secrets—and even then only indirectly—, namely 1 Enoch 68:1, which reads as follows:

> After that, he gave me instructions in all the secret things (found) in the book of my grandfather, Enoch, and in the parables which were given to him; and he put them together for me in the words of the book which is with me. (Charlesworth:I, 47)

That the combination concerned in Mark 4:11 is unusual is further emphasized by Matthew and Luke's insertion of "to know" before "the secret" so as to form a more conventional syntagm (Matt 13:11; Luke 8:10). In this light it must be considered highly unlikely that the text of Mark refers to the revelation of the secret in question.

Neither is it clear why "the secret of the kingdom of God" in Mark 4:11 should refer to the hidden kingdom of God (Pesch:239; Gnilka:165), which was to be revealed. In the context of Mark 4 there are few or no clues for this interpretation. The context rather suggests a connection between the secret on the one hand and the similarities or equivalences implied in the parable of the seed on the other. As in 1 Enoch 68:1, it is therefore more likely that in addition to a first meaning the parable in Mark also has a second, as yet hidden and uncomprehended meaning, as a result of which we can possibly speak not only of a secret but also of a riddle. This is a) an auditive or visual construct, b) which has an unknown meaning, c) is constructed precisely to reveal that meaning, d) as a rule also holds the key to this revelation, and e) is presented by someone who knows the solution to someone who does not. But is this possibility not excluded by the interpretation of the parable story in 4:14–20? The meaning of the parable story seems to be fully disclosed there through a consistent decoding, with the key provided by 4:14 which equates "the seed" (which, strangely enough, remains unmentioned) with "the word." But is that really the case? Is the series of secondary meanings really fully revealed there? One could say, after all, that only the second level of meaning concerned with the seed is revealed and that this does not exclude the presence of yet another level of meaning which is still unknown to the reader. But even of the disclosed level of secondary meanings not everything is in fact disclosed. It is true that equivalences are given of practically all elements in the order in which they occur in the parable story, each time introduced by the phrase "this is..." (grammatically adapted, of course). But there is one exception, namely the character of the sower. This leads sometimes to the conclusion that he is unimportant (Boucher:49). But the opposite conclusion is possible as well and is in fact drawn by L. Marin (124):

> ...la seule figure du récit-parabole qui n'ait pas reçu le commencement d'un décodage est le semeur lui-même qui a tout entier glissé dans la semence-parole. On aperçoit l'importance capitale de cette remarque: si une place reste vide dans l'espace décodé-transcodé du récit secondaire dans le discours explicatif, c'est celle-là même que tient celui qui parle ce discours, Jésus, qui s'y désigne métaphoriquement par cette absence dans l'espace du texte....

It is not at all impossible that Marin is right. After all, the interpretation of the parable does explain the various listening and reading positions, as Delorme (5–23) has stated, but the position of the speaker remains implicit. Thus only half of the communication process is illuminated, namely the part relating to the *addressee*; the complementary part relating to the *addresser* remains obscure and is not revealed. One could also put it in this way: the interpretation given in 4:14–20 does decode the parable story about the seed and the soil it falls on for the reader, but by remaining silent about the figure of the sower it encodes at the same time for the reader a secret which refers to the identity of the sower. This secret affects the reader as a riddle that is propounded to him in order to make him look for the solution. Whether he can find this at the denotative or connotative level of meaning is an open question as yet. Both are equally possible.

2.1.2. If we continue on the basis of this information, it appears that this signal within Mark 4 is intensified by a number of other sets of signals, so that the repetition of these signals makes it almost impossible for the reader not to concern himself with the enigmatic quality of the story.

2.1.2.1. The first set of signals itself shows the same phenomenon of repetition and intensification. The "Listen!" (4:3) at the beginning of the parable is paralleled with a more elaborate and considerably stronger ending: "He who has ears to hear, let him hear" (4:9). Within the story Jesus calls on the listeners, but at the level of the Gospel of Mark these words call on the reader to pay special attention, which implies that possibly something out of the ordinary is said here which is not immediately clear to the reader. This need not, but could relate to a second level of meanings that is not revealed yet.

But there is more than repetition and intensification. The same elements recur in 4:23–24, and they are given special emphasis again through "Listen!" being expanded into "Take heed what you hear." The position of this textual element is marked by inversion, for in the former case the exhortation is put as a framework around the parable of the seed, whereas in the latter it is placed in the center and framed between the sayings of the lamp and the corn measure.

2.1.2.2. In the second case we also find a set of signals characterized by repetition and intensification, for the quotation from Isaiah (6:9–10) in Mark 4:12 speaks of people who look but do not really see, and of people who hear but do not understand what they hear. This does not refer to those who are given the secret, but to those to whom everything happens in puzzling riddles; it is made quite clear to the reader that there are ways of seeing and hearing that do not lead to insight and understanding. This theme of hearing without understanding recurs at the end of the parable chapter in 4:33–34, but it obtains its full meaning only after a third set of signals which must be discussed first.

2.1.2.3. The third set of signals is to be found in the sayings of 4:21–25 which are put between the first parable of the seed with its interpretation and the other parables of the seed. What is concealed in the first parable and its interpretation is then compared to the oil lamp which is not to be put under a bushel or a bed but because of its very nature demands to be brought out and set on the lampstand (4:21). If in the first instance the story conceals something from the reader, it does so precisely in order to disclose and bring it to light in the second instance. (In 4:22 the twofold ἵνα indicates that the concealment is intentional.) The reader has therefore every reason to expect that the secret will be revealed.

However, the text makes it clear immediately to the reader that this expectation will not be fulfilled automatically; the expectation will only be realized after the reader has made a concentrated effort to listen most attentively (4:23–24a). The measure of listening of the reader is the basis for the measure of the reader's understanding of what has been said; according to that measure the secret will be revealed to him and the riddle solved, and he will be able to see even more than he could expect on account of the attention given by him (4:24b). The reader who is attentive is given understanding, but the reader who is not is robbed even of the understanding he has (4:25).

This interpretation of the sayings in 4:21-25 may at first sight seem arbitrary. It is quite possible that in another context they could or even should be interpreted differently. But the fact that the two sayings of 4:21-22 and 4:24b-25 are structured in a concentric manner around 4:23-24a (which calls on the reader to prick up his ears and listen closely to what he hears) justifies this interpretation. The urgent request to listen carefully made to the reader before and after the parable of the seed (4:3,9), precisely in the outer part of the concentric structure, acquires additional significance through the repetition in 4:23-24a. Accordingly, the passage not only calls on the reader to open his mind to meanings that are not clear at a first reading of the parable, but also points out that when listened to attentively the parable of the seed says even more than what is elucidated in the interpretation in 4:13-20.

2.1.2.4. In this context the verses 4:33 and 4:34 concluding the parable chapter also merit attention, as has already been said at the end of 2.1.2.2. They say in brief that Jesus only proclaimed his message through such parables for the benefit of the crowd so that they could understand it, but that he explained everything only to his disciples, when he was alone with them. With Gnilka (191) I am of the opinion that "to hear" means here "to understand" because of the presence of ἠδύναντο ("they were able"). If this is correct, then the information given by the narrator makes the reader at the end of the parable discourse realize that apart from the meaning understood by the crowd the parables have a second meaning which Jesus only reveals to the disciples.

2.1.2.5. As a consequence the chapter appears to be interspersed with indicators telling the reader that a straightforward first reading cannot bring to light all meanings. In addition to being carriers of announcements that can be understood by everyone, the parables of the book are also carriers of a message that can only be understood after special attention and effort. That this applies particularly to the parable of the seed (4:3-8) appears from the fact that the signals relating to a hidden meaning are most numerous exactly around this parable. On the other hand 4:13 emphasizes there is an interaction between the understanding of this parable and that of all parables.

2.2   *The parables of the seed and the vineyard*

Although the word "parable"—as appears particularly from 3:23; 4:11; 7:17; and 13:28—has a much wider meaning in Mark than the specific parable stories, and could therefore refer to a great many more parables than that of the seed (4:3-8) and that of the vineyard (12:1-12), the study of Y. Almeida has shown convincingly that these two are related to each other in a special way and taken together have a typical and significant function in the book.

2.2.1. The most striking equivalences and contrasts are summarized by Almeida in a survey (251–252) which may suffice for our present purpose:

Figure 4: Equivalences and oppositions between the parable of the seed and the parable of the tenants

PARABLE STORIES

	THE SOWER	THE TENANTS	
1	**euphoric** trajectory	**dysphoric** trajectory	1
2	isotopy of **word**	isotopy of **body**	2
3	isotopy of **plants**	isotopy of **plants**	3
*	sowing	reaping	*
*	fig.: grain (food)	fig.: wine (beverage)	*
4	isotopy of **space**	isotopy of **space**	4
*	proxemic	topographic	*
*	outside	inside	*
5	position	position :	5
	in the **first** part of Mk	in the **last** part of Mk	

In addition to these superficial relationships, a remarkable system of correspondences is disclosed by an analysis of the deep structures. These can be summarized in the following two formulas:

SOWER: isotopy of plants $\simeq$ isotopy of space $\simeq$ isotopy of word
TENANTS: isotopy of plants $\simeq$ isotopy of space $\simeq$ isotopy of body

The two formulas show *isomorphy* between the *isotopy of the plants* and *space* but at the same time they show a striking substitution between the two parables. The *isotopy of word* in the parable of the seed is replaced by an *isotopy of body* in the parable of the winegrowers, which Almeida represents with the formula (253):

<u>PARABLE OF THE SEED</u> $\simeq$ <u>PARABLE OF THE TENANTS</u>
   isotopy of word   isotopy of body

This visualizes both what the two parable stories have in common and how they differ.

2.2.2.   In view of point 5 in figure 4 above it is also clear that the position of both parable stories in the text of the Gospel is such that the parable of the seed is in the first and that of the tenants is in the second main part.

Moreover, each of them functions as a mirror story of Jesus, expressing by means of a metaphor what either part tells about Jesus. The first part deals with the proclamation of the word and is predominantly euphoric, the second part deals with the violent way in which Jesus' adversaries put an end to this, and is mainly dysphoric. Together the two mirror stories represent in miniature what the two main parts of the book and of the whole story tell about Jesus.

2.2.3. Two considerations must be added to this. First, Almeida does not make a connection between what the parables tell and the attribution of a second system of meanings, something clearly called for precisely by the contextual relationship of the parable of the seed. Secondly, Almeida does see connections between the secret of Jesus' identity and certain passages in Mark—including the stories about the two feedings (6:35–44 and 8:1-9) and that of the last supper (14:22-25). But he discusses these connections exclusively within the analysis of a semiotic system and not as the result of a synthetic operation on the part of the reader (265–304).

2.3   *The two stories of feeding (6:35–44 and 8:1-9)*

2.3.1. The two stories of feeding, also, are accompanied by signals drawing the reader's attention to a second, as yet incomprehensible meaning. The first signal is to be found in the passage relating the second crossing of the lake, where the theme of the misunderstanding—already obscurely present in the story of the first crossing (4:40–41)—is brought to a crisis in the story of the miraculous feeding which has taken place before: "For they did not understand about the loaves, but their hearts were hardened" (6:52). The signal is repeated and considerably intensified after the second feeding when at the third crossing Jesus troubles the disciples with awkward questions (8:17). In the first place he asks them why they worry about the fact that they have not brought any loaves with them, and then says to them: "Do you not yet perceive or understand? Are your hearts hardened?" And after this, in words that largely repeat what in 4:12 had been said about the outsiders: "Having eyes do you not see, and having ears do you not hear?" (8:18). After reminding them of the numbers of baskets full of broken pieces collected after the two miraculous feedings, Jesus finally repeats once more: "Do you not yet understand?" In what way do these words function as a signal for the presence of a second, yet unknown meaning? In that the reader becomes aware of being in exactly the same position as the disciples. At least at a first reading the reader also fails to see what the disciples do not understand about the baskets filled with broken pieces left over. In the stories of feeding the reader has read that the remaining broken pieces serve as a symbol for the abundance of bread. But it is clear from the questions Jesus asks the disciples that they must have another meaning as well.

2.3.2. But what meaning? The reader who wants to have an answer is referred back by the text to three preceding passages. First to the two stories of a miraculous feeding (6:35–44 and 8:1–8), which are still fresh in the reader's memory. Next, through the striking similarity between the two quotations about seeing but not understanding in 8:18 and 4:12, the reader is also referred back to the parable of the seed in 4:3–9. If he follows these indications, the reader will soon come to the conclusion that there are connections between this parable and the miraculous feedings which had escaped detection at first. The following indications attract the reader's attention at once, but for the moment it is not clear what they can contribute to the meaning of the book.

2.3.2.1. The most trivial but also the *first* and most recognizable indication is the relation suggested by the text between the crop of grain in the parable of the seed and the loaves as the main part of the two meals. The grain is, after all, needed for the baking of the loaves. In other words, grain and bread belong to the same semantic field of the production and consumption of food. Besides, the syntagmatic sequence in which these terms occur in the passages mentioned corresponds to the sequence in which they occur in the process that begins with sowing and ends with eating, and thus to their paradigmatic sequence.

2.3.2.2. A *second* connection may be seen in a structural similarity. In both cases there is an initial situation that can be characterized as "little" and a final situation that can be characterized as "much" and even "abundant." The relatively little seed that falls in good soil yields an abundant crop, and with only a few loaves a great many people are fed abundantly.

2.3.2.3. A *third* connection could be that in the case of the seed and the loaves a quantity remains that is many times larger than what was available at the outset.

2.3.2.4. A *fourth* connection is of a different order. On rereading the parable chapter the reader will find there is not just one parable concerned with sowing and harvesting, but two. Next to the longer parable about the seed and its uncertain fate there is a shorter one about the seed that grows by itself (4:26–29). A longer and a shorter parable about the seed and its produce appear to correspond to a longer and a shorter story about a miraculous feeding with bread.

2.3.2.5. Finally, there is perhaps a *fifth* connection, this time between the second parable of the seed and the two stories of feeding. The absence of any activity on the part of the farmer after the seed has been scattered over the field might have an equivalence in the absence of any specific activity of Jesus as a result of which so few loaves can satisfy the hunger of so many people. He does nothing else than what any head of the family would do before a meal: ask a blessing and break the bread. On distribution there appears to be more than enough for everyone.

2.3.3. The relevance of these five connections is as yet unclear. But the reader must reckon with the possibility that the passages form a network of connotative references of *connotators* and that the failure to understand in 8:15–21 bears on these connotative references.

By now the reader has understood from the context that this failure to understand may at least partly have to do with Jesus' identity. This would appear first of all from the fact that the questions of 8:17–21 are asked during a crossing of the lake and that both the fundamental attitude of the disciples and their complete lack of understanding of Jesus come up in a similar way at the two other crossings, as appears with a comparison of 4:40; 6:52; and 8:17–21:

Figure 5: Similarities between the stories of the crossing

4:40	οὔπω ἔχετε πίστιν;		
6:52	οὐ	συνῆκαν ἐπὶ τοῖς	ἄρτοις
8:17-19	οὔπω νοεῖτε οὐδὲ συνίετε...	τοὺς... ἄρτους;	
8:21	οὔπω	συνίετε;	

τί δειλοί ἐστε;	4:40
ἀλλ' ἦν αὐτῶν ἡ καρδία πεπωρωμένη	6:52
πεπωρωμένην ἔχετε τὴν καρδίαν ὑμῶν;	8:17

The relationship of the failure to understand with Jesus' identity appears also in the next part of the book. Immediately after the third discussion in the boat, comes the central part in which appears Jesus' own answer to the question of who he is (8:27–29). This is the threefold announcement of his arrest, execution and resurrection as the completion of his way of life. How much this is connected with the theme of seeing and understanding can be inferred from the fact that this central part is provided with a framework which consists of the only two stories relating the healing of a blind man in Mark (cf. van Iersel, 1982:131–32, 1983). The theme of the first story (8:22–26) is the development of "seeing" into "looking intently" and the doubly qualified "seeing everything clearly." And the story supposes that there are various degrees of seeing: from a way of seeing which causes one to misinterpret what one sees to a way of seeing which is both clear and comprehensive. The theme of the second story (10:46–52) is the connection between seeing on the one hand and following Jesus on the way on the other.

2.3.4. So we come to the following tentative conclusions: (1) the two parables of the seed and the two stories of a miraculous feeding are connected in Mark in a very specific way; (2) it is quite probable that both these parables and the two stories of feeding speak about the identity of Jesus but in a way that is still hidden; (3) the passages mentioned and the identity of Jesus not only puzzle his disciples within the story but also the reader outside it, although it would seem that the reader has been fully informed by the words of the Baptist and the voice from heaven on the first page of the Gospel.

2.4 Eating and drinking

2.4.1. If in the first half of the Gospel regular mention is made of eating (1:6; 2:16,26; 3:20; 5:43; 6:31,36–44; 7 2–5,27–28; 8:1–9), drinking is not mentioned in the book before the second half (9:41; 10:38–39). In that second half we also find the parable story of the vineyard, of which Almeida has demonstrated so clearly and convincingly that it is the counterpart of the parable of the seed. Both parable stories pertain to the isotopy of the production of what people consume for the preservation of life. The parable of the seed relates to the production of the food required, and the parable of the vineyard relates to the production of the drink which people usually prefer to have with their food, namely wine.

2.4.2. There are a few other important oppositions. The first is a contrast in atmosphere. The parable of the seed is predominantly euphoric, that of the vineyard dysphoric, at least if we leave out of consideration the parable (quoted from Ps 118) about the stone rejected by the builders but chosen by JHWH to become the cornerstone (12:10–11). A second contrast bears on the metaphoric reference, which in the case of the parable of the seed is of a verbal and in the case of the parable of the winegrowers of a somatic nature; for, according to the interpretation following it, the former is brought to bear on the various effects of the word when it is listened to by people of different dispositions, while the latter is connected with the murder plotted and later successfully carried out by Jesus' adversaries.

2.4.3. It also seems to be of major importance that in contrast to the first the second parable story clearly confronts the reader with the question of Jesus' identity. Within the story of Mark, the high priests, scribes, and elders realize in the end that this parable is aimed at them, and therefore attempt to arrest Jesus (12:12). The reader, however, has already understood that the story refers to what is going to happen to Jesus. After all, the reader knows on the basis of 1:11 and 9:7 the identity of the "one beloved son." In addition the reader also understands that there is a clear equivalence between the triple announcement of the rejection of the son of man, the rejection and discarding of the stone by the builders, and the condemnation of Jesus; between the triple announcement of the murder of the son of man, the murder of the son of the owner by the tenants, and the execution of Jesus; and finally also between the announcement of the resurrection of the son of man, the placing of the stone as the corner- or keystone of the building by JHWH, and the raising of Jesus from the dead. Thus is brought together in this parable what the reader has been told in 1:11 and 9:7 about the identity of Jesus as the son of God and, in the central part of the book, about the way of the son of man Jesus, which leads to the resurrection through the valley of torture and murder.

2.4.4. Meanwhile the riddle of the loaves, which neither the disciples nor the reader have understood, has faded into the background. Nevertheless, it begins to dawn on the reader where the solution is to be found. Field, seed, grain, bread, and eating had already proved to be interrelated by way of a network of possible *connotators*. This network finds an extension in the second half of the book where it has a counterpart relating to wine, namely the vineyard and the grapes. But with this is not yet given the key that enables the reader to read the connotative system and thereby solve the riddle of the book and unlock the secret of the parable of the seed.

2.5   The key

2.5.1. That key is to be found in 14:22–25, the passage which is usually referred to as the institution of the Lord's supper. This name is incorrect, however, for, unlike Luke 22:1–19 and 1 Cor 11:24–25, Mark 14:22–25 does not mention a single word about a later repetition of what Jesus does here. So there is no question of an institution. The words used rather point in another direction. Within the confined space of a few lines the reader not only reads about the bread and the cup with the crushed fruits of the vineyard, about the breaking and pouring, the eating and drinking, but the reader also recognizes the words which are used elsewhere in Mark to indicate the meaning of something or someone: "This is..."

2.5.2. This formula is recognized as a regular feature of the questions "What is this?" (1:27) and "Who is this?" (4:41), "Is not this the carpenter, the son of Mary and brother of James and Joses and Judas and Simon?"

(6:3), "Who do men say that I am?" (8:27), and finally "Who do you say that I am?" (8:29), which without exception concern the identity of Jesus. The reader also recognizes them as a variant of the explanatory formula in 7:2 and furthermore as the basic form of the phrase which in the interpretation of the parable of the seed is used four times to indicate the equivalences between elements of that parable and situations in real life (4:15,16,18,20). Finally, the reader also recognizes them in answers that are given to the basic question of the book who Jesus is: "This is my Son" (9:7), and "This is the heir" (12:7).

But the reader can therefore also deduce from this what function the double "this is" has at the last meal of bread and wine. It explains to the reader the equivalence of the broken bread with Jesus' murdered body and of the poured wine with his blood shed innocently. If this is correct, then it is here in Jesus' own words that eventually the key is offered with which the secret can be unlocked. These words of Jesus are related to what happens to his body and blood. And for that reason the verbal reference of the parable of the seed and the somatic reference of the parable of the vineyard completely coincide here. The offered key consists in two equivalent series of *connotators*, which refer to a *connotative* system. These connections can be simply visualized in a graphic representation, as in figure 6.

Figure 6: The key: two series of *connotators* and their *connotations*

FIELD				VINEYARD
CORN				GRAPES
BREAD	:: BODY	BLOOD	::	WINE
TAKING				TAKING
BREAKING	:: KILLING	SHEDDING	::	POURING OUT
GIVING				GIVING
TAKING				TAKING
EATING				DRINKING

The reader who realizes the connection will find it difficult to deny the connotative system a certain measure of obviousness. Most probably this obviousness has to do with the nature of the relationship between the *connotators* and the *connotative* system. This relationship is iconic, meaning that it departs from a visual reality, as is represented in the broken bread and poured wine at the last supper of Jesus with his disciples. And it seems obvious that it is easier for the reader to recall this visual image than to recall a purely verbal expression.

2.5.2.   It has now become clear what the disciples and the reader failed to understand with regard to the loaves. Within the stories of the miraculous feedings reference is made in a denotative manner to the food so abundantly provided by Jesus and his disciples that a great many baskets are left. Within the network of connotations reference is made at another level, to the identity of Jesus. This reference is comprehensible only to the reader who has taken pains to understand. The identity of Jesus cannot be understood unless the broken bread is seen from the outset as a reference to Jesus' murdered body. Precisely the paradoxical combination of the following three aspects is part of Jesus' inalienable identity: (a) that Jesus is the beloved son of God; (b) that therefore he is tortured and murdered; (c) that he does not escape this even though he could if he wanted to (15:29–32). Therefore, in 1:11 Jesus' identity is only partly revealed to the reader by the voice from heaven.

2.5.3.   In this connection it should also be noted that from the story of the last supper retrospective light falls on the curious announcement in 8:14 that the disciples have forgotten to bring loaves: "And they had only one loaf with them in the boat." This comment by the narrator has everything to do with what the disciples and the reader fail to understand. The only loaf they have with them in the boat is none other than Jesus himself (Pesch: 4:14; Gnilka: 311–12). Not for the disciples—because the narrator is speaking—but for the reader the solution to the secret of Jesus' identity was already present here, be it in veiled terms.

2.6   Once more the parable of the seed

2.6.1.   Although the question of the secret of Jesus' identity may have been answered, the problem of the secret of the parable of the seed remains yet unsolved. Still, the answer is no longer difficult to give. For, if we consider the structural equivalences between the parable stories and the story of Mark in which they are embedded (in Figure 7), the parable story of the seed can be read from two perspectives: from the perspective of what Jesus does in Galilee and from the perspective of what happens to him in Jerusalem, or, in other words, from the beginning of the book and from the end, or also, from the verbal and from the somatic aspect.

104   Semeia

Figure 7: Structural equivalences between the parable stories and the main parts of Mark

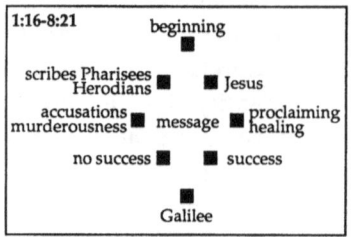
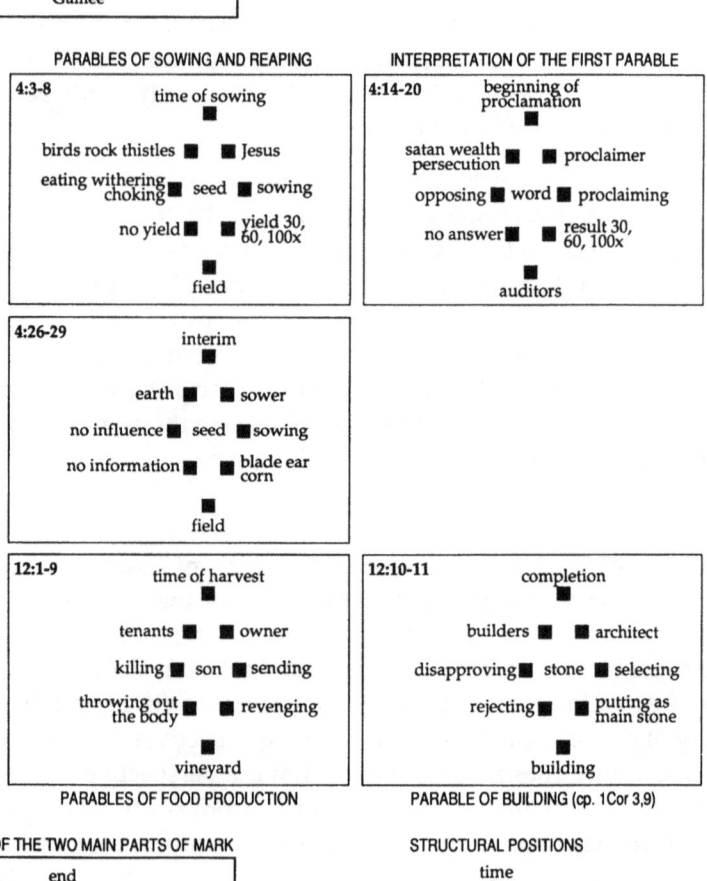
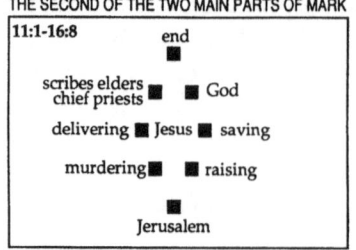
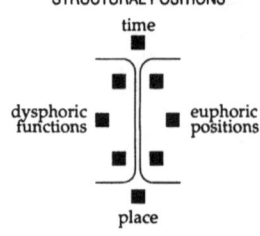

What happens to the seed in the parable is—seen from the first series of perspectives—an equivalence of the different effects of the word proclaimed by any preacher but in particular of the word proclaimed by Jesus. From the second series of perspectives, the failure of a considerable portion of the seed is an equivalence of the violent death of Jesus in Jerusalem, the small remainder of seed an equivalence of the buried body of Jesus, and the abundant harvest from that remainder an equivalence of Jesus' resurrection. Marin, therefore, is right in saying that it is of paramount importance that in the interpretation of the parable given in 4:14–20 the figure of the sower remains unnamed.

It is left to the reader to supply the equivalences here. The use of the plural is intentional because there are now two systems of equivalences that cross one another. In the first there is equivalence between Jesus and the sower, in the second between Jesus and the seed. It is with the sower Jesus as it is with his word; only after considerable losses, including the loss of his freedom, his physical integrity, and his life, is he put in the right by God in that he raises him from the dead. That the seed and its sower should suffer the same fate is the paradoxical riddle which is the reference of the parable of the seed.

2.6.2.   And the enigma of the loaves? On rereading 8:14–21 the reader notes that only the disciples speak of loaves (8:16). Precisely this causes Jesus to reproach them bitterly for what they fail to see, and to draw their attention to the pieces (κλάσματα) left over (8:17–21). In retrospect the reader recognizes in "pieces" one of the key words of the *connotative* system (κλάω, "break"). Outside of 8:14–21 verb and noun only occur in the stories of the miraculous feedings and the last supper (6:41,43; 8:6,8,19,20; 14:22). /To break the bread/ is an equivalent of /to murder Jesus/, which corresponds with /to shed Jesus' blood/. The reference to the Pharisees and Herod (8:15) confirms that the pieces of broken bread refer to Jesus' violent death (cf. 3:6; 6:16–29).

2.6.3.   Within the scope of the Gospel of Mark the riddle is solved by no one. That is only logical because the narrator has incorporated the riddle in the Gospel in behalf of his readers and only the readers have access to the connotations woven into the text of the story from the book in its entirety. Accordingly, the readers do not, and need not, receive an answer from anyone, not even from the narrator, to the key question of the book "Who do you say that I am?" (8:29). Instead they are challenged to find an answer themselves. Thus it is left to the reader to find a solution to the riddle which is contained in the book. The narrator only provides those elements which to his mind should not be lacking in any answer: That the name which suits Jesus best is "son of God," that the only attitude which does justice to him is to follow him on his way with unfaltering steps, and that both the utterance of that name and the imitation of his way of life are only valuable if one does not forget that faithfulness may lead to arrest, torture, and execution.

2.6.4.   Naturally the solving of this riddle demands a specific effort on the part of the reader, as is the same with the spectator of *Oidipous Tyrannos* and the reader of the stories about Samson and of a modern detective story or crime fiction, which also deal with secrets and riddles. They are usually about a violent death, and are especially concerned with ascertaining the criminal and his or her motives. It is exactly the other way round in Mark. The identity of the murderers as well as their motives are known. Although the reader knows the name of the victim, however, his fundamental identity remains a secret, and his motives call for further explanation. There is a fundamental difference also in another respect. When the reader of the Samson stories or any good detective novel has solved the riddle the book can be closed because the reading has been rounded off satisfactorily. But when the reader of Mark has found the answer there is an awareness that it is only a partial and provisional answer; although it touches upon the secret of Jesus' personality, it does not exhaust it, and only means something if the reader follows Jesus on his way.

But what about the reader who does not have this competence? In so far as information is concerned, such a reader need not fear being at a disadvantage as compared with other readers. In 8:27–9:8 alone all the information produced by the connotative operation is available as content at the level of the denotative meaning. Why nevertheless this connotative level as well? Could it be that precisely as a result of the many operations connected with that level the reader becomes considerably more involved in the meaning which is produced?

3   Reconsideration of the Theory

3.0   We now return to the theory and do so in three stages. In the first stage an attempt is made to adapt the model represented in Figure 3. Next the new model will be tested with reference to the two basic models of Figures 1 and 2.

3.1   The steps unfolded in the proposed model of Figure 3 should be connected with the equivalence series which have been presented in Figure 6 as the key to the secret of Mark. Since the two models are constructed along different lines, this is not possible without an intermediary step which makes clear how the equivalence series fit into a model constructed on the basis of the relationship between a denotative and a connotative level of meaning. In Figure 8 this relation is visualized in the following model.

Figure 8: The equivalences between /bread/ and /wine/ on the basis of the connotation-model

ἄρτος /bread/		/body/	/blood/	wine/ποτήριον		connotations
field					vineyard	
corn					grapes	a double
BREAD	::	BODY	BLOOD	::	WINE	network of
taking					taking	equivalent
BREAKING	::	KILLING	SHEDDING	::	POURING OUT	connotators
giving					giving	
eating					drinking	
		connotational system		signified /pouring out wine	ἐκχύνω οἶνον	metonymy
signifier κλάω ἄρτον	signified /breaking bread/			signified /[filling] a cup/	signifier (γεμίζω) ποτήριον	denotations

This is the first model which shows, at the denotative level, the metonymy in which the wine is referred to. The primary denotation (the cup) functions by virtue of an iconic relation as a metonym (the wine), which however has been used so often that it has ceased to be thought of as such. Next, the denotative meanings in their turn appear to function as a connotative system within which (through 14:22-24) the reader's attention is drawn to the parallel structure of the two equivalence series around bread and wine. The equivalences between the broken bread and the poured wine, on the one hand, and the murdered body—compare Matt 10:28 and Luke 12:4 for this somewhat peculiar term—and the shed blood, on the other, are based on an iconic relationship, and because of that convince the reader directly. The equivalence has become customary in the Christian congregation and consequently the ultimate connotations are symbolical, which again enhances its effect on the reader considerably.

3.2   After this intermediary step the model of Figure 3 can now without difficulty be fitted into Figure 9.

Figure 9: The steps in which the reader produces the connotations of /bread/

	A TWOFOLD NETWORK OF CONNOTATORS				SYSTEM OF CONNOTATIONS	
2	ἀγρός /field/	καρπός /corn/	ἄρτος /BREAD/	λαμβάνω /taking/	κλάω /BREAKING/	δίδωμι /giving/	ἐσθίω /eating/	:ἀμπελών /vineyard/ :καρπός /grape/ :οἶνος /WINE/ :λαμβάνω /taking/ :ἐκχύνω /pouring out/ :δίδωμι /giving/ :πίνω /drinking/	BODY : BLOOD : : KILLING : SHEDDING	3
1	signifiers :	/secrecy/ /riddles/ /lack of understanding/			PRESENCE OF A LEVEL OF CONNOTATIONS	
		/bread/			JESUS	4
0	signifier ἄρτος	signified /bread/				

Here are unfolded the steps by which the reader realizes the first connotation, that between the bread and Jesus. The model is more complete than that of Figure 3 and shows that the reader makes a circular movement. Apart from the three steps of the model designed first there is a fourth step, in which the connotative meaning of /bread/ is really produced (step 4). In step 0 the reader makes the connection between *signifier* and *signified* at the denotative level. The connection at the connotative level is not made immediately. Only in the second instance (step 1) does the reader, on the basis of a number of *signifiers*, come to the conclusion that attention must be paid to connotative meanings without such meanings becoming clear. Only when the reader also recognizes a double and equivalent series of *connotators* (step 2) in a number of elements (which fully retain their first meaning at denotative level) and connects the connotative system with it (step 3), can the performance of meaning at the connotative level take place (step 4). That the steps follow a circular movement is not without importance. It has to do with the fact that the reader does not acquire the complete series of *connotators* as well as the key enabling the switch to the system of connotations until the reader starts reading the last chapter but one. With retrospective effect the reader can then produce the connotative meaning with regard to the bread.

3.3.   The model represented in Figure 9, however, does not go beyond the production of the connotative meaning of the bread. The way the reader produces the connotative meaning of the sower from the parable of the seed can be visualized by means of another extension of the basic model, as represented in Figure 10.

Figure 10: The steps in which the reader produces the connotations of /sower/ and /seed/

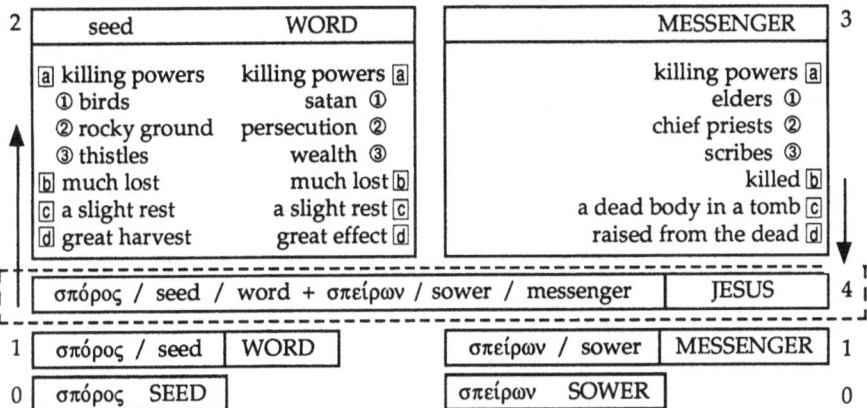

Again, the steps taken by the reader follow a circular movement. And here, too, this has to do with the way in which, in the syntagmatic structure of the text, a paradigm becomes gradually visible which affords the reader such a retrospective vision of the character of the sower that he recognizes the fate of the seed as a metaphorical description of the fate of the proclaimer par excellence Jesus. Step 0 represents the denotative connection made by the reader between the two relevant *signifiers* and their *signifieds*. Step 1 relates to the first connotation of the two sememes /seed/ and /sower/. Step 2 shows that from the syntagmatic connection of what is told in the parable of the seed and in its interpretation in 4 11–20 a paradigmatic structure is derived which in step 3 is recognized as the paradigmatic and syntagmatic structure of what happens to the proclaimer of the word or the messenger: he is murdered and afterwards raised from the dead. In step 4 the reader finally assigns the second connotative meaning to the figure of the sower: he appears to refer to Jesus.

The last operation is considerably more elaborate than the preceding ones and partly for that reason it is also more difficult to perform. The relation between /seed/ and /word/ is largely iconic and is presented to the reader directly and explicitly in the text itself through v. 4:14. But the transition represented by step 3 can only be effected when the reader picks up the new iconic relationships of step 2 and connects them by means of indexical relationships with characters and events from the second half of the story. Finally, in step 4 the reader performs a synthetic operation whereby all the previous symbolic, indexical, and iconic relationships are brought together to form a new iconic relationship between /the sower of the seed/ and /the proclaimer of the word/ and also /the sown seed/ and /the proclaimed word/, on the one hand, and Jesus, on the other.

3.4   If the above is converted into the basic model of R. Barthes, it may be represented as in Figure 11, which as a summary of the interrelations of *signifiers* (left) and *signifieds* (right) visualizes the complex whole of connotations to which the steps analyzed above lead.

Fig. 11 The four connotations of /seed/ in Mark 4:3–8

σπόρος / seed / word / messenger / Jesus					SOWER	Level of connotation 4
σπόρος / seed / word / messenger				JESUS		Level of connotation 3
σπόρος / seed / word			MESSENGER			Level of connotation 2
σπόρος / seed		WORD				Level of connotation 1
σπόρος	SEED					Level of denotation

It appears from this that by separating the *signifiers* and their *signifieds* Barthes' model can visualize in a simple way how a complex whole of connotative meanings is structured. At the same time it becomes clear how fruitful the model is; because of its open construction it is able basically to represent a connotation process even if it has no end.

It is true that the other extended models are not generally valid, but with regard to the simple multiplication of the connotative meanings at increasingly higher levels (as realized in the example of Figure 11), it is at least possible to question whether this model may not be applicable to all connotative meanings.

How do the relatively complicated schemes represented in Figures 9 and 10 relate to Barthes' representation? This relationship may become clear if one realizes that these schemes show the operations the reader has to perform in order to produce the connotative meanings. There is no room for these steps in the model of Figure 2, which, after all, only illustrates how the *signifier* and the *signified are* connected but not how they *are being* connected. For that we must return to the model of Figure 1 (represented in the formula (ERC)RC), which not only comprises the *expression* (or *signifier*) and the *content* (or *signified*) but also the *relation*. And it is precisely this relation to which these diagrams of reader's steps refer. Making the connections between *signifiers* and *signifieds* is precisely the specifically semiotic, and sometimes very complex, operation which the reader must perform if the connotative meanings of a text are to come to light. The phase referred to as step 1 in Figure 9 is, as it were, the engine setting the reader in motion.

3.5   It is not without significance that the results of the operations carried through in part 2 above are already visible in the biblical tradition, especially in John 1:1-14; 12:23-24; and 1 John 1:1-3, even though the text of Mark was not necessarily influenced by that tradition. After all, these places actually pronounce the equivalence between the word and Jesus, on the one hand, and the son of man Jesus and the lost seed that bears fruit, on the other. But going into this now would mean entering the field of intertextuality which is intended to be the subject of a later study.

WORKS CONSULTED ON CONNOTATION

Barthes, R.
- 1964   "Eléments de Sémiologie." *Communications* 4: 91-135.
- 1967   *Elements of Semiology*, London: Jonathan Cape.
- 1970   *S/Z*. Paris: Editions de Seuil.
- 1975   *S/Z*. London: Jonathan Cape

Eco, Umberto
- 1976   *A Theory of Semiotics*, Bloomington: Indiana University Press.

Greimas, A.J. and J. Courtés
- 1979   *Sémiotique; Dictionnaire Raisonné de la Théorie du Langage*. Paris: Hachette.

Grossklaus, G.
- 1981   "Konnotative Typen alltäglicher Weltverständlichung." *Zeitschrift für Semiotik* 3:143-70.

Kanyo, S.
- 1976   "Stil und Konnotation." *Zeitschrift für Literaturwissenschaft und Linguistik* 6:63-77.

Kloepfer, R.
- 1975   *Poetik und Linguistik*. Uni Taschenbücher 366. München: W.Fink.

Lyons, J.
- 1977   *Semantics I*. Cambridge: Cambriclge University Press.

Molino, J.
- 1971   "La connotation." *La Linguistique* 7:5-30.

Patte, D. and A. Patte
1978   *Structural Exegesis: From Theory to Practice*. Philadelphia: Fortress.

Rössler, G.
1979   "Konnotationen, Untersuchungen der Mit- und Nebenbedeutung." *Zeitschrift für Dialektologie und Linguistik*, Beiheft N.F. Nr.29.

Scholes, R.
1982   *Semiotics and Interpretation*. New Haven: Yale University Press.

Schulte-Sasse, J. and R. Werner
1977   *Einführung in die Literaturwissenschaft*. Uni Taschenbücher 640. München: W.Fink.

Stierle, K.
1975   *Text als Handlung*. Uni Taschenbücher 423. München: W.Fink.

Titzmann, M.
1977   *Strukturale Textanalyse*. Uni Taschenbücher 582. München: W.Fink.

Ullmann, S.
1972   *Semantics: An Introduction to the Science of Meaning*. 2nd ed. Oxford: Basil Blackwell.

SPECIFICALLY EXEGETIC LITERATURE

Almeida, Y.
1978   *L'opérativité Sémantique des Récits-Paraboles*. Louvain/Paris: Éditions Peeters/Éditions Du Cerf.

Boucher, M.
1976   *The Mysterious Parable*. CBQMS 6. Washington: The Catholic Biblical Association of America.

Charlesworth, J. H.
1983   *The Old Testament Pseudepigrapha*. Garden-City, N.Y.: Doubleday.

Delorme, J.
1982 "Savior, Croire et Communication Symbolique." *Actes Sémiotiques-Documents* IV 38:5–23.

Gnilka, Joachim
1978 *Das Evangelium nach Markus.* I.Teilband. EKK 11/1. Zürich/Einsiedeln/Köln/Neukirchen-Vluyn: Benziger/Neukirchener Verlag.

Iersel, B. van.
1982 "De betekenis van Marcus vanuit zijn topografische structuur." *Tijdschrift voor Theologie* 22:117–18.
1983 "Locality, Structure and Meaning in Mark." *Linguistica Biblica* 53:45–54.
1985 "Marcus vierdimensionaal." *Schrift* 100:124–59.
1986 *Marcus.* Boxtel/Brugge: Katholieke Bijbelstichting/Tabor.
1987a "Het geheim in Marcus nader bezien." *Tijdschrift voor Theologie* 27:356–69.
1987b "Les Récits-Paraboles et la Fonction du Secret pour le Destinataire De Marc." *Sémiotique et Bible* 45:23–25. Also in *Parole-Figure-Parabole.* Ed. J. Delorme, 189–206. Lyon: Presses Universitaires de Lyon.

Marin, L.
1974 "Essai d'Analyse Structurale d'un Récit-Parabole: Mt. 13, 1–23." Pp. 93–134 in *Le Récit Evangélique.* Ed. Claude Chabrol and Louis Marin. Bibliothèque de Sciences Religieuses, Aubier Montaigne/Éditions du Cerf/Delachaux & Niestlé/Desclée de Brouwer.

Pesch, R.
1976 *Das Markusevangelium.* I. Teil. HThKNT 11/1. Freiburg/Basel/Wein: Herder.

Räisänen, H.
1973 *Die Parabeltheorie im Markusevangelium.* Schriften der Finnischen Exegetischen Gesellschaft 26. Helsinki.
1976 *Das "Messiasgeheimnis" im Markusevangelium.* Schriften der Finnischen Exegetischen Gesellschaft 28. Helsinki.

Tuckett, C., ed.
1983 *The Messianic Secret in Mark.* Issues in Religion and Theology 1. Philadelphia/London: Fortress/SPCK.

Wrede, W.
  1963   *Das Messiasgeheimnis in den Evangelien*. 3rd ed. Göttingen: Vandenhoeck & Ruprecht.

THE RHETORIC OF DIRECTION AND INDIRECTION IN THE GOSPEL OF MARK[1]

Robert M. Fowler
Baldwin-Wallace College

ABSTRACT

The aim of this essay is to use reader-response criticism to talk about the experience of reading the Gospel of Mark, and at the same time to sharpen and clarify the critical vocabulary of reader-response criticism. With regard to the latter, the terms *story* and *discourse, direction* and *indirection, reliable commentary, uptake,* and *inside view* are introduced and used. With regard to the former, passages in Mark are examined in which rhetorical strategies of direction and indirection are employed by the narrator of the Gospel. Under the rubric of direction, the experience of reading two clear and unmistakable instances of reliable commentary by means of *parenthetical comments* is discussed (Mark 10:22 and 12:12), as well as two less-than-clear instances of parenthesis (Mark 2:10 and 2:28). Under the rubric of indirection, the difficult passage Mark 4:11–13 is discussed, in which indirect narrative strategies of *opacity, intertextual allusion, ambiguity, verbal* and *dramatic irony,* and *unanswered, "rhetorical" questions* are used by the narrator. The conclusion is drawn that Mark's Gospel is designed less to *say* something to the reader than to *do* something to the reader, as the reader encounters the twists and turns of the direct and indirect narrative discourse of the Gospel in the act of reading.

My task in this essay is to use reader-response criticism to talk about the experience of reading the Gospel of Mark. I presume a basic familiarity with the standard moves of reader-response criticism, which are described in a growing number of anthologies and general introductions to this brand of criticism (Tompkins; Suleimann and Crosman; Freund). Even though reader-response criticism has obtained the status of a standard approach to literary criticism, and has been applied with success to biblical literature (Detweiler; Fowler, 1981; [1991]; Moore; Resseguie), there is still the need to sharpen and clarify the use of this critical approach to the reading experience. In this essay I want to point out and discuss two broad rhetorical strategies employed in the discourse of Mark's Gospel, strategies that I have called *direction* and *indirection*. I shall discuss these and several other critical terms that can help us to articulate better what we experience as we read Mark's Gospel.

A good place to begin is with the common narratological distinction between the *story* and the *discourse* of a narrative. Seymour Chatman (15–42) explains this terminology clearly and succinctly. The *story* is the *what* of a narrative—the characters and the events that make up the content of the narrative. The *discourse* is the *how* of a narrative—the way in which the narrative is narrated or the way in which the available means of narrative rhetoric are employed by the narrator[2] that we may suppose to be telling the story. So far, so good, but we must hasten to observe that the great bulk of modern criticism of biblical narrative, whether primarily historical or literary in aim, has focused primarily upon the story level of biblical narrative and the events or ideas to which it is thought to refer, whereas reader-response criticism invites us to shift our attention primarily to the experience of encountering the discourse level of biblical narrative in the act of reading. I have argued elsewhere that biblical narrative generally, and the Gospel of Mark particularly, is designed primarily to accentuate the effects of the discourse rather than the contents of the story, but that argument cannot be presented here (see Fowler, [1991]). Suffice it to say here that reader-response criticism is a salutary way to learn how to focus critical scrutiny upon the discourse level, as opposed to the story level, of biblical narrative. With these few words of introduction, we may now look briefly at several instances of direction and indirection at the discourse level of Mark's Gospel.

When I speak of the rhetoric of direction in Mark, I think first and foremost of what Wayne Booth calls "reliable commentary" (Booth: 169–209). The reliable commentary provided by the narrator directs the thinking and understanding of the narratee in relatively clear and determinate ways. By means of this sort of direction the narrator places into the possession of the narratee those unquestionable "facts" that she or he simply must embrace and make use of if she or he wishes to continue reading the narrative with any degree of understanding. In Mark's Gospel the commentary that is issued by the reliable, omniscient, third-person narrator of the Gospel comes to us frequently in the form of explanatory, parenthetical remarks upon elements of the story. Chatman calls this kind of narrative commentary "interpretation": "the open explanation of the gist, relevance, or significance of a story element"(228). The parenthetical comments made in the discourse about elements of the story are legion in Mark and invite exhaustive study (Fowler, 1981:157–179; [1991]). Nevertheless, I propose here to examine only two very clear instances of parenthesis, both of them introduced by the linguistic signal γάρ ("for"), one in Mark 10:22 and the other in 12:12. Then I shall examine Mark 2:10 and 2:28, two other instances of parenthesis that are less clear, since they are usually thought by critical readers *not* to be parentheses at the level of discourse, but rather explanatory comments made within the story by Jesus.

Mark 10:22[3] is the last verse of the episode that is often labelled "The Rich Man" (Mark 10:17–22). In this story a man comes to Jesus and asks him what one must do to inherit eternal life. Jesus responds by reciting the commandments of the Decalogue, and the man replies by saying that he has always observed these commandments. The story reaches its denouement when Jesus instructs the man to go and sell all that he has, and to give the proceeds to the poor. Upon hearing these words, the man departs, "sorrowful." Why? "For (γάρ) he had great possessions" (10:22).[4]

That this episode has been given the handy title of "The Rich Man" speaks volumes about the neglect of the experience of reading this story among non-professional and professional readers alike. Why do I say this? Let us take care to note that we do not know that the rich man is a rich man until after the story is over. The story itself contains no mention at all of the wealth of the man. It is only at the level of discourse, and then only after the story itself has ceased, that the narrator informs *only* the narratee that the man has great wealth. Then, in retrospect, the narratee can think back through the episode and see the whole episode in a new light. The reader of the Gospel (who is encouraged by the Gospel always to imagine himself in the role of the narratee) can actually re-read the story. The reader is enticed to re-read, re-view, and re-interpret everything in the story from the vantage point of having read this episode through once already to its revelatory conclusion. We will re-read the episode, in short, knowing this time from the very beginning that the man is a rich man. In re-reading we will re-consider and re-evaluate his motivations in coming to Jesus. Whatever we thought of him upon a first reading, probably upon a second reading we will evaluate him less favorably, considering him this time less of a seeker of truth and more of a self-aggrandizer. We will also re-consider and re-evaluate Jesus' response to the man, perhaps finding new evidence of Jesus' unusual perspicacity. And so on and so forth. Thus does reliable commentary provided by the narrator "direct"—i.e., it both instigates and constrains—the development of a progressive series of re-interpretations in the course of reading and re-reading.

Mark 10:17–22 is an excellent example of an episode in biblical narrative that has been "read" and "re-read," clarified and concretized, so many times that hardly anyone really "reads" it anymore; we just go through the motions of reading it. We may even label the story "The Rich Man" in our Bibles, thus encouraging future readers to skip right past a first reading of the story, to leap ahead, as it were, into an enlightened re-reading. Why not make the work of reading easier for others than it was for ourselves? As a result, first-time readers now anticipate the outcome of the story even before they begin to read it. The standard title given to the episode tells us the punch line of the story before it can be delivered by the narrator in his discourse. Of course, this robs the punch line of its punch. Consequently, we have lost sight of the surprise that the revelation of the man's wealth must have brought to the earliest readers of this episode. And that has meant in turn that the possibility of being all but coerced by the narrative commentary into a re-visionary re-reading of the episode has also been obliterated. The episode is perhaps neither "read" nor "re-read" in any significant sense today.

But not only have we lost the ability to read this episode and to be surprised and powerfully directed by the discourse, we have at the same time lost sight of what is and is not happening in the story. On the one level, at least the narratee does grasp that the man is rich, in the very last phrase of the narrator's discourse in 10:22. On the other level, absolutely no one at the story level ever demonstrates clear and unmistakable knowledge of the man's wealth. A term introduced by J.L. Austin, the father of "speech act theory," is useful here. As Austin might say, there is no indication at the level of story that there is any "uptake" for the statement that the man was rich (Austin:117–18). But how could there be any uptake in the story, since the statement is made only at the level of discourse? To be sure, in retrospect it may appear that Jesus, as is so typical of him in Mark, reads the heart of the man and discerns the man's fatal weakness. But Jesus does not *say* that he knows that the man is rich; readers *infer in retrospect* that Jesus knows that the man is rich. Then, typically, readers read their discourse-level inference back into the story and "find" it there on subsequent re-readings. In other words, we have often mixed up what is or is not understood in the story with what is or is not understood at the level of discourse. Since biblical critics have tended not to draw the distinction between story and discourse, we have seldom been able to keep the two straight, in spite of the fact that most modern critics of the Bible have tacitly professed a critical focus upon the story level.

Another clear instance of an explanatory parenthesis, one that also comes at the end of its episode and is also introduced by the narrator with γάρ, is found in 12:12. Mark 12:12 is the final verse of an episode often labelled "The Parable of the Vineyard and the Tenants" (Mark 12:1–12). In this episode we have not only direction but much indirection as well, for the bulk of this episode is inherently indirect, being a parable or a riddle (παραβολή) supposedly uttered by Jesus at story level. Let us not fail to observe, however, that indirect, parabolic discourse uttered within the story is simultaneously indirect, parabolic discourse at the discourse level of the narrative. When Jesus speaks indirectly, our narrator speaks indirectly. In this particular instance, Jesus issues a patently indirect narrative puzzle within the story, but it is only the narrator at the discourse level who provides the crucial key for solving the puzzle.

In the story told by Jesus, a man plants a vineyard and rents it to tenants, while he goes into another country. The man sends a succession of servants to collect the rent, all of whom are treated shamefully by the tenants. At last the man sends his "beloved son," whom the tenants kill and cast out of the vineyard. The end of the story finds the owner returning to the vineyard, "destroying" the tenants, and renting out the vineyard to others.

Since the story is introduced as a "parable" in the narrator's discourse in 12:1, the reader is alerted from the beginning that the story should not be taken literally. It is thoroughly metaphorical or figurative, which is to say that it needs to be "figured out." Jesus himself begins the process of figuring out the parable at the level of story (12:10–11), but his explanation ("the very stone which the builders rejected has become the head of the corner") is itself figurative and therefore it too needs to be figured out. The substitution of one figurative riddle for another does not solve anything for us.

The crucial comment that allows the reader to solve the riddle of the vineyard and the tenants comes from the narrator in 12:12, at the level of the narrator's discourse, after the words spoken within the story have ceased: "And they tried to arrest him, but feared the multitude, *for* [γάρ] *they perceived that he had told the parable against them*; so they left and went away." The first matter of business for the reader encountering this concentrated moment of narrative exposition intertwined with narrative commentary is to clarify who the "they" is. Who is the "they" who tried to arrest Jesus, who feared the multitude, who perceived that the parable was aimed at them, and who then went away? *Ambiguity* is a favorite strategy of indirection employed frequently in the Markan discourse, but the ambiguous "they" in 12:12 is not among the more challenging of the Markan ambiguities. The reader will recall that in the episode immediately preceding the vineyard parable Jesus was disputing in the temple with "the chief priests and the scribes and the elders" (11:27). That same setting and those same interlocutors seem to be presupposed as we move into 12:1, which is the narrator's introduction to the vineyard parable: "And he began to speak *to them* in parables." Because of our experience of reading 11:27 and 12:1, as we read Jesus' vineyard parable in 12:2ff. it will not be difficult to infer that the parable is a figurative attack upon the interlocutors introduced back in 11:27 and mentioned again in 12:1, namely, the chief priests, scribes, and elders. We infer that it is they who are the "tenants" in Jesus' story. This identification must remain only a supposition, however, until the narrator confirms our supposition by means of the parenthetical γάρ clause in 12:12. Once the identification *tenants = chief priests + scribes + elders* is confirmed by the narrator in 12:12, all the rest of the pieces of the puzzle fall more or less neatly into place, in retrospect. To be sure, most of the riddle is not exceedingly difficult for the reader to figure out even upon a first reading. Besides having a strong suspicion from the beginning of the parable about who the "tenants" are, who the "beloved son" must be (12:6) is also not too difficult to figure out, if we remember reading Mark 1:11 and 9:7. However, it is the incontrovertible identification of the "tenants," reliably provided by the narrator, that guarantees that the puzzle will be solved correctly by the reader, albeit in retrospect.

It should be noted also that the γάρ clause in 12:12 is a particular kind of narrative commentary, an "inside view" (Booth:163–64 et passim) into the hearts and minds of story characters. In fact, in 12:12 we are granted altogether no less than three different inside views. We are told the *intention* of Jesus' opponents ("they tried to arrest him"), we are told of their *emotion* ("they feared the multitude"), and we are informed of their *knowledge* ("they perceived that he had told the parable against them"). Because we are usually too busy making use of this remarkable gift of insight into the hearts and minds of story characters, we have usually neglected to observe where the gift comes from. It comes to us directly and openly from the narrator, in the narrator's discourse. Moreover, we have tended to overlook that this gift of insight in 12:12 just so happens to place into our hands the one sure key that is indispensable for figuring out what the vineyard parable is all about. This is wonderfully indirect direction. We are all but coerced into understanding *Jesus'* parable, by being directed momentarily into the hearts and minds of his *opponents*, all of which encourages us to overlook that our grasp of everything in story and discourse alike is being carefully orchestrated by our *narrator*. Paradoxically, the more omniscient, the more intrusive, the more insistently direct our narrator becomes, the easier it becomes to overlook him.

Having now examined two fairly clear and noncontroversial instances of direction by means of parenthetical comments emanating openly from the narrator of Mark's Gospel, I now want to look at two more instances of narrative commentary that are less obviously parentheses by the narrator. The two Son of man sayings in Mark 2:10 and 2:28 are usually taken as explanatory comments uttered by Jesus at the level of story, but I want to argue instead that they are actually parenthetical comments uttered by the narrator at the level of the narrator's discourse. I also want to argue that it makes absolutely no difference at all whether Jesus speaks these lines in the story or whether the narrator speaks these lines as parenthetical interruptions of the story, as long as it is recognized that the only one who definitely takes up these comments is the narratee of the story. In tackling two parentheses whose function in story and discourse may at first appear less than clear, I am tackling turns of narrative discourse that lie somewhere between the clearest turns of direction and the shadowiest turns of indirection.

The Son of man sayings in Mark 2:10 and 2:28 are noteworthy, among other reasons, for being the only two Son of man sayings in the first half of the Gospel. Together 2:10 and 2:28 assert that the "Son of man" possesses "authority to forgive sins" and is in some sense "lord of the sabbath." This leaves much about the Son of man open to future development in the narrative, but that the Son of man possesses authority and lordship in Mark's Gospel is hereafter hardly to be disputed. Although it is often noted that Jesus is the only character in the Gospel to use the expression "Son of man," and oddly enough only in the third-person, it is too seldom observed that Jesus never identifies himself explicitly as the Son of man anywhere in the Gospel. Mark 10:32 ("he began to tell them *what was to happen to him*") comes the closest to being an explicit identification, but it is an oblique and not an explicit identification, and it is a statement by the narrator in the narrator's discourse and is not uttered at the level of story. Who the Son of man is, is one of many puzzles given to the reader of this Gospel, and like many of Mark's puzzles, this one is easily figured out. Who else could the Son of man be, other than Jesus? But the most important point to be made here is that who and what the Son of man is, is a puzzle that is handed to the reader to be solved.

Regardless of who gets credit for speaking the Son of man comments in 2:10 and 2:28, it should be fairly clear that they are both parenthetical comments. They are both "interpretations," in Chatman's terminology, of an element of the story. They both interrupt the story in order to offer a comment on the story. Literal translation and judicious use of typography may help us to see this better:

"Which is easier, to say to the paralytic, 'Your sins are forgiven,' or to say, 'Arise, take your bed, and walk'?"—*but [δέ] so that [ἵνα] you may know that the Son of man has authority to forgive sins on earth*—he says [λέγει] to the paralytic: "I say to you, arise, take your bed, and go to your home" (2:9–11; my translation).

And he said to them, "The sabbath was made for man, not man for the sabbath"—*so [ὥστε] the Son of man is lord even of the sabbath* (2:27–28; my punctuation of the RSV's translation).

Both parenthetical comments abruptly interrupt the flow of the narration in order to shed some light on an element of the story, namely, to say something illuminating about the Son of man. Both parenthetical comments are introduced by linguistic signals that are commonly used elsewhere by the narrator to signal his parenthetical comments. For example, the introduction of the parenthesis in 2:10 is signaled both with ἵνα and an adversative δέ. The conclusion of the parenthesis is signaled as the narrator shifts his focus back to the level of story and *re*-introduces Jesus as the speaker within the story: "he says [λέγει] to the paralytic..."

One possible problem with my suggestion that the parenthesis in 2:10 is spoken only at discourse level and not in the story is that the parenthesis is addressed to a second-person plural "you," and therefore one might argue that in 2:10 Jesus continues to address the interlocutors he first addressed in the story back in 2:8-9. It is possible to construe that in 2:10 Jesus is still talking to the scribes, but this could just as well be one of a number of places in the Gospel where an assembled audience *for the Gospel itself* is presupposed. I think particularly of Mark 13, where second-person plural pronouns and verbal forms occur with such exaggerated emphasis and frequency that discourse completely overwhelms story. I would argue that the "apocalyptic discourse" in Mark 13 is aimed less at Peter, Andrew, James, and John in the story (13:3), and more at the narrator's audience of assembled narratees outside of the story. Mark 13:37 makes rather clear that the apocalyptic discourse supposedly uttered by Jesus within the story is actually aimed primarily at Mark's narratees: "And what I say to you [Peter, Andrew, James, John] I say to all [Mark's narratees]: Watch."[5] If a reader is still disposed to take 2:10 as a parenthetical comment made by Jesus within the story, then she or he must assume the burden of explaining where the "he says to the paralytic" phrase comes from and what its function is. This is obviously not Jesus speaking; it can only be the narrator who speaks these words. But if the narrator feels the need to use these words to introduce Jesus all over again in 2:11, it may well be because the narrator had broken off from the words of Jesus in the story in 2:8–9, in order to give us his own commentary on the story in 2:10. At least that is how I read 2:10.

The Son of man comment in Mark 2:28 is also signaled linguistically as a parenthetical comment. The chief linguistic signal is ὥστε ("for this reason, therefore, so"), which serves here to introduce an independent clause. The independent clause in 2:28 is a comment from the narrator that stands apart from the comment by Jesus that immediately precedes it. A parenthetical comment by the narrator that breaks off from a statement by Jesus that immediately precedes it was exactly what we had also in 2:10, but 2:28 is the less obvious parenthesis of the two, for in 2:28 the parenthesis comes at the very end of the episode, and therefore it does not dramatically interrupt the flow of the narration half-way through an episode, the way 2:10 does. That our narrator should choose in 2:28 to delay an explanatory comment until the very end of an episode is a practice with which we are already familiar, from having examined the parentheses at the end of episodes in 10:22 and 12:12.

Consequently, regardless of who gets credit for speaking them, it should be fairly obvious that the Son of man statements in 2:10 and 2:28 are both parenthetical comments on the story. In addition, I would argue that they are properly understood as parenthetical comments *made by the narrator* on the story. They are, after all, signaled in the same fashion that other parenthetical comments by the narrator are signaled in Mark's Gospel. But be that as it may, the most important point to be made here is that even if it is Jesus who speaks the Son of man comments in 2:10 and 2:28, there is no indication whatsoever that anyone in the story hears and understands these comments. There is no demonstration of uptake for the Son of man statements in 2:10 and 2:28 at the level of story. Indeed, *no Son of man statement in Mark's Gospel ever receives clear and unmistakable uptake at the level of story.*[6] But if the characters in the story do not hear or understand the Son of man statements, who does? The narratee, obviously. There has never been a recipient of Mark's narrative discourse who has not heard every single Son of man statement in the Gospel and understood them all, at least to some extent. Even though the identity of the one who is the Son of man is never made explicitly clear in either story or discourse, there has never been a reader who has not been able to figure that the Son of man can only be Jesus. What readers have *not* been sufficiently cognizant of is that no one in the story hears and understands what we hear and understand. Once again, we have grasped neither what characters in the story understand nor what we as readers are led to understand by the narrator's discourse. The workings of story and discourse in Mark's Gospel remain largely a mystery to us. The orchestration of story and discourse in this narrative is so masterful that we are utterly enchanted by the spell it weaves over us as we read. In narrative commentary such as that in 2:10 and 2:28, the narrator has directed our thinking in ways we have not yet fathomed.

I want to turn now from direction to indirection in Mark's rhetoric. That is not to say that direction and indirection can always be easily distinguished and disentangled in the discourse of the Gospel. Sometimes one has the sense that various strategies of direction and indirection shade gradually over into each other and therefore are difficult to try to distinguish. At other times turns of direction and indirection are distinguishable but are tangled up in each other, indirection playing off against direction and vice versa. The experience in criticism gained above, learning how to identify and describe the more overt turns of direction by the narrator, stands us in good stead now as we turn to more covert and indirect guidance from the narrator. With indirection the narrator ceases to speak openly and directly and steps momentarily behind the curtain, as it were, in order to orchestrate the workings of story and discourse covertly from offstage, in the wings. Whereas in direction he speaks to us directly, in his own voice, in indirection he "speaks" to us tacitly, through what the characters in his story say or do, or through the way that the events and situations in the story are structured and plotted. "Speaking" to us indirectly through both characters and the orchestration of circumstances and events in the narrative, the narrator employs verbal and dramatic turns of irony, metaphor, paradox, and ambiguity. Like direction, indirection often leads us to insights and understandings. At other times, indirection does not lead us to a particular destination. In such cases it is offered to us as an experience to be experienced for its own sake. Indirection permeates Mark's Gospel, from beginning to end, but there are some places in the Gospel where the rhetoric of indirection is particularly concentrated, and I would like to look at one such passage here.

The passage I would like to consider is the difficult and much-discussed scene that occurs between the riddle of the sower in Mark 4:3–9 and its story-level explanation by Jesus in 4:14–20. I want to concentrate especially on 4:11–13:

> And he said to them, "To you has been given the secret of the Kingdom of God, but for those outside everything [τὰ πάντα] is in riddles [παραβολαῖς]." (So that [ἵνα] in seeing, they may see and not perceive, and in hearing they may hear and not understand, lest they should turn and be forgiven.) And he says [λέγει] to them, "Do you not know this riddle? How then will you understand all [πάσας] of the riddles?" (4:11–13; my translation).

Few verses in Mark have perplexed scholars more than 4:11. The problem here can be stated simply: Jesus says to his disciples that they have been given "the secret of the Kingdom of God," but the narratee does not know what this secret is or when it might have been given to the disciples in the story. When critical readers encounter this verse, they often flip back through the preceding pages of the Gospel, hoping to discover when and where this secret might have been given to Jesus' disciples, but to no avail. We have found it most difficult to accept that in 4:11 the discourse alludes to something that apparently occurred in the story, but the narrator chose not to narrate it to us. I call this narrative strategy *opacity*. Whatever the secret might be, and whenever we may suppose it was given in the story, it lies behind an opaque veil as far as we are concerned. We might say that the giving of the secret apparently occurred at the level of story, but was omitted from the narrator's discourse, thus excluding the narratee from this moment in the story.

If we have had a hard time recognizing and coming to terms with the opacity in 4:11, it may be because we have assumed that narrative is invariably supposed to enlighten the narratee, not to put him or her in the dark. But 4:11 does put the narratee in the dark, or, more accurately, it reveals to the narratee that he or she has for some unknown period of time been in the dark concerning the existence of a "secret." To be sure, more typically Mark will portray the characters in the story as victims of opaque veils that blind their eyes, deafen their ears, and keep them from understanding the events in the story that are taking place in front of their noses. Opacity is another way of talking about the absence of uptake in the narrative. In Mark there is much opacity—absence of uptake—at the level of story, veils that seem to keep the characters in the story in the dark (e.g., all Son of man sayings are smothered by an aural veil of opacity in the story). But what is most interesting to the student of narrative rhetoric, however, is that the narrator of this story is not afraid to put the narratee occasionally in the dark as well. Of course, by the very nature of opacity, we cannot know that we are being excluded by an opaque veil as long as the veil is in place. But the narrator will occasionally reveal to us, in moment of retrospective illumination, that we had been excluded from an earlier moment in the story that the characters apparently had experienced. That is, occasionally the narrator will tear away a veil that had previously blinded us.

In narratological terms, opacity occurs when either the story or the discourse halts and the other level proceeds by itself. Opacity occurs whenever the narrator introduces a gap into either the story or the discourse, thus excluding either characters or the narratee from understanding a portion of the story. As powerful as the various covert twists and turns of Markan indirection can be, opacity is the ultimate strategy of indirection, since it is the outright denial, to either a character or a narratee, of the opportunity to experience and understand fully the story that is being told.

Lest we fall into despair over the narrator's denial to us of the secret of the Kingdom of God, we need to continue reading. Surprises may lie ahead. But before we proceed with our reading of 4:11–13, we need to observe the opposites that are introduced to us in 4:11. On the one hand, we have those who have been graced with the secret of the Kingdom of God. On the other hand, we have the outsiders, for whom *everything* (τὰ πάντα) is in riddles. Putting this language together and filling in the missing terms, apparently there are insiders, who possess the secret of the Kingdom of God and who understand Jesus' riddles, and there are outsiders, who do not possess the secret and who do not understand the riddles. Using this language we would have to say that in 4:11 it would seem that Jesus' disciples are insiders, who possess the secret of the Kingdom, while the narratee is an outsider, not possessing the secret. At this point in the passage the reader seems to stand on the outside of the privileged circle of insight and understanding, and laments that she or he has been so excluded. But matters do not rest there. We must read on.

In Mark 4:12 we come across yet another of our beloved parenthetical comments. Like the parentheses in 2:10 and 2:28, the parenthesis in 4:12 is usually regarded as a comment by Jesus uttered at the level of story. And like the parentheses in 2:10 and 2:28, I would argue that 4:12 should be understood instead as a parenthetical comment by the narrator. And, furthermore, like the parentheses in 2:10 and 2:28, it really does not matter whether we understand that Jesus or our narrator is the principal speaker of the parenthesis in 4:12, as long as we recognize that there is no indication of uptake for the comment in the story. This is yet another of those parenthetical comments that we only know for sure that the narratee hears and responds to. Even if Jesus does speak the parenthesis at story level, there is no indication at story level that anyone there hears it and takes it to heart.

That 4:12 is a parenthetical comment should be fairly obvious. It interrupts the speech by Jesus about understanding parables that both precedes and follows it, in vv. 11 and 13. Furthermore, the parenthesis is introduced by the linguistic signal ἵνα, just like the parenthesis in 2:10. Also like 2:10, the narrator's parenthesis in 4:12 concludes with the *re*-introduction of Jesus as the principal speaker in the story: "and he says [λέγει] to them…"

In form, therefore, this parenthetical comment resembles the other parenthetical comments in the Gospel. In function, however, this parenthesis differs from the others we have seen so far in several respects. For one thing, it is an allusion to, if not a direct quotation from, the Old Testament. It is an allusion to Isaiah 6:9–10, to be precise, but precise our narrator is not. The quotation, if that is what it is, is not an accurate quotation, nor is it even introduced as a quotation by either Jesus or the narrator, nor are we told what we should make of it. What relevance does it have to the topic under discussion in the story? Unlike the other parentheses we have examined, this one is more of a question than an answer, more of a puzzle than a solution, more of a challenge of indirection than a piece of clear, reliable direction.

It should be noted that the narrator on a number of occasions offers to the narratee gratuitous allusions to Old Testament passages. The Gospel in fact begins with a parenthetical comment in Mark 1:2–3 that loosely "quotes" a pastiche of passages from Exodus, Malachi, and Isaiah. What we are to make of that scriptural allusion is also difficult to determine. Suffice it to say that as a result of these and other allusions to Jewish scripture, the reader of Mark's Gospel must read the Gospel intertextually. The textual fabric of Mark's Gospel is intertwined with the fabric of these precursor texts, which makes this narrative one that is perpetually open to the influence of its precursors. Allusions to the Old Testament may cast some light upon Mark's story, but the lighting is often at best indirect and inconclusive.

Besides observing that the parenthetical comment in 4:12 is an unheralded, unexplained, ambiguous allusion to a precursor text, we should also note that this allusion is thoroughly figurative, indeed, *metaphorical*. "Seeing" and "hearing" are introduced here as grand metaphors that will appear again and again in the narrative that follows. Hereafter, whenever we encounter "seeing" or "hearing" (or their opposites, "blindness" or "deafness") in either story or discourse, we must suspect that these are figures not to be taken up too literally. In spite of the openness and ambiguity of the Old Testament allusion in 4:12, the reader can surely figure out minimally that this comment is suggesting that some who think they "see" really do not perceive anything at all, and some who think they "hear" really understand nothing. What we are to do then with this insight remains far from clear, but one thing it may do is to encourage us to begin to re-consider the understanding we developed back in 4:11 that the disciples are insiders and we are outsiders. Maybe, just maybe, those in 4:11 who seemed to "see" and "hear" certain things did not "see" or "hear" as much as we thought.

As if it were not enough that 4:12 is an ambiguous intertextual allusion, and a metaphorical one at that, it is also *ironic*. The irony comes at the beginning of the parenthesis, in the infamous "so that" (ἵνα) clause, and especially at the end of the parenthesis, in the shocking conclusion, "lest they should turn and be forgiven." The ἵνα is infamous, because it seems to suggest that the parables are told with the express purpose of excluding people from understanding them. Whether they will admit it or not, most modern readers are deeply offended by Mark's ἵνα, and consequently they prefer Matthew's substitution of ὅτι ("because"; Matt 13:13) for Mark's ἵνα, because this suggests that the purpose of telling parables is to enlighten people, not to exclude them from enlightenment. None of us likes to feel excluded, so we like Matthew's ὅτι much better than Mark's ἵνα. However, were we able to face up to the opacity that does indeed exclude us in 4:11, we might be less astonished and offended by the apparent implication in 4:12 that a storyteller would ever intentionally shut someone out of the inner circle of understanding.

The ἵνα is definitely perplexing, but the key to identifying the parenthetical comment as an ironic statement is the final clause, "lest they should turn and be forgiven." This tips us off that the whole verse has been recited with tongue in cheek. We can figure this out because it is clear from our reading experience that both our narrator and his protagonist wish to persuade their respective audiences to hear and believe their respective discourses, and to repent or turn their lives around accordingly. The narrator already begins to reveal his goal of swaying his audience in the very first verse of the Gospel: "The beginning of the gospel of Jesus Christ, the Son of God." This tells us already before the Gospel gets under way certain things the narrator hopes we will be willing to say about Jesus as a result of reading this narrative. Within the story, Jesus makes clear his rhetorical aims as well: "The time is fulfilled, and the kingdom of God is at hand; repent, and believe in the gospel" (1:15). Jesus offers this epitome of his preaching at the beginning of his ministry, as he takes up the mantle of John the Baptist, who had also preached repentance, specifically "for the forgiveness of sins" (1:4). All of this the reader reads in the first fifteen verses of the Gospel. Then when we arrive at 4:12, are we actually supposed to believe that either the narrator or Jesus would actually tell a story *so that* people would *not* turn their lives around, *so that* they would *not* be forgiven? The literal sense of Mark 4:12 is patent nonsense, quite incongruous with the clear and unmistakable rhetorical goal of both the narrator, at discourse level, and Jesus, within the story. Consequently, Mark 4:12 simply cannot be taken literally. It should not be taken in a straightforward, direct manner, because it is not uttered directly; it is uttered indirectly. It is spoken (by the narrator, I believe, but neither I nor the narrator would mind if Jesus got credit for it) with tongue in cheek. One might even dare to say that it is a little bit humorous. The narrator (or Jesus) may be pulling someone's leg, either the leg of the narratee at the level of discourse, or the leg of certain characters within the story, or maybe both simultaneously. So, just as the metaphors of "seeing" and "hearing" within the parenthesis are not to be taken literally, the whole parenthetical comment is not to be taken literally either. Two major turns of indirection work together here, metaphor and verbal irony. It is only fitting, after all, that a metaphorical statement that suggests that "seeing" and "hearing" are not always what they seem to be, should itself be uttered in a manner that is not what it seems to be.

Let us read on to verse 13. Jesus is re-introduced by the narrator and he poses two questions to the disciples: "Do you not know this riddle? How then will you understand all of the riddles?" These are "rhetorical" questions, in the sense that they serve the narrator as an effective rhetorical strategy for guiding the thinking of the narratee indirectly. Since they receive no explicit answer either in the story or in the narrator's discourse, the narratee is encouraged to try to answer the questions, or at least to explore their implications, on his or her own. The first of the two unanswered questions seems to imply that Jesus thinks that the disciples do not understand the riddle of the sower (4:3-9). The narratee may already have suspected this in 4:10, when the disciples[7] of Jesus "asked him concerning the parables," but why they were asking about the parables was left artfully ambiguous by the narrator. Now in 4:13, however, we know for sure that they did not understand the sower riddle, but we learn this from the narrator indirectly, through an unanswered question uttered by a character at the level of story. The second of the two questions suggests rather emphatically that if the disciples do not understand this one riddle, then *all* (πάσας) of the riddles will be a mystery to them. Apparently they stand in imminent danger of failing to understand everything that Jesus teaches, and perhaps everything that he stands for.

This is quite a turnabout. Back in 4:11 we were surprised and maybe a little offended to learn that the disciples had been given the secret of the Kingdom of God without our knowing anything about it. But now it appears that these touted insiders are really outsiders, after all. And the narratee, the one excluded by the veil of opacity in 4:11, now suddenly understands that the disciples do not understand, which turns the narratee into an insider, at least to a modest degree. We may not know much, but we know at least that the disciples do not know. In revealing to us that the "insiders" of 4:11 are in fact "outsiders," we the "outsiders" of 4:11 are turned into "insiders." The tables are turned; positions are reversed; the veil of opacity has now excluded new victims while ushering the old victims into a modest enlightenment.

Reading Mark 4:13 is an experience of *dramatic irony* for the reader. Dramatic irony is sub-category of situational irony, which is built upon a provocative incongruity of situations or events. One might say that dramatic irony is situational irony used as rhetorical strategy in narrative discourse. Dramatic irony occurs when there is a sharp incongruity between various situations or events within the story, or more dramatically still when there is a sharp incongruity between what is known or understood at the level of story and what is known or understood at the level of discourse. In the theater, for example, dramatic irony occurs when Oedipus does not know his origins, and therefore stumbles "blindly" into his fate, while everyone in the audience knows full well from the beginning of the play both what his origins are and what his fate must be. Mark's dramatic irony in 4:13 is even more powerful than this classic example, because Mark first sets up an incongruous opacity that favors the characters and excludes the audience in 4:11, and then he reverses the positions, by suddenly favoring the audience and excluding the characters behind the opaque veil in 4:13. Each of the two turns of opacity is dramatically ironic by itself, but there is the further dramatic irony that the narrator replaces one dramatically ironic opacity with another that is diametrically opposed to it. The two ironic moments of opacity are ironically, maybe even paradoxically, opposites of each other.

Like so many moments in the reading of Mark's narrative, the dramatic irony of 4:13 is a matter of re-visioning the reading experience in retrospect. The reader cannot detect the dramatic incongruity between 4:11 and 4:13 until 4:13 is read and its indirect challenge taken up. When it is read, Mark 4:13 functions as an indirect invitation from the narrator to re-read and re-vision the preceding verses. Not only may we detect for the first time a dramatic irony reverberating between 4:11 and 4:13, we may also begin to suspect that the verbal irony that we encountered in 4:12 had already begun back in 4:11. Perhaps 4:11 participates not only in dramatic irony, but also verbal irony as well. Maybe Jesus (or the narrator) was already pulling the leg of the disciples (or of the narratee) back in 4:11. Maybe Jesus never seriously intended to suggest that the disciples had actually received the "secret of the Kingdom of God." If the reader could suspect already in 4:10 that the disciples really did not understand the parables, and that that is why they asked Jesus about them, could not Jesus also have been this shrewd, and have begun to chide the disciples ironically for their lack of perception already in 4:11? Whether or not Jesus is chiding the disciples ironically in 4:11, by the time we reach 4:13 it is without doubt that he chides the disciples and sharply so. By that point his tone has become unmistakably severe, for the stakes are high. If the disciples cannot figure out this one riddle, then *everything* (πάσας) will be a mystery for them. *Their position in 4:13 is that of the outsiders who were mentioned in 4:11, those for whom everything* (τὰ πάντα) *is in rid-*

dles. The reader can only hope that she or he will not also end up as an outsider, but our experience of reading 4:11–13 leaves us less than sanguine about the possibilities of this happening, for we know by our own experience that it is possible for us, even us, to be "blind" and "deaf" to what is happening in Mark's narrative.

The experience of reading Mark 4:11–13 can be summarized briefly. The temptation here is to say that the text tells us that those who "see" often are in fact "blind," and those who "hear" often are in fact "deaf." The text, especially the parenthetical comment in 4:12, does say something like that, but far more important than what the text *says* is what it *does*. We are not merely *told* about those who "see and yet do not see," *we are given the opportunity to experience this for ourselves*. The reader lives through the experience of being shut out of insight and understanding by an opaque veil, followed by the gift of a modest amount of sight and understanding, in a surprising reversal of position with those who had started out on the favored side of the veil.

The experience of reading Mark 4:11–13 is illustrative of the experience of reading Mark's Gospel as a whole in several respects. For one thing, reading Mark is less a matter of being informed of certain facts and ideas and more a matter of being given the opportunity to live through certain kinds of experiences. And those experiences typically proceed on paths that are both direct and indirect, but with a special inclination toward indirection. The experience of reading this narrative is characterized by frequent twists and turns, by surprises and reversals. This narrative does not just *say* that insiders are outsiders, and outsiders are insiders; it *performs* this reversal upon us time and time again. But as often as it might cast us out into the dark, it more often casts us into the inner circle of privileged insight and understanding. The overall tendency of this narrative is gradually to make of the narratee, by direct and indirect means alike, an inveterate insider.

Mark 4:11–13 is also illustrative of the whole Gospel insofar as we encounter here, in a remarkably brief span of narrative, examples of many of the favorite Markan turns of indirection. We encounter different moments of *opacity* that exclude at one point the narratee and at another point the characters; we are given an *intertextual allusion* that signals the openness of this narrative and that seems to reflect the narrator's willingness to live with *ambiguity*; several major *metaphors* are offered to us; we encounter both *verbal* and *dramatic irony*;[8] and we take up the challenge of *unanswered, "rhetorical" questions*. When this critical vocabulary is used along with the other terms I have introduced and employed in this essay (*story* and *discourse, direction* and *indirection, reliable commentary, uptake, inside views*, etc.), we are well on our way toward the development of the critical tools necessary to describe and discuss the experience of reading Mark's Gospel.

The latter describes well my goal in this paper and in the larger project of reader-response criticism in which I have been engaged for the last decade. My goal is to learn to attend as closely as possible to the experience of reading. I want to understand better what is or is not happening in Mark's story as I read it, and especially what is or is not happening in me at the same time, thanks to the narrator's discourse. I want to observe and understand the workings of the gamut of rhetorical moves made by the narrator, as I encounter them in the act of reading, ranging from the most overt and direct turns, to the most covert and indirect turns. For me, this is the proper goal of a reader-response criticism of the experience of reading Mark's Gospel.

NOTES

[1] This essay is dedicated to Bob and Mary Lou Thomson, who made possible my participation in the SNTS seminar on "The Role of the Reader in the Interpretation of the New Testament." I am greatly indebted to them for their encouragement and support.

[2] I am presuming familiarity with the common narratological distinctions between, on the one hand, the real author, the implied author, and the narrator, and on the other hand, the real reader, the implied reader, and the narratee (see Chatman: 147–151; Fowler, 1985:10–15). For all practical purposes, in Mark the implied author is virtually indistinguishable from the narrator, and the implied reader is virtually indistinguishable from the narratee.

[3] For this example I am indebted to the article by Resseguie (312–313).

[4] Unless indicated otherwise, the English translation I am using is the Revised Standard Version.

[5] I pursue this argument at greater length elsewhere (Fowler, [1991]). Suffice it to say here that there are a number of places in Mark where second-person plural forms seem to imply an assembled audience for the Gospel. To give only one example, see the brief parenthetical comment in 9:41, which should also, I believe, be credited solely to the account of the narrator: "because you are of Christ" (ὅτι Χριστοῦ ἐστε).

[6] The closest thing to a Son of man statement that receives uptake in the story is perhaps the Son of man statement in Mark 14:63, in the scene where Jesus is questioned before the high priest. But I would argue that this, too, is a parenthetical comment that is spoken by the narrator and heard only by the narratee. There is no clear demonstration by the high priest that he hears and responds to the Son of man statement that the narratee of the Gospel undoubtedly hears and responds to.

Mark 14:63 interrupts the story in order to offer a comment on the story, and it functions only at the level of discourse.

Nevertheless, let us be clear that Jesus does indeed utter many Son of man statements in the story. See, for example, the three passion predictions in 8:31, 9:31, and 10:33. However, not one of these receives clear and unmistakable uptake within the story. The narrator confirms this lack of uptake explicitly in 9:32, after the second passion prediction, when he says that the disciples "did not understand the saying."

[7] To identify "those who were about him with the twelve" in 4:10 is difficult. I suspect we have a scribal gloss here that was introduced into an early manuscript of Mark's Gospel to save the twelve from the embarrassment of having to ask for Jesus' help in understanding the parables. Ultimately, it does not matter much to whom Jesus is speaking in 4:11 and 4:13. It is enough to know that he is speaking to disciples intimately associated with him, a group of supposed "insiders."

[8] Elsewhere I have discussed both verbal and dramatic turns not only of irony, but also of metaphor, paradox, and, to a limited extent, ambiguity (Fowler, [1991]).

WORKS CONSULTED

Austin, J.L.
   1975   *How To Do Things With Words*. Ed. J.O. Urmson and Marina Sbisà. 2nd ed. Cambridge: Harvard University Press.

Booth, Wayne C.
   1983   *The Rhetoric Of Fiction*. 2nd ed. Chicago: University of Chicago Press.

Chatman, Seymour
   1978   *Story and Discourse: Narrative Structure in Fiction and Film*. Ithaca: Cornell University Press.

Detweiler, Robert, ed.
   1985   *Reader Response Approaches to Biblical and Secular Texts*. Semeia 31. Decatur, GA: Scholars Press.

Fowler, Robert M.
   1981   *Loaves and Fishes: The Function Of the Feeding Stories in the Gospel of Mark*. SBLDS 54. Chico: Scholars Press.
   1985   "Who is 'the Reader' in Reader Response Criticism?" *Semeia* 31:5–23.
   [1991]   *Let the Reader Understand: Reader-Response Criticism and the Gospel of Mark*. Forthcoming.

Freund, Elizabeth
    1987   *The Return Of the Reader: Reader-Response Criticism.* London and New York: Methuen.

Moore, Stephen D.
    1986   "Narrative Homiletics: Lucan Rhetoric and the Making of the Reader." Ph.D. Thesis, Trinity College, University of Dublin.

Resseguie, James L.
    1984   "Reader-Response Criticism and the Synoptic Gospels." *JAAR* 52: 307–324.

Suleimann, Susan R. and Inge Crosman, eds.
    1980   *The Reader in the Text: Essays on Audience and Interpretation.* Princeton: Princeton University Press.

Tompkins, Jane, ed.
    1980   *Reader-Response Criticism: From Formalism to Post-Structuralism.* Baltimore: Johns Hopkins University Press.

Response to W. Schenk, Die Philipperbriefe des Paulus

H. J. Bernard Combrink
University of Stellenbosch

ABSTRACT

The commentary of Schenk on Philippians is to be commended for its consistent application of linguistic and literary approaches within a semiotic framework. The author furthermore gives specific attention to the pragmatic dimensions of the text, and in this respect a careful analysis of various textual signals appealing to the reader is made. Intertextual material is also utilized to illumine the context of the letter. Yet, in certain aspects this commentary still displays some similarities with "traditional" procedures. The different categories of readers, as well as the distinction between text and work, are not dealt with adequately. This article then calls attention to the relocations of the implied referential actions in the poetic sequence of the letter and the effect of this on the reader.

1. *Positive Contributions of the Commentary*

This commentary is to be welcomed and commended for its comprehensive approach and consistent effort to supplement traditional exegetical approaches by implementing recent linguistic and literary research in a study of the letter to the Philippians. Due to the author's specific linguistic and semiotic approach, his work includes not only textual commentary, but also discussions on the theory of exegesis, on its implication for current theological reflection, and on the implementation of semantic studies in a syntagmatic (context semantics) as well as paradigmatic (semantic domains) manner.

Other points to be commended are: the basic approach which takes as its point of departure the view that a sign only functions as a sign in a code; the implementation of syntax, semantics, and pragmatics as the basics of semiotics; and the emphasis that a text is to be taken as the primary linguistic sign. This last point means that *langue* is to be found only in the form of *parole* and, therefore, that semantics is basically text-semantics: sentences have meaning only within the TEXT. Schenk's distinction between the reader and the researcher/critic is also important and functions in a positive manner when dealing with the variety of empirical responses to a text (cf. Steiner; Fowler:6f.).

Especially significant is the author's consistent attention to the pragmatic dimensions of the text as a series of connected speech acts in the context of a communication model. This is, of course, typical of a reader response approach which is by definition pragmatically oriented. There can be no doubt about the great value of finally having a commentary available which consistently deals with the text from this perspectives.

There are numerous valuable insights to be gained from Schenk's perceptive analysis and reading of the text. Here one could note his conclusions from the use of vocatives with imperatives (3:17; 4:1) with reference to the fact that what Paul said about himself as example also had relevance for the readers—although one is tempted to ask: which reader? (see below 2.4).

One could also point to his discussion of the concentric nature of the text in Phil 3, marked by the circular occurrence of *you* (3:2; 4:1) / *we* (3:2; 3:20) (Schenk:254ff.). His remarks on the role of the first person with a view to the readers, are also challenging and significant. It actually presupposes the correlation between the role of the corresponding textual factors on the rhetorical axis of the communication model (for example narrator / narratee, addresser / addressee). Not only is the *we* in 3:3, 20 clearly opposed to the opponents in 3:2, 18ff., but the use of *we* in 3:20 is anticipated by the *we* in 3:17, in this manner enclosing the mentioning of the enemies in 3:18f.

> Meint ἡμᾶς hier semantisch zwar "meinesgleichen" als Vorbild für die Adressaten, so ist doch die Setzung von ἡμᾶς als morphologisch-syntaktisches Signal im Blick auf den Einsatz von 3,20 mit vorangestelltem ἡμῶν als bewusste Klammerbildung gewählt, da Pl 4,9 den Vorbildgedanken durchaus wiederum singularisch formuliert (Schenk:256).

Shenk also identifies various other textual signals pertaining to the appeal of the text to the reader. By way of example one could point to the text-pragmatical appeal function of the use of the first person personal pronoun in 3:13, as well as to the appeal function of the present tense ἐπιλανθανόμενος 3:13 (Schenk:261ff.).

The way in which material from the intertextual level (Sirach, for example) is used to elucidate the context of Philippians is stimulating and very valuable. From the point of view of methodology this is also significant, especially since there is a real danger in literary orientated exegesis of becoming trapped in a text-immanent exegesis. However, questions must be raised in this respect.

2. *Points for Discussion*

2.1   A first question would be whether Schenk, who professes to work with a linguistic and literary method from the perspective of a model of communication, really breaks new ground. To my mind there is no doubt that this question must be answered affirmatively. Yet, one cannot escape the impression that in certain respects his work shows a remarkable similarity with "traditional" approaches of contemporary criticism. One could point here to the traditional theory of three letter fragments in Philippians. It may further be interesting to recall that Holub also points to the fact that even reception theory in a sense remains quite conventional when compared with post-structuralist models (154). Even when full justice is done to the role of the reader in the text, the following remark of Holub remains illuminating: "Trying to circumvent the text by displacing the critical focus onto another agency only amounts to a postponement of the confrontation with determinacy" (157).

2.2   A next question—or rather statement—is that Schenk does not really deal adequately with the role of the reader in the text of Philippians. This must be seen against the important distinction of the physically objective *text* and the mentally subjective *work* (Petersen 1984:42). It would be fair to say that Schenk deals extensively with the objective text, the cultural and linguistic codes known to the reader, yet the *work* as the result of the interaction of these factors with the personal experience of the reader could have benefited from more explicit attention to the role of the reader.

2.3   Another fundamental question is whether Schenk makes enough allowance for the polyvalence of a text, or at least for the multi-functionality of literary signs. It seems as if he assumes a textimmanent authorial reception.

> Der grundlegende methodische Charakter der sorgfältigen und gewissenhaften Befragung des Gegenstands entnimmt die wissenschaftliche Befragung der Beliebigkeit und zielt auf Verbindlichkeit und Allgemeingültigkeit der so erfragten Antworten und Aussagen (Schenk:21).

Is this possible? Should it not be said that we are irrevocably non-authorial readers who cannot get out of the box of the text? We are not participants in the text's communicative and interpretive context and we are limited in our competence.

> That is to say, because non-authorial readers cannot get out of the textual box, they can only know about the communication what the *intra*textual actors disclose to them. They cannot know, apart from what is in the box, what the extratextual actors intend in or construe from the communication (Petersen, 1984:40).

This surely does not imply that one may not use intertextual information, as Schenk so often does when referring to Sirach, etc. That he does this repeatedly is in accordance with the necessity for continuous switching between the various levels of a text, specifically between the intentional and extensional levels (Eco:14). This could also be taken to be the realization of a repertoire of extratextual factors.

2.4   Something should also be said in connection with the different categories of readers proposed, without going into all the detail. If one takes as point of departure the basic differentiation by Link (25) as well as a proposal by Petersen (1984:39f.), it is necessary to differentiate between actual (extratextual) and textual readers.

2.4.1   Actual readers

One could differentiate here between various kinds of readers (Grimm:38–9), but relevant to our discussion is the intended reader as extratextual category (= real reader), but with a textual residue (in that sense part of 2.4.2). Is this what Schenk had in mind when he pointed to the way in which, for example, the keywords of the opponents function in the text? The *authorial* readers (Petersen, 1984:40) should be able to recognize themselves in the text, whereas other real readers in different situations and times are prone to decode the text wrongly.

2.4.2   Textual readers

2.4.2.1   The *implied* or abstract reader has to be seen as a textual category which actually aims at the active participation of the reader in the reading process. According to Iser:

> This term incorporates both the prestructuring of the potential meaning by the text and the reader's actualization of this potential through the reading process. It refers to the active nature of this process—which will

vary historically from one age to another—and not to a typology of possible readers. (xii)

Schenk does not really discuss this aspect of the role of the reader, although one could perhaps say that it is implied, for example, in his discussion of the role of the first person or the appeal-function of the present tense (Schenk:260ff., 263ff.).

2.4.2.2 The *explicit* reader (= encoded reader of Petersen?) is linguistically present in the text by means of first and second person personal pronouns. On this level Schenk extensively outlines the implications of the imperative, vocative, and so forth, and at the same time linking this to the intended reader.

2.5 One of the most fundamental questions deals with Schenk's view of *the composite nature of the text* of Philippians (335). He remarks that 2:19–30 points to the closing of a letter starting with 1:1 (334), and that there are valid grounds for posing various letter fragments. He then classifies Phil 3 as of the form: *genus judiciale*, and closely related to Gal and 2 Cor 10–13. He is of the opinion that his arguments are textpragmatic, and not only intuitive pragmatic (335). This has to be questioned from at least two perspectives.

2.5.1 The first is the perspective of the symbolic and narrative world of a letter (cf. Petersen, 1985:17ff.). Even though a common rhetorical model may be posited for different letters, this does not imply that they all represent the same symbolic universe. Although the notion of the autonomy of the text can be overemphasized, Petersen underlines the fact that a textually intrinsic sociological analysis can take us further than we have gotten without it (1985:20f.,30f.). It can also be accepted that in a literary approach, even if a composite origin of a letter may be posited, the role of the reader would definitely be to actualize the *work* from the *text* as a whole before him. And from this work, the symbolic *world* in which the authorial and non-authorial readers find themselves has to be surmised.

2.5.2 The second perspective is that of letters as stories. From this point of view one could say that it is very important to be aware of the fact that a letter not only contains a message, but that in the letter, the story is in the message. "Letters have stories, and it is from these stories that we construct the narrative worlds of both the letters and the stories" (Petersen, 1985:43).

It is therefore important to realize that the poetic sequence of the letter as a whole has to be compared with the referential sequence of the letter as a whole in order to fully understand the impact of the poetic reordering of actions in this "story." As a contribution to the discussion in this respect, the poetic sequence of actions will be outlined here, followed by the referential sequence of actions construed from the first series. The implications of the differences between the two sequences will then be drawn out. It is hoped that in this manner it will become clear that it is not valid, especially when approaching a letter such as this from the point of view of the role of the reader, to divide the letter into various fragments.

3. *Poetic Sequence of Philippians*

PoetS		Refer S
1	Philippians worked together with Paul from the beginning of Paul's work (1:5).	6
2	God who began this good work, will complete it on the Day of Christ! (1:6, 10).	5, 31
3	Paul longs for the Philippians and prays for their true knowledge (1:8–11).	14
4	Paul in prison (1:12f.).	9
5	Brothers have confidence to preach, even though with wrong motives (1:14–18).	11
6	Despite his wish to be with Christ, Paul wishes to visit them again, or at least to hear reports concerning them (1:27).	27
7	Paul urges them: live in accordance with the Gospel, with a common purpose, battling together (1:28–30).	16
8	Living according to the Gospel (2:1–4) means having the same attitude as Christ (2:5): the story of Christ's service and obedience as Servant of the Lord (2:6–11).	17
9	If they live in unity and like stars, Paul will be proud on the Day of Christ (2:12–18).	30
10	Paul will send Timothy to them, and wants to go there himself too (2:19–24).	26
11	Paul wants to send Epaphroditus back to Philippians (2:25f.).	15
12	Epaphroditus had been very ill (2:27).	13
13	Paul appeals to Philippians: accept Epaphroditus—he represented Philippians to Paul (2:28–30).	25
14	Appeal of Paul: be joyful in the Lord (3:1).	18
15	Paul warns against "fleshly" (σαρκικός) people (3:2f.).	19

16	Paul's own "fleshly" story (3:4–6).	2
17	Paul discarded his "fleshly" life as refuse to be united with Christ (3:7–11).	3
18	Paul strives to attain the goal (Christ has won it already) that is ahead (3:12–14).	4
19	Philippians ought to be imitators of Paul, citizens of heaven awaiting the return of Christ (3:15–17, 20).	21
20	Shameless opponents think only on things of the earth, 20 enemies of Christ (3:18f.).	20
21	Christ will come, will transform weak bodies (3:20f.).	32
22	Paul appeals for standing firm in the Lord: having unity (Euodia, Syntuche), and helping the women (4:1f.).	22
23	Women have worked together with Paul and others for the Gospel (4:3).	8
24	Paul appeals for joy, friendliness, no worries, prayer (4:4–6, 7–9)	23
25	God's peace will keep them safe (4:7).	28
26	Philippians once more proved that they cared for Paul (4:10).	12
27	Paul has learned to be "content" (αὐτάρκης), to live through power of Christ (4:11–13).	10
28	Philippi only church to help Paul in the past (4:14–17).	7
29	Paul gives Philippians receipt for their gift brought by Epaphroditus. They receive the letter (4:18).	24
30	God will supply all their needs in future (4:19).	29

4. *REFERENTIAL SEQUENCE*

ReferS		**PoetS**
1	Story of Christ as servant (2:6–11).	8
2	Paul's own "fleshly" story (3:4–6).	16
3	Paul discarded his "fleshly" life (3:7–11).	17
4	Paul strives to attain the goal (3:12–14).	18
5	God started good work in Philippians (1:6f.).	2
6	Philippians worked together with Paul from the beginning of Paul's work (1:5).	1
#	Implied: Paul's action in the church of Philippi.	
7	Philippi only church to help Paul in the past (4:14–17).	28

8	Women have worked with Paul and others (4:3).	23
9	Paul in prison (1:12f.).	4
10	Paul has learned to be "content," to live through power of Christ (4:11–13).	27
11	Brothers have confidence to preach (1:14–18).	5
12	Philippians once more proved they cared for Paul, by sending their gift with Epaphroditus (4:10).	26
13	Epaphroditus had been very ill (2:27).	12
14	Paul longs for the Philippians and pray for their true knowledge (1:8–11).	3
15	Paul wants to send Epaphroditus with letter (2:25f.).	11
16	Paul urges them: live according to the Gospel, with a common purpose, battling together (1:28–30).	7
17	Living according to Gospel (2:1–4) means having same attitude as Christ (2:5–11).	8
18	Appeal: be joyful in the Lord (3:1).	14
19	Paul warns against "fleshly" people (3:2f.).	15
20	Shameless opponents, enemies of Christ (3:18f.).	20
21	Philippians ought be imitators of Paul (3:15–17, 20).	19
22	Paul appeals: stand firm, having unity, helping the women (4:1f.).	22
23	Paul appeals for joy, friendliness, prayer (4:4–6, 7–9).	24
24	Paul gives Philippians receipt for their gift brought by Epaphroditus. They receive the letter (4:18).	29
25	Paul appeals: accept Epaphroditus (2:28–30).	13
26	Paul will send Timothy soon (2:19–24).	10
27	Paul wants to visit Philippians again, or at least hear reports (1:27).	6
28	God's peace will keep them safe (4:7).	25
29	God shall supply all their needs in future (4:19).	30
30	If they live in unity and like stars, Paul will be proud on the Day of Christ (2:12–18).	9
31	God will complete his work in Philippi on the day when Christ comes again (1:6).	2
32	Christ will transform weak bodies when He comes (3:20f.).	21

5. *Discussion of Poetic Sequence*

Paul starts his poetic sequence of actions by mentioning the important fact that the Philippians worked together with Paul from the beginning (1:5). In view of the urgent warnings given in chapter 3, the moving forward of referential actions[1] 5, 31, and 14 underlines that what happened in Philippi is God's work, and that Paul had for quite a time been longing to see them. This special relationship with them, and his longing to see them, is emphasized again by PS 6, which significantly relocates RS 27. Against this background the urgent appeal of PS 7 and 8 (RS 16 and 17) is understandable and acceptable.

It is interesting that the main thrust of the referential actions which remain in their relative chronological order in the poetic sequence (for example RS 9, 11, 16, 17, 18) constitutes the main line of Paul 's argument: they have to live according to the gospel, to follow Christ and to be joyful in the Lord.

The relocation of RS 30, 26, 15, 13, 25 in PS 9–13 underlines the interrelation of their living according to the gospel, and Paul's relationship to them.

The next phase in the poetic sequence of action, as well as the referential sequence of actions, deals with Paul's call to joy, immediately followed by his stern warnings to the readers (PS 14, 15, 19f.). Again, this is interrupted by some relocated actions, which nevertheless follow the same sequence: PS 16, 17, 18 (RS 2, 3, 4) . Note that PS 18 also implies and recalls Christ's story in PS 8 (RS 17). It is clear that while Paul is warning them against the opponents, he is also advising them to be real τέλειοι, imitators of himself, and giving them the hope that Christ will come to transform their mortal bodies. It should be noted that by and large, Paul's basic argument is constituted by the sequence of actions where a similar sequence between poetic action and referential actions can be observed.

As has been pointed out already, after PS 15 (RS 19) the referential sequence differs again from the poetic sequence, though again basically retaining the same order. PS 16–19 represents RS 2–4, 21. It is significant that Paul, after having introduced the theme of the "fleshly" people, immediately recalls RS 2–4 which are of such basic significance in his own life, yet also very important with a view to his discussion of the opponents.

After returning to the theme of the opponents in PS (and RS) 20, another relocation of the referential action takes place, but this time not from the beginning of the referential sequence, but from the end—the coming of Christ and the transformation of the weak bodies (RS 32). After Paul's appeal to unity in PS 22 (RS 22), he recalls an example from the referential sequence (8) as an illustration of the fact that it had been done already.

The poetic sequence then continues (24) with a call for joy, friendliness, and prayer. The following actions in the poetic sequence again relocates referential sequences, assuring the readers of the safekeeping by God's peace in future, but also calling to mind their help to Paul (RS 12) in his situation of need (RS 10). The fact that Paul reverts even further back in PS 28 (RS 7) to the fact that the Philippians was the only church to help him in the past, emphasizes the importance of PS 26 and 28. PS 29 follows logically, whereas PS 30 also remains close to the referential sequence.

6. *The Suspense in the Story*

The letter opens (PS 1) with Paul's reference to the fact that the Philippians worked together with Paul from the beginning of his work. It is thus clear that the relation between Paul and the Philippians is of the utmost importance from the beginning of this letter. This is underlined by the following poetic actions which are relocated from their referential sequence positions and which also deal with the work in Philippi and Paul's longing to be with them.

The suspense in this respect is heightened when Paul declares in PS 6 that, despite his longing to be with Christ, he would rather remain in the flesh with a view to be able to be available to them. But that would then imply a lot for the addresses too, *inter alea* the authority to address them in a stern manner! Throughout the letter it would appear that the relocated referential sequences more often than not underline the relationship between Paul and the Philippians.

In the middle of the poetic sequence (13) Paul appeals to them to accept Epaphroditus. Why is it necessary to exhort them to accept Epaphroditus? It should be noted that this appeal is placed after the call to follow Christ as Servant, the call to unity and to be like shining stars, and before the warning against the opponents. And yet, Epaphroditus represented the Philippians with Paul. Was the need for this call related to a breach in the relationship between the Philippians and Epaphroditus (and Paul)? When Paul refers at the end of the poetic sequence (28 & 29) to their help and a receipt for it which is to be delivered by Epaphroditus, this may imply that he trusts that any tension would be cleared away, as well as any distance between the positions of Epaphroditus and the Philippians. That could mean then that the Philippians have taken up the position of the authorial readers, that is, people who follow Christ and imitate Paul, as indicated earlier in the letter.

It is also important that the imitation of Paul and the following of Christ play such a crucial role in this letter, because in the referential sequence the story of Christ and of Paul (who had to discard his "fleshly"life), is closely tied up with the warning against the opponents. When the letter closes with the promise that God will supply all their needs, it could be inferred that that could also imply that the readers would also have learned to be "content" (as Paul). To this, of course, the letter gives no answer.

It is therefore evident that, amongst other things, the implications of the relocations of the referential actions in the poetic sequence of the letter and the way in which this facilitates the heightening of the suspense for the implied readers, are factors which have to be reckoned with in a discussion of the role of the reader in Philippians.

NOTES

[1] Hereafter abbreviated as PS (poetic action/sequence) and RS (referential action/sequence).

WORKS CONSULTED

Eco, Umberto
    1979   *The Role of the Reader. Explorations in the Semiotics of Texts.* Bloomington: Indiana University Press.

Fowler, Robert M.
    1985   "Who Is 'the Reader' in Reader Response Criticism?" *Semeia* 31:5–23.

Grimm, Gunter
    1977   *Rezeptionsgeschichte. Grundlegung einer Theorie. Mit Analysen und Bibliographie.* Uni Taschenbücher 691. München: Wilhelm Fink.

Holub, Robert C.
    1984   *Reception Theory. A Critical Introduction.* London: Methuen.

Iser, Wolfgang
    1978   *The Act of Reading.* London: Routledge and Kegan Paul.

Link, Hannelore
    1976   *Rezeptionsforschung. Eine Einführung in Methoden und Probleme.* Mainz: Kohlhammer.

McKnight, Edgar V.
    1985   *The Bible and the Reader. An Introduction to Literary Criticism*. Philadelphia: Fortress.

Petersen, Norman R.
    1984   "The Reader in the Gospel." *Neotestamentica* 18:38–51.
    1985   *Rediscovering Paul. Philemon and the Sociology of Paul's Narrative World*. Philadelphia: Fortress.

Schenk, Wolfgang
    1984   *Die Philipperbriefe des Paulus. Kommentar*. Stuttgart: Kohlhammer Verlag.

Steiner, George
    1979   "'Critic'/'Reader'." *New Literary History* 10:423–452.

Suleiman, Susan R.
    1980   "Introduction: Varieties of Audience-Oriented Criticism." Pp. 3–45 in *The Reader in the Text: Essays on Audience and Interpretation*. Ed. Susan R. Suleiman and Inge Crosman. Princeton NJ: Princeton University Press.

THE IMPLICIT AND EXPLICIT READERS AND THE GENRE OF PHILIPPIANS 3:2-4:3, 8-9: RESPONSE TO THE COMMENTARY OF WOLFGANG SCHENK

Detlev Dormeyer
University of Münster

ABSTRACT

Analysis of the persons (first, second, and third persons) of verbs provides a general approach to the Letter to the Philippians. The persons of the verb represent the positions attributed to the sender (first person), the receiver (second person), and the message (third person).

This model has to be coordinated with the levels of author-reader-relationships as presented by Link. The differences between levels of readers (real/explicit/implicit) lead to a sociological and aesthetical interpretation of the letter C as belonging to the genre "friendship-letter," as classical literary theory called it.

The store of knowledge possessed by the Philippians is investigated. Through Paul the Philippians have learned the whole Old Testament and evolved from the status of the uneducated lower class to the educated Christian community. This Christian religion has to be connected to the levels of the act of reading. Paul's friendship-letter C presupposes advancement from the naive to the critical reader. Through a reading-process of this kind, all the Christians of Philippi are able to become explicit, critical readers.

1. *Structuring of the text according to syntactical signs of the person of the verb (deixis).*

    Schenk bases his proposal for the structure of the letter upon the use of different persons with verbs. In section 9.2.9 of *Die Philipperbriefe des Paulus*, Schenk gives an overview:

Simply stated, Phil 3:2ff. has the following structure, orientated toward subjects.

1. Indicative 1. Person Singular	2. Indicative 1. Person Plural	3. Cohortative 1. Person Plural	4. Imperative 2. Person Plural general	5. Imperative 2. Person Plural special	6. 3. Person
			3:2		
	3:3				
3:4–14			(3:13a)		(3:4b) 3:15a
		3:15b		3:15c-d	
	3:16a	3:16b			
			3:17		
3:18-19					
	3:20-21		4:1	4:2-3	
			4:8-9		

The main parts are those in the I-speech of 3:4–14; the inner framework is marked by the summarizing we-indicative of 3:3, 20f. and by the outer imperative framework of 3:2 and 4:1ff. In the central column 4 the main part of the I-speech is recognizable only by the parenthetical addressing of brothers in 3:13a. But if all reader-oriented signals in 3:4c, 8a, 8b, 8d, 9, 12a, 13a, 13b were placed in the I-speech, the diagram would be less schematic. Thereby the relation between the I-speech and the orientation to the receiver becomes more significant. It becomes clear the extent to which the relationship of the I-speech to the receiver is a regularly recalled relationship. It also becomes clear that the regular change which seems to be significant for 3:15ff. and which is made stronger in the surface structure was already present in the semantic and pragmatic deep-structure. If the relations between the I-speech of column 1 and the opponent-references of column 6 (indicated by the parenthetical hints in 3:4b) are completed through the references to the pre-Passover past of Paul, an appropriate picture is gained. To a great extent, in his disagreement with opponents, Paul fights against positions which he once took himself; in other words: he fights against his own past in Phil 3:5–6, 7a, 9b, 12a, and 13a. To a certain degree this explains the unusual detailed I-speech of Paul (Schenk: 273f.).

A sound theory underlies this procedure. According to H. Weinrich (not cited by Schenk) the syntactic function of the person of verbs is regulated most uniformly and plausibly in all languages. "As far as I know there is no language that diverges from the basic model of first, second, and third person" (Weinrich: 29). The function of the person is as follows: "The first person 'I' obviously signifies the speaker. The second person (sing.) 'you' signifies the addressee, who is the hearer. (Of course the polite forms 'Sie', 'Usted', 'Lei' are the second, not the third person!). The third person (no matter whether it is he, she, or it) signifies the world of the speaker and hearer as far as it is an object of the speech. The third person is a 'remainder category'" (Weinrich: 29). The differentiation between the first, second, and third person makes possible a creation and arrangement of communication between author (I), reader (you), and world (it). It is necessary to pay attention to additional distinctions which Schenk also considers in his table (Schenk: 274). "'We' is not always a synonym for 'I' plus 'you' plus 'he'. It can be as well: 'I' plus 'you', excluding 'he.' Or: 'I' plus 'he', excluding 'you'" (Weinrich: 29). Schenk is justified in distinguishing between the first person singular and the first person plural. He symbolizes the inclusion of "we" and "you" (pl.) by an arrow (Phil. 3:2 to 3:3) and the exclusion of "we" from "you" by leaving the arrow out (Phil. 3:16a; 15b; 16b). A special case is the "we" in 3:20–21. Although it is formulated as exclusive, it is intended to fuse with "you" (pl.) in 3:20–21; 4:1, 2–3, 8–9. This coherence between "I/we," "we/you" (sing./pl.), "he..." as a deep-structure of text is convincing.

The table of Schenk further divides the first person plural into the indicative and cohortative (hortatory subjunctive) modes. The second person plural is divided into "general" and "special." But these divisions are arbitrary and are either not significant or not sufficiently distinctive. The differentiation between indicative and cohortative does not affect perception. This mode is not significant for the arrangement of the text in this letter.

A special semantic problem is indicated by the "imperative second person plural special" in 3:15c–d. But a special group is not to be recognized on the basis of syntax. On the other hand, in 4:2–3 single persons are addressed by proper names or special titles. This is indeed a matter important for arranging the text, but it has to be defined more exactly as "imperative second person plural with addressees named." This imperative is not a special syntactical category. It is included in the category: "imperative second person general." The three persons of verbs according to Weinrich are a sufficient basis for analyzing the structure of text.

The present tense as an appeal with the first person singular, which Schenk considers important (Schenk: 263–266), does not appear. If the function of "appeal" is linked to the present with "I," this mode is not a special case, which dissolves the semantic information to πάντα in v. 7f. and transfers the *rhema* into the "present-relationship" of the verb (so Schenk: 264).

According to Bühlers organon-model (1965), cited by Schenk, each speech-act has a relation to "matters [*Gegenstände*], sender, receiver" (Schenk: 25). From that perspective the present ἡγοῦμαι ("I count" 3:8) is a statement concerning the activity of the sender, whereas πάντα refers to the textexternal area. The conjunction of sender-activity and reference implicitly includes an "appeal" to the hearer without which the reference may be ignored. Contrary to ἅτινα, the word πάντα signifies a universalization as scholars to this time have correctly considered it. The present in the first person does not represent a special case because it often has an implied function of appeal.

2. *The role of the reader in Phil. 3:2–4:3f., 8f.*

Schenk does not distinguish between the explicit and real reader. It is possible to suppose that he refers I/we-you-speech directly to the real reader and the he/they-statements to the real opponents. That is not generally the case. But before mentioning Schenk's preparatory work concerning the implied level of communication ("implied author-reader-matters"), some preliminary remarks about the relation between the role of the reader and the letter in the New Testament are necessary.

2.1 The instances of author-reader-relation according to Hannelore Link (25):

author	A = author	reader	E = area
real author	A1 (empirical historical person)	real reader	E1 textexternal area
abstract author = implicit author	A2 (abstract instance = theoretical construction)	abstract reader = implicit reader	textinternal area: E2 abstract situation of communication ('normativ')

fictional author (narrator, speaker) explicit author	A3 (fictional person = figure in the text)	fictional reader explicit reader	E3 fictional situation of communication
Many communicative situations (among others) in text-worlds (dialogues, speeches...)—all other events of the "narrative"			E4 "world in text"

This scheme must now be adapted to communication in the New Testament letter.

2.2   *The role of the reader in the New Testament letter.*

Michael Bunker introduces the distinction between *social* and *sociological* interpretation: "While social interpretation analyses the literary work with regard to socially created problems, events, and conflicts, sociological interpretation concentrates exclusively upon the work by reading it as a social fact and by asking for the reasons why it was created and produced, under which condition it is received by someone (a group), why it adjusts to this or that form, and how it is related to the respective overall culture" (16).

In relation to social interpretation, Bünker mentions G. Theißen among others (Theißen: 1979). On the other hand, the sociological interpretation aspired to by Bünker is a new way based on W. Iser's search for the implicit reader (Bünker: 17). Nevertheless Bünker makes a momentous mistake by confusing the explicit reader with the real community. It has to be stated that Paul, for example, intends the whole community (the explicit readers) as addressee in 1 Cor. 1:10–4:21—which is proved by the frequent address to "brothers" (1:10,26; 2:1; 3:2, and so on). Nevertheless Paul's special protagonists are the leaders of parties and in all probability "they belonged to the relatively upper class in the community" (Bünker: 17).

It is gratifying that Bünker maintains the concept of the "implicit reader" in spite of the direct addresses. If the "explicit reader" is recognized as fiction, the misunderstanding that the implicit reader still has to be proved is avoided. Without the creation of the implicit reader, it is impossible to draw a conclusion from the explicit, fictive addresses and also from the giving of proper names to the real reader.

For the sociological program of defining production and reception of the *literary* letter, comparison with the classical letter form becomes central for Bünker. Instead of Theißen and the older form history, the *aesthetic function* of the letter is once again given its proper place.

2.3   *Starting-point for the description of communication between implicit author and implicit reader in Philippians.*

2.3.1   *The classical friendship-letter as a genre of Phil C (elsewhere "Warnbrief" = genus iudiciale; Schenk: 277–286) 3:2–4:3, 8f.*

In section 9.2 ("The rhetorical situation and structure") Schenk examines the classical letter genre. He compares it with Phil 3:2–4:3, 8f. (1984: 277–280). His results correlate in a striking fashion with the earlier textsyntactical structure. I want to elucidate this correlation with the following scheme, which uses the model of Weinrich:

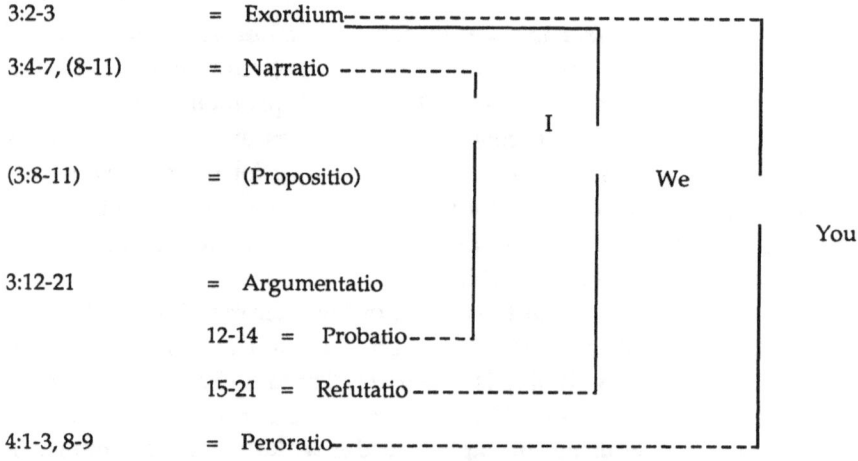

The textsyntactical signals of the person of the verbs were obviously arranged by Paul according to the scheme of the genre of the philosophical friendship-letter of antiquity.

This result permits far-reaching conclusions. Paul had textbook knowledge of letter writing. In viewing Pseudo-Demetrius and Pseudo-Proclus as creators of theories concerning the letter (Schenk: 227) caution must be taken since their dates are either uncertain or after the time of Paul and furthermore knowledge of them is no precondition of qualification for letter writing (Bünker: 21ff.). Rather "letter writing as a form of rhetorical school exercises (προγυμνάσματα) with the intent of ἠθοποιιά [formation of character or manners] is proved" only since the time of Theon (first century C.E.) (Bünker: 23, n. 40). In the *Progymnasmata* no special genre scheme was developed, but the letter had to be arranged according to the "dispositio" of the "oratio."

These considerations may refute the assumption of A.J. Malherbe that Paul's letters reflect the "third level of the system of education": the study of rhetoric in "stylistic conventions" (221). *Progymnasmata* were set even on the second level, the level of the study of grammar, and unspecific instructions for letter writing were realized on that level. In my opinion, Bünker's theory that the *function* determines the arrangement of the letter (cultivation of friendship, private communication, fictional *production* of literature...) is worthy of continued attention (23). Schenk's considerations of the three "genera dicendi" of the rhetoric of Aristotle are also moving in the right direction:

> Since Aristotle, three different kinds of speeches (*genera*) can be distinguished (based on the area of practice) which were at the same time valid as models with possible influence on genre:
>
> a) *genus iudiciale* (forensic) for indictment and defence at law-court and everywhere in the case of disputes;
>
> b) *genus deliberativum* (symbuleutic [advisory]) for persuasive statements (pro and con) at public meeting;
>
> c) *genus demonstrativum* (epideictic) for praise and censure of persons, things, and events before a general audience (277f.).

Nevertheless I doubt that Galatians and this Philippian letter can be ascribed to genus iudiciale (but see Schenk: 278). As a friendship-letter it is a "mixed sort" (Deißmann: 160), which cannot be assigned to the three genera. Berger makes a similar judgment, even though, according to H.D. Betz, he ascribes to Galatians the iudical apology (1984: 1289ff.; H.D. Betz: 1975). Schenk's decipherment of structure does not touch the question of classification of genre. The individual "letter" genre lies on a level above the basic genre of Aristotelian rhetoric because of its intersubjective, nonforensic nature. Even the iudicial letter is a matter of a world of fiction and not a real court-situation.

In Phil C it is also a question of a friendly "school-situation," not of public legal proceedings. From the literary structure of Phil C it becomes clear that the real author and real reader must have been educated on that level (study of grammar) in order to be writing the letter and reading it with understanding.

The peroratio 4:1–3 calls two women and one man by their proper names and at least paraphrases the proper name of another man (perhaps calling him by name). Common sense indicates that these names refer to real and not fictitious readers. But is it possible to learn from the scanty admonition anything about the real situation at Philippi? Like most commentaries Schenk goes much too far here.

He is right when he refuses to accept the view that a quarrel between the two women can be established on the basis of the sentence repetition v. 2b (271ff.). But how can Schenk say that Paul is thinking of "leaders of house communities who opened their meetings for heresies" (272) and who are responsible for the composition of Phil. 2:6ff. (327)? Paul's terms are much too common and general to be able to draw out of them conclusions relative to exact activities (Gnilka: 166).

Paul has four confidants at Philippi in whom he can confide especially. From these he supposes that *they* at least *coincide* with the critical *implicit reader*. More should not be said about the community situation on the basis of this letter fragment.

Is it possible to draw further conclusions concerning the educational level of the real author and real readers?

2.3.2 *The history-of-religions comparison and the education level of the community.*

The explicit, fictive level of the letter comes into form immediately at 3:2 with the triangle "brotherly reader, opponents, and present author." Up to v. 14 this conflict constellation keeps unchanged. With v. 15 a difference between author and reader becomes a possibility, but at the same time the neutralization of this difference by God's act of revelation is announced. This narrowing of view point has consequences for the author-reader relation, because the conflict with the opponents is discussed again in v. 18. Its connection with the readers is closer than suggested by the polemic at the beginning.

Schenk is justifiably on his guard in the decision whether Paul's opponents were Jews or Jewish Christians. The closeness of v. 18 and the appeal to God's fictive separation between readers and opponents suggests a lively relationship between followers and opponents. What is the basis of the conflict? Exegetes agree that the conflict concerns the value of the Jewish law. Is the problem of the law brought in from outside the community? The ending 4:9 speaks about "what you have learned and received and heard and seen." Does this (with "teaching" and "tradition") only mean the gospel as "Easter message" and some parts of the Jesus-Halacha and ethical orientation (Schenk: 318f.)? Or is one to suppose, like von Campenhausen, that until the end of the second century the total Old Testament was studied as the Holy Scripture (see Campenhausen: 29ff.)?

Such knowledge is a basic precondition for understanding the represented conflict and the narratio of the author. If the Old Testament is not studied by the *real* community, its knowledge is at least imputed to the implicit readers. The letter authorizes them indirectly to interpret the letter, in opposition to those who do not know the Old Testament. But did

Paul consider the education of such a "scholastic school" as desirable (Judge: 164)? I question such an assumption.

One must ascribe to the Pauline mission an intensive scholarly activity which forms the preconception that all real readers of Paul's community understand the implicit level of the letter. All conclusions from the represented conflicts which omit the reception-qualification of readers are capricious. Schenk's assumption of the "wisdom teacher" as representing the self-understanding of the implicit author (274-277) and the "righteousness proselyte" the implicit addressee of the opposing agitation (302ff.) leads in the right direction. If the opponents desire a proselyte who keeps the total law perfectly, they must find in Philippi hearers who at least understand. If the agitation requires a refutation, the implicit hearers must know the pretension to full observance of the law and consider it as a meaningful way of Christianity.

Has Paul, perhaps because of his own biography, only fought windmills against the projection of his own shadow? Concerning that we do not learn anything, and that is why we must accept the manifest level of the connection. We must assume that Paul was not mistaken completely about the knowledge of his real readers at Philippi and that Paul could assume their knowledge of the Old Testament and comprehension of the Jewish law. But from whom have the Gentile-Christian hearers received their knowledge?

Is the reason for the overwhelming missionary success of Paul the fact that he was able to offer the lower class (which did not have an elementary and grammar education) an education in the Christian version of the Israelite religion? Did he bring to the Gentile Hellenists at Philippi what Max Weber considers to be the main achievement of postexilic Judaism: the transformation of folk religion into confession, into acknowledgement of the individual (Weber: 400)?

I consider Schenk's continual emphasis on the aspect of knowledge against the empty attitude of confidence to be quite right. But he only sees one side of the problem when he rejects metaphor as "pseudosemantic" (276f., 310–314). The new religious knowledge of the Philippians requires religious metaphor even if the content is transformed decisively by Jesus' resurrection. A number of semantic problems are settled by the assumption of metaphor (Dormeyer: 1987a). If all converted Philippians have learned the Old Testament, self-evidently they have also learned the metaphor of the Old Testament.

Under this condition, the implicit reader is no longer the educated among the uneducated (as Theißen, Bünker and others suppose), but the whole community. It is restored by the "teaching" according to the Pharisaic ideal (interpreted in a Christian fashion) of *knowledge* of the

Old Testament law as a way of life and a way of practise (Phil. 4:9). Herder and "Formgeschichte" have seen this line thoroughly: the Old Testament which is untouched by Hellenism transmits its popular native originality to Christianity (Herder: 195f.).

Except for romantic implications, this line must be followed further. The Christian message interprets the Old Testament in a new way and becomes a philosophy of life only as an interpretation of the Old Testament. Because of this indissoluble relationship, the Christian message for contemporary interpretation of Jewish Hellenism and Jewish Christianity remains reversionary—but not in a way that (according to Schenk) always can or must be differentiated semantically between terms of agitators on the one hand and interpreters of Paul on the other hand. Judaism and Hellenistic Christianity continue to share many codes.

Although Schenk thematizes the difference between researcher and reader (27f.) he equates the decoding-reading of the critical reader (Dormeyer, 1979: 90–113) with the analytical-reading of the researcher. But it is important to distinguish between these two levels of reading. The starting point of reading is a third level: the naive reading.

Reader-attitude

act of reading	naive reader	critical reader	critical researcher
activity of conscious	experience	reflection	analysis
activity of text	confirmation of attitude of reader	change of attitude of reader	neutralized objectivity
synthesis	delight a./o. displeasure	hermeneutic a./o. dialectic	distance of metalevel

The levels "naive reader," "critical reader," and "critical researcher" are constructed according to Ingarden (18ff.).

These three levels constitute a circle of reading. The naive reader begins with the naive reading and may go forward to critical reading and research reading. After that, the circle of reading begins afresh with a deeper understanding. The naive reading may stop on the first level. Such a reading does not involve critical reading and research reading. Critical reading may omit the naive reading, in which case there is a blocking of feeling and delight. The reading process may also be stopped on this second level. The research, historical-critical reading may omit naive and critical reading, in which case there is a blocking of feeling, delight, and hermeneutic and dialectical factors. The researcher, therefore, tries normally to engage in naive and critical reading. But often he or she fails to operate at these two levels. A number of new methods in the human sciences are necessary for the activation of naive and critical reading (Dormeyer, 1987b: 119f.).

Which reader does Paul have in mind? I think that he has addressed his emotional statements and arguments to the naive and critical reader, not to a research reader. Perhaps he has found a few rhetorically educated readers (so too the Corinthian community according to Hollenweger). But Paul shows no interest in that kind of hearer. Nevertheless the author of 2 Peter declares Paul's letters to be an object of research reading (2 Peter 3:16). Paul has not been transparent for naive reading and partly unintelligible for the other levels of the reading process.

It is also important for the later history of the Holy Scripture that when the writings of the New Testament became a unity paralleling those of the Old Testament (from the time of Irenaeus) the letters of Paul gave precedence to the Gospel writings (Dormeyer, 1989: 20–25). This continues until today in many churches. On the other hand, the revision of Paul by Luther brought the Old Testament to bear again. You cannot have Paul without the Old Testament, but it seems to be possible to have the Gospels without the Old Testament—and Paul also when you prefer naive reading with the exclusion of critical and research reading.

WORKS CITED

Berger, Klaus
    1984   *Hellenistische Gattungen im Neuen Testament.* ANRW II 25.2. Berlin:1031–1432.

Betz, Hans Dieter
    1975   "The Literary Composition and Function of Paul's Letter to the Galatians." *NTS* 21:353–79.
    1987   *Der Galaterbrief. Ein Kommentar zum Brief des Apostels Paulus an die Gemeinde in Galatien.* (English tr. 79), München: Kaiser.

Bühler, Karl
    1965   *Sprachtheorie: Die Darstellungsfunktion der Sprache.* Stuttgart (1st ed. 1934).

Bünker, Michael
  1984 *Briefformular und rhetorische Disposition im 1. Korintherbrief.* Göttingen.

Campenhausen, Hans Frhr. von
  1968 *Die Entstehung der christlichen Bibel.* BhTh 39, Tübingen.

Deißmann, Adolf
  1908 *Licht vom Osten. Das Neue Testament und die neuentdeckten Texte der hellenistisch-römischen Welt.* 1st ed. Tübingen.

Dormeyer, Detlev
  1979 *Der Sinn des Leidens Jesu: Historisch-kritische und textpragmatische Analysen zur Markuspassion.* SBS 96, Stuttgart.
  1987a "Die Kompositionsmetapher 'Evangelium Jesu Christi, des Sohnes Gottes' Mk 1,1. Ihre theologische und literarische Aufgabe in der Jesus-Biographie des Markus." *NTS* 33:452–68.
  1987b "Das Verhältnis von 'wilder' und historisch-kritischer Exegese als methologisches und didaktisches Problem." *Jahrbuch der Religionspädagogik* 3:111–27.
  1989 *Evangelium als literarisch und theologische Gattung.* Erträge der Forschung 263. Darmstadt: Wissenschaftliche Buchgesellschaft.

Gnilka, Joachim
  1968 *Der Philipperbrief.* HThKNT 10/3, Freiburg.

Herder, Johann Gottfried
  1967 *Vom Erlöser der Menschen. Nach unseren drei ersten Evangelien* (1796). Herder SW 19. Ed. B. Suphan. Berlin 1980, Hildesheim:135–252.
  1984 "Der Galaterbrief und das Verhältnis von antiker Rhetorik und Epistolographie." *ThLZ* 109:241–450.

Hollenweger, Walter J.
  1978 *Konflikt in Korinth und Memoiren eines alten Mannes*: Zwei narrative Exegesen zu 1 Kor 12–14 und Ez 37, München.

Ingarden, Roman
  1976 *Gegenstand und Aufgaben der Literaturwissenschaft. Aufsätze und Diskussionsbeiträge* (1937–1964), Ed. R. Fieguth, Tübingen 1976: 1–28.

Iser, Wolfgang
1976   Der Akt des Lesens: Theorie ästhetischer Wirkung. Uni Tashenbücher 636. München.

Judge, Edwin A.
1979   "Die frühen Christen als scholastische Gemeinschaft." Pp. 131–65 in Zur Soziologie des Urchristentums. Ed. N.A. Meeks. ThB 62. München.

Link, Hannelore
1976   Rezeptionsforschung: Eine Einführung in Methoden und Probleme. Stuttgart: Kohlhammer.

Malherbe, Abraham J.
1979   "Soziale Ebene und literarische Bildung." Pp. 194–222 in Zur Soziologie des Urchristentums. Ed. W.A. Meeks. ThB 62. München.

Meeks, W.A., ed.
1979   Zur Soziologie des Urchristentums. Ausgewählte Beiträge zum frühchristlichen Gemeinschaftsleben in seiner gesellschaftlichen Umwelt. ThB 62. München.

Roller, Otto
1933   Das Formular der paulinischen Briefe. BWANT 58. Stuttgart.

Schenk, Wolfgang
1984   Die Philipperbriefe des Paulus. Kommentar. Stuttgart: Kohlhammer.

Theißen, Gerd
1979   "Soziale Schichtung in der korinthischen Gemeinde. Ein Beitrag zur Soziologie des hellenistischen Urchristentums." Pp. 237–72 in Studien zur Soziologie des Urchristentums. WUNT 19. Tübingen.

Weinrich, Harald
1971   Tempus. Besprochene und erzählte Welt. 2nd ed. Stuttgart: Kohlhammer.

Weber, Max
1923   Gesammelte Aufsätze zur Religionssoziologie. III. Das antike Judentum. Tübingen.

"SOME THINGS OLD, SOME THINGS NEW"
A RESPONSE TO WOLFGANG SCHENK,
DIE PHILIPPERBRIEFE DES PAULUS

James W. Voelz
Concordia Theological Seminary

ABSTRACT

Wolfgang Schenk's interpretation of Philippians adopts a reader-oriented approach, embracing modern communication theory and concerning itself, not only with the semantic, but also, and, especially, with the *pragmatic* dimensions of a text. Thus, the *function* of semantic units—which is not related to their form—is shown to be of crucial importance. Unfortunately, Schenk's effort is inadequate in several respects. It proceeds from the assumption that a text *contains* meaning; that this meaning is to be ascertained by a "scientific," investigative procedure; and that such a procedure consists in the analysis of an objective structure of text. This approach is wholly incongruent with one which is reader-oriented, which asserts that readers (not investigators) make (not discover) meaning in the process of reading (not in detached analysis).

For his efforts in his commentary on Philippians, Dr. Wolfgang Schenk is only to be commended. Despite the (quite proper) disclaimer that "the production has in all its aspects the character of a draft" (14), his "provisional attempt," as it were, is a bold and effective one, indeed. There is so much to commend in this work.[1] In general terms, the format is effective (especially the summarizing and interpretive paraphrases at the end of each section); there is extremely close attention to detail throughout; and the actual interpretations which result seem to me to be effective.[2] As far as features which impinge directly upon reader-oriented[3] considerations are concerned—which are more directly to the point of this paper—there is, on the one hand, in *Philipperbriefe*, proper contextualization of many basic issues: a) features of text are discussed within the framework of communication theory (14–15); b) written signs are understood against the background of "signs" in general (16–18); and c) text and word are seen in the proper relation one to another, with the complete text understood as the basic unit of discourse (18–19).[4]

On the other hand, however, there is a most helpful discussion of the three dimensions of semiotics (19–20), particularly the semantic (23–25) and the pragmatic (25–26) dimensions of a text. Especially valuable from a reader-oriented point of view is, I believe, the semantic treatment of "word-fields" (semantic fields) (24), which, in turn, enables Schenk to draw the proper connections between related vocabulary in the text of Philippians.[5] But even more useful, because it is most specifically reader-oriented, is Schenk's treatment of a number of pragmatic dimensions of the text. He clearly and properly supports and proceeds from the insight that language has function—a function which embraces both the sender and the receiver:

> Pragmatics describes the relationship between the signs and the people as users of signs. Here the question is addressed: What is to be accomplished with what is said? What is intended? (19)

He also demonstrates that, for both senders and receivers of signs, form does not determine function, but, rather, that quite different forms may express quite the same function (cf. Thiselton:77). Especially effective is his treatment of ἀδελφοί and ἐγώ in 3:13:

> As, therefore, Paul in 3:18, with the inserted relative clause, introduced the imperative aspect as a warning, so does he possess, in fact, other means besides imperative and cohortative grammatical forms of verbs to bring to expression this pragmatic accent in the text. In 3:17, as in 4:1, this becomes apparent, as the imperative was strengthened by the direct address ἀδελφοί. This direct address occurs...in 3:13. There this ἀδελφοί of the addressees is followed directly by a redundant, explicitly expressed, ἐγώ of the sender. By this means, the exemplary and pictorial nature of that which Paul says of himself is already signalled, also for the addressees. What in 3:17 is explicitly stated as imitation/exhortation is here given in anticipation. The address ἀδελφοί possesses, likewise, an imperatival function (259).

In addition, he demonstrates, not only in the above-quoted treatment of 3:13, but also in the treatment of οὐχ ὅτι in 3:12, that the function of words and other textual units is signalled (one might add: particularly when they are special) for the reader (in a text in writing, in spoken discourse by extra-linguistic elements):

The expression used here, οὐχ ὅτι, possesses, in 4:11 as in 4:17, as far as the pragmatics of the text is concerned, a continuing, forward-moving function, and the same thing can be recognized in the same forward-thrusting usage in 2 Cor 1:24 and 3:5, where, as here, it is always linked with the first person. Therefore, its function, as far as the pragmatics of the text is concerned, is not that of a text-segmenting insertion *de novo*, but of an appeal oriented to the addressees, which marks the "I" discourse as conveying an example, and which thus corresponds to the words constituting an appeal in 3:13a and b. (262).

All of these insights are, it would seem, especially important for interpreters of the Pauline correspondence, especially for a proper understanding of the pragmatic function of (cf. "appeal") and the orientation of (e.g., toward the receptor as well as toward the sender[6]) the "I" sections of these writings.

Because I have found *Philipperbriefe* so valuable, it is difficult for me to say that it has, unfortunately, serious shortcomings. This must, however, be said, especially when one views it from a reader-oriented perspective. Simply put, while this commentary does speak to many reception theory or reader-response criticism concerns, it very much proceeds from a traditional point of view, viz., it normally argues from grammar, and from author's usage elsewhere,[7] not from the standpoint of how a reader reads (cf. Fish, 1970: 123–62) or how a reader creates understanding (cf. Crosman:149–64). In fact, in some respects, the close attention to textual details borders on a structuralist approach similar to that taken by R. Jakobsen and C. Levi-Strauss (204–16) in their analysis of Baudelaire's "Les Chats". Why is this so? It stems, I believe, from several fundamental assumptions made by Schenk in his first, introductory chapter. While he does assert that a text is not simply an aggregate of words or sentences but is, chiefly, a whole,[8] a text is, for him, an "ordered mass of verbal signs" (18), and these "signs" have both a specific structure and a specific content:

> "Syntactics" describes the relationship between signs and other signs. Here the questions is answered: How is what is said formulated/structured? (19)
>
> "Semantics" describes the relationship between the form of signs and their content (meaning). Here the question is addressed: How should/must what is said be understood? What is that which is meant? (19)

Now this is a very traditional viewpoint—that the text has a definite structure and that its signs have a specific (cf. "should/must...be understood") meaning. It does not raise the question of the reader's role, as reader-oriented criticism would raise it, *viz.*, does the reader make meaning in a text, or, even, does the reader determine what the text itself is (cf. Fish, 1976:484)? And, not surprisingly, this viewpoint is carried over into his understanding of what it means to interpret any text: "The goal of exegesis is the translation into a communicative equivalent of a New Testament text" (20). Or: "The investigative goal is the analysis and description of the content and structure of meaning of a text. This makes possible a semantically adequate translation" (23). Again, there is no thought that readers make meaning in texts, or even have a role in determining the nature and structure of texts. Rather, according to this view, the shape of the text is determined, and "content of meaning" must (simply) be unloaded or unpacked, much as one would empty a container of its contents.[9]

The basis for these assumptions is, I believe, another assumption more fundamental still, *viz.*, the "reader-researcher" distinction (27–28). Schenk is insistent that a "major error" in interpretation is the

> identification of reader with researcher. The removal of this confusion consists in the insight that both are different "subjects" or, indeed, different procedures, in so far as scientific inquiry into a text is distinguished from a naive, uncontrolled reader stance (27).

Indeed, today's "researcher," he maintains, can understand a text more adequately than an author's contemporary readers. He quotes Hirsch approvingly: "...the learned people of today understand [an early Christian author] better than he was understood by any of his contemporaries" (27). This viewpoint, it would seem, adopts a rigorous scientific rather than literary approach.[10]

But to proceed to a text from such a scientific rather than a literary viewpoint is inimical to a reader-approach. On the one hand, it is inimical *theoretically*. First of all, it ignores the insight of reader-response criticism regarding authorial reader (Petersen:40), *viz.*, that "authorial readers know more than non-authorial readers about what is or is not pertinent to the understanding and interpretation of a text. They know how to read between the lines." If this assertion by Norman Petersen is correct—and I believe it is—Schenk's "reader-researcher" distinction should be stood precisely on its head. Second, and relatedly, Schenk's viewpoint ignores the role and function of the community—an important factor in a reader-oriented approach—in the interpretive task. We have been reminded (Lategan:14), e.g., that "signals function only within the conventions of an interpretive community," and (Culler:116) that a poem—or any literary piece—"has meaning only with respect to a system of conventions which the reader has assimilated." Or, in the words of J.G. Davies (53): "The separate authors were members of a community and they wrote for that community. The meaning of their words is not just what they had consciously in mind, but what the community made of them." Schenk's viewpoint isolates the text, as it were, from the receiving (and believing) community.

On the other hand, to adopt a strictly "scientific" rather than literary approach when one interprets a text is inimical to a reader-oriented approach *practically*. Because it is not really concerned with real readers reading a text—either contemporary or current readers—but is, rather, concerned with a more traditional grammatical (indeed, almost structural) approach, it looks, first of all, at detailed syntactical and morphological characteristics and ignores, for all practical purposes, the function of the continuation of, or the progression of, thought within a text. With regard to Phil. 3:18, e.g., Schenk says that one can see

> a semantic relationship between the "many" of 3:18–19 and the known personages introduced in 3:2. This is...brought to one's attention...in an obvious way also through the faulty sentence structure in 3:18, which, through the medium of the plural accusative objects in the relative οὕς and the article τούς refers back to the double τούς of 3:2. For, between these two textual locations such a plural masculine accusative is found only in 3:17—once again to give an antithesis to Paul and his party—and for this reason, [such a plural masculine accusative] is conceivable only as a purposeful reintroduction of the enemy agitators mentioned at the beginning [of the section] (255).

Similarly,

> The plural of the quantitative relative pronouns ὅσοι (= "all who")...at this location [3:15] refers back to the personal plural objects of 3:2. For they never explicitly appear in between [these verses], but certainly in the πολλοί in 3:18, which corresponds to the ὅσοι in this verse, they are repeated, by which connection the quantitative characteristic of this verse is [also] clearly repeated (267).[11]

In all of these cases, the conclusion regarding linkage is probably correct, but not because of the correspondence of the plural number of each later morpheme with the plural number of the people mentioned earlier (in 3:2), but because of the natural connection of the thoughts involved.[12]

Second, Schenk's traditional, grammatical approach to the text also does not consider the literary nature of a document.[13] It is asserted, e.g., that the τέλειοι of 3:15 must be linked to the τετελείωμαι of 3:12 (267), that the ὅσοι of 3:15 cannot include Paul (267), and that "because of the move to the first person plural in 3:3, it is totally out of the question that the imperatives [of 3:2] are meant in a positive but ironic sense" (253). In each of these cases, a literary possibility is ruled out by the presence of morphological/syntactical congruencies in the text. Such judgments, it would seem, are questionable as such, since the recipients of the text would have been able to "read between the lines"(cf. Petersen), and they would, therefore, have been able to understand properly a statement by Paul which asserted, e.g., that all true followers of Christ and of his own example are the "real τέλειοι," rather than the opponents. Indeed, Schenk himself seems to veer in this very direction procedurally, on occasion.[14] Third, the approach presented in this commentary does not allow for a loose structuring, perhaps occasioned by the *ad hoc* nature of a piece of correspondence. I will mention here only the treatment of the reference to "Clement" in Phil 4:3.

> The wider reference to the man with the Roman name Clement, named in the prepositional phrase in 4:3c, seems to be a detour without purpose ("funktionslose Abschweifung"), if he is part of the [subordinate] relative clause. If the μετά followed by the striking adverbial καί is connected to the main clause, however, then Clement and the others are to help Timothy, who is addressed.(272)[15]

Is a "detour" such an impossibility? And would it, in any case, be "without purpose" or function? Given an understanding of the pragmatic dimensions of texts, one can hardly regard the mention of a specific individual as having no function, even if that function is simply "cohesive."[16]

Do the shortcomings, as they appear to me, vitiate the value of Wolfgang Schenk's *Die Philpperbriefe des Paulus*? I believe they do not. Not only are the conclusions (the actual interpretations, considered by themselves) very attractive and appealing, but this book does make one acutely aware, not only by its theoretical introduction, but also by the actual exegesis presented, of reader-oriented concerns, especially those that have to do with the pragmatic dimensions of communication. This can only enhance the treatment of texts, as it is practised by any one of us. And for this, we can only be most thankful.

NOTES

1 While the whole commentary is in view, the focus of this paper will be upon Schenk's handling of the material of Philippians 3:2–4:3.

2 Interested readers may wish to see his treatment of the problems of Chapter 3 as unified (267), the question of the female co-workers (271–2), and the relationship between Paul and "judgment" (260ff.).

3 This paper will address aspects of this book from the standpoint of both reception theory and reader-response criticism, because, while these two approaches are not identical, they are related, and each does seem to apply at points.

4 "A text is...a complex verbal sign" (18).

5 Schenk shows (257) that στήκω (4:11), περιπατέω (3:17,18), and στοιχέω (3:16) were related in terms of semantic field at Paul's time when understood ethically, encompassing teaching, thinking, and acting. So also (263) were ἡγέομαι (2:3;3:7,8), φρονέω (2:2,5;4:15) and σκοπέω (2:4;3:17).

6 Schenk says, e.g.: "Because the 'I' of 3:4ff. from the very first plays an 'example-giving' role, so the often strikingly-stressed singular construction 'my,' instead of 'our,' Lord (cf. 3:8), which one meets no where else in Paul, is not to be characterized as idiosyncratic. For this reason the determining factor for the expression is pragmatics as far as the sender is concerned, rather than, as would be necessary following the syntactic flow of the text, [pragmatics] as far as the receivers are concerned" (266).

7 See note 6 above.

8 See above, especially note 4.

9 It may be observed that Schenk does refer to Ingarden and to his idea of the "concretization" of a work (27), but it is noteworthy that he makes virtually nothing of Ingarden's concept of "spots of indetermination" ("Unbestimmtheitsstellen"); he concentrates, rather, on the problem of the adequacy of concretization. See Holub:24–28.

10 Schenk speaks of the "Black Box Method" (21–3).

11 In the same way Schenk links the plural neuters of σκύβαλα in 3:8 and τὰ ἐπίγαια in 3:19 with ἅτινα, ταῦτα, and πάντα in 3:7–8 (265).

12 It may be noted that the approach Schenk employs is not followed consistently. On several occasions the same form is seen to bear no relationship in terms of referent to one which is identical. Compare the following analyses:

It is clear that 3:3 and 3:20–21 are not to be torn apart from one another. Therefore, it is not possible to reference the "we" of 3:3 to Paul and his party but in 3:20 to see Christians as such characterized—in a natural way, as it were....Against this is the decisive point that 3:3 like 3:20 begins with the construction ἡμ(εῖς) γάρ and, therefore, establishes these "we" sections as the indicative foundation for the preceding imperatives (254).

...anticipating verse 20, [Paul] clearly closed 3:17 with such a striking, contrasting "we," and in this manner he framed verses 18 and 19 with the "we" references, even if this ["we"] does not include the addresses but contrasts with them, flowing, as it does, from the first [person] singular of the sender in 3:17a (256).

[13] But it is clear that Schenk does consider rhetorical criticism, albeit briefly (cf. 277–8).

[14] Two examples are instructive. Schenk says, with reference to the imperatives of 3:2 (βλέπετε):

> The word βλέπετε, which occurs only here in Philippians, is followed by the accusative and has the sense of "be on your guard against," although neither a μή (cf. Gal 5:15; 1 Cor 8:9; 10:12; Mark 13:5), nor an ἀπό (cf. Mark 8:15; 12:38) follows, but, rather, the simple accusative (as in 1 Cor 1:26; 10:28—where, however, no warning is conveyed). The warning function of verbs of fearing, etc. with the simple accusative is possible and from that fact to be understood here…(253).

His analysis of the first five words of 3:15 (ὅσοι οὖν τέλειοι, τοῦτο φρονῶμεν) runs thus:

> Here no thought of "Christian maturity" is developed, and one will have to be careful not to insert the first person plural, which belongs properly in the second half of the sentence, in the first half of the sentence, even in the translation. Because the second half of the sentence, which is stressed with the first person plural, looks back principally to 3:3, it is not amazing that the first half of the sentence—also in parallel—looks back to the three forenamed persons who are the antithesis in 3:2. Considering the given relational situation, which was known to the addressees at that time, as far as matters of reference are concerned, an adversative particle is not necessarily to be demanded here, as a condition for the validity of this interpretation (268).

[15] Schenk understands Timothy as the referent of the phrase γνήσιε σύζυγε earlier in 4:3 (272).

[16] This is what has been called by Malinowski (Caird:32) the language of "phatic communion," which is "designed primarily to establish rapport, to set another person at his ease, to create a sense of mutual trust and common ethos."

WORKS CITED

Caird, George Bradford
    1980   *The Language and Imagery of the Bible*. Philadelphia: Westminster Press.

Crosman, Robert
1980 "Do Readers Make Meaning?" Pp. 149–164 in *The Reader in the Text*. Ed. Susan R. Suleiman and Inge Crosman. Princeton, NJ: Princeton University Press.

Culler, Jonathan
1975 *Structuralist Poetics: Structuralism, Linguistics, and the Study of Literature*. Ithaca, NY: Cornell University Press.

Davies, John Gordon
1983 "Subjectivity and Objectivity in Biblical Exegesis." *BJRL* 66:44–53.

Fish, Stanley
1970 "Literature in the Reader: Affective Stylistics." *New Literary History* 2:123–162.

Holub, Robert C.
1984 *Reception Theory: A Critical introduction*. London: Methuen

Jackobsen, Roman and Claude Levi-Strauss
1970 "Charles Baudelaire's 'Les Chats'." Pp. 202–21 in *Introduction to Structuralism*. Ed. Michael Lane. New York: Basic Books.

Lategan, Bernard
1984 "Current Issues in the Hermeneutical Debate." *Neotestamentica* 18:1–17.

Petersen, Norman R.
1984 "The Reader in the Gospel." *Neotestamentica* 18:38–51.

Schenk, Wolfgang
1984 *Die Philipperbriefe des Paulus: Kommentar*. Stuttgart: Kohlhammer.

Thiselton, Anthony
1977 "Semantics and New Testament Interpretation." Pp. 75–104 in *New Testament Interpretation: Essays in Methods and Principles*. Ed. I. Howard Marshall. Exeter: Paternoster.

Tompkins, Jane P., ed.
1980 *Reader-Response Criticism: From Formalism to Post-Structuralism*. Baltimore: Johns Hopkins University Press.

LEVELS OF READER INSTRUCTIONS IN THE TEXT OF GALATIANS[1]

Bernard C. Lategan
University of Stellenbosch

ABSTRACT

The so-called encoded or textually defined reader refers to a composite image which depends on the integration by the prospective reader of a variety of directives operating on different levels of the text. Examples of these reader instructions on four levels of the text of Galatians are briefly discussed—the syntacto-rhetorical level, the level of cultural codes, the semantic universe of the text, and the development of a participatory ethics.

1. Introduction

The development of the concept of "the reader in the text," and its use as a heuristic device to facilitate the reading process, have been discussed from different perspectives in the preceding contributions. In addition to what has been said so far, it is important to keep in mind that this "reader" is of a composite nature, is so far as its construction depends on the integration of information from all over the text. The image of the implied reader gradually emerges through a process in which the (real) prospective reader assembles a series of hints and directives provided on different levels of the text. Eco (7) stresses the pedagogic function of these directives: they not only supply the reader with information, but in doing so, create the competence needed to read the text. In this essay, we shall be examining the form and function of some of these instructions to the reader, as well as the level on which they operate.

Although reader instructions are present in all kinds of texts, there are some differences in how they are used in narrative and non-narrative material. In his study of a narrative text like Mark, Van Iersel shows how a system of connotations is used in the development of the story. In the case of Galatians, we are dealing with a non-narrative text, which poses its own problems. Two interrelated issues—the type of rhetorical discourse used by Paul and the rhetorical structure of the letter—have been at the center of recent discussions (cf. Betz, 1975; 1979; 1987; Hübner; Hester; Smit; Hall). It is not the intention of the present essay to pursue these intriguing and complex questions. The aim is much more modest: to illustrate, with the help of certain selected examples, how the argument of the letter is developed on different levels and how the participation of the reader is invited by the use of various techniques. The focus, therefore, will be on the reading instructions themselves and how they are designed to steer and influence a potential reader (cf. Verschuren:49). In the introductory essay, it was pointed out that these instructions are of two kinds. On the one hand there are directives in the text itself, which may be more or less explicit. On the other hand, there is a substratum of assumptions which forms the basis on which the directives are activated. The text of Galatians offers interesting examples of the interaction between these two levels.

Without attempting further subdivisions, we shall, for the purpose of our analysis, consider Galatians to be an argumentative text—that is, a text written with the aim to convince, to persuade, to move its reader from one position to another. The fact that the argumentative mode is used so often in the New Testament does not mean that faith is rational, but that matters of faith can be presented in an argumentative mode in order to convince the reader or the listener. In our analysis the focus will be on how the first readers of Galatians were likely to interpret these instructions. In order to do so, two remarks about the wider argumentative context of Galatians are important.

First, from the evidence of the text itself it is clear that Paul is facing a formidable challenge from both the Galatian churches and certain representatives from Jerusalem. He finds himself in a totally disadvantaged position. His erstwhile followers have been persuaded by recent envoys from Jerusalem to accept a different interpretation of the gospel They apparently argue that faith in Christ is important—they subscribe to that themselves—but that it is not enough. The Galatians should strengthen their spiritual life by becoming part of a much wider group and a much longer religious tradition. They are urged to accept the Jewish way of life, which has stood the test of time and which has a practical moral system ideally suited to people coming in from a Hellenistic background with no guidelines as to how to structure their lives as Christians. What adds force to this argument is the fact that these people work with the approval and blessing of Jerusalem, the center of authority of the young developing church. But in Paul's understanding, the move back to the law amounts to a fundamental abrogation of the gospel; it will make the Galatians dependent on the law again and rob them of their freedom.

Second, Paul meets this challenge in two ways. He begins by defending the proposition that the gospel is not dependent on human authority or on human consent (1:11) and illustrates this by examples from his own life and that of Peter. Then, in order to move his readers to accept his central proposition, Paul uses all the pragmatic techniques at his disposal. This makes Galatians a complex and very concentrated text. Numerous strategies are mobilized on all levels to strengthen the central theme. But, in doing so, he has to start where his readers are, take their *Erwartungshorizonte* into consideration, and work within their codes. It also means that the shifting of positions is not achieved in one move, but by a *gradual* process in which a series of intermediate positions is spelled out. To illustrate the apostle's argumentative technique, we shall look at some examples on different levels of the text.

2. The syntacto-rhetorical level

On this level, a wide range of techniques is at the author's disposal. To give some idea of the field, we shall concentrate on three rather arbitrarily chosen aspects, namely the use of pronouns to demarcate textual space, rhetorical questions and their audiences, and the phenomenon of the double reader.

2.1 Pronomina and textual space

Pronomina can be used very effectively to demarcate textual space and to enable the author to manoeuvre within the room thus created. Paul is not the first to mark positions in the text by means of pronomina and to attach a certain value to each of these positions in their relationship to one another. Prior to Paul Dionysos Thrax (190–70 BC) in his *Ars Grammatica* (par 13.20) discusses the three forms of personal pronouns and defines them as follows: The first person is the one from whom the word comes; the second the one to whom the word is directed and the third person is the one about whom the utterance is made. In terms of textual space, it is clear that the first and second persons are closer to each other than the second and third, or the first and the third. The third is a step further removed from the direct interaction presupposed between the first and second pronomina. Furthermore, textual distance can become associated with specific values—or rather, certain positions are marked as being preferable to others. Preference is usually expressed in terms of proximity. An increase in distance between narratee and addressee serves as a negative sign, while a decrease marks a preferred position—culminating in solidarity or identification. In contrast to most other religious codes where the accent is on transcendence, biblical texts are characterized by emphasizing solidarity between God and human beings. In fact, fundamental change becomes possible only by the divine willingness to identify with human existence, as exemplified by incarnation.

In Galatians, Paul uses textual distance and proximity as part of his persuasive strategy. Throughout the letter, the second person pronoun "you" vacillates between two positions—it can either be grouped with Paul's opponents (5:1 "You foolish Galatians! Who has bewitched you?") or with the apostle's own group (4:12 "I plead with you, brothers..."). The middle position of the second person pronoun is perhaps best seen in an example like 1:8:

> But even if *we* or an angel from heaven should preach a gospel other than the one *we* preached to *you*, let *him* be eternally condemned!

The object of Paul's plea is to move the Galatians from a position of exclusion (allied with his opponents) to one of inclusion (allied with himself). He does this by subtly diminishing the textual distance and by suggesting how this mediation can take place: "I plead with you, brothers, become like me for I became like you" (4:12). By combining the possessive with the personal pronoun, the gravitational force of the writer's own group is increased: '*My* dear children...how I wish I could be with *you* now...' (4:19). At the same time the kinship connection (children) and the explicit expression of solidarity reinforces the argument. The final stage of inclusion is reached when the second person pronoun is subsumed under the first and any textual distance between the apostle and his followers is eliminated: 'Therefore *brothers, we* are not *children* of the slave woman, but of the free woman' (4:31). Little doubt is left to the reader as to the position which Paul expects him or her to assume.

In his commentary on Phil 3:2–4:9, Schenk comes to very similar conclusions (254–74). In an extensive discussion of the use of pronomina in these verses, he not only analyzes the movement to and fro between first, second and third person, but also the related shifts in mode, between indicative, cohortative and imperative (cf. especially the diagram on p. 274). His analysis reveals how strongly reader-oriented the pronomina are, especially the "paradigmatic 'I'" (260–63). With regard to changes in textual space, the same tendency can be found as in Galatians. For example, the first person plural used in Phil 3:3 clearly has inclusive force, binding author and readers together and providing the basis for the imperatives which are to follow (Schenk:254).

2.2 Rhetorical questions and their audiences

Recent studies in this field have stressed the important role of rhetorical questions in the dynamics of argumentation (cf. Wuellner). At the same time, it is important to distinguish more carefully between the different audiences for whom these questions are intended. Perelman has made it clear how important the role of the audience is in determining the effect of a rhetorical strategy. With biblical material the tendency is to think almost exclusively in terms of historical, real audiences, while there are also clear instances of questions addressed to a universal audience or to a single interlocutor (the "you" of many biblical passages—cf. for example Matt 5:23: "If *you* are bringing your gift to the altar..."; Matt. 5:25, 29, 40; 6:2 and many similar statements). Another variation is the author as self-deliberating—examples are the famous "I" passages in Romans 7 or the "we" references where Paul identifies himself with his readers in general or with the consciousness of the whole Christian community (cf. Wuellner and Schenk:260–63).

For our purposes, the most important aspect of rhetorical questions is the way in which they can be used to structure reality. These questions rest on social values or norms, which can be either challenged or confirmed by such procedures. Their main function is to concentrate attention on one point and to effect crucial changes in the flow of the discourse. Often rhetorical questions are used to sum up the argument, to state a conclusion, and to move to the next issue. A good example is Gal 1:10. Here Paul has to get himself out of a difficult corner. His opponents have used a main theme of his preaching (the abandonment of the Jewish torah) to cast doubts upon his intentions. Their argument runs more or less as follows: Paul rejects the law—therefore, he attempts to make life easier for his followers—therefore, he wants to be popular—therefore, he is uncertain of himself—therefore, he should not be trusted—therefore, his preaching should be rejected—therefore, the Galatians should accept the message of Paul's opponents and adopt their position.

It is very difficult to avoid this conclusion once the premise is accepted that Paul wants to be popular. The only way to break the flow of the argument is by means of a drastic intervention. Paul does this by uttering a curse: "Let him who preaches a different gospel be damned" (1:8—cf. the quotation above). By deliberately repeating the curse in 1:9, Paul emphasizes that it is not a slip of the tongue, but intentional. Such a shocking statement can be interpreted in different ways, but Paul now uses a rhetorical question to draw out the right conclusion for his purpose: Someone who is prepared to curse outright anybody who differs from him, is certainly not trying to curry favor with his audience:

> Am I now trying to win the approval of men, or of God? Or am I trying to please men? If I were still trying to please men, I would not be a servant to Christ (1:10).

By combining the effect of the curse with the interpretation of the rhetorical question, Paul is able to turn the argument around to reach a different conclusion in the minds of his audience: Paul obviously does not try to be popular—therefore, he is not uncertain of himself—therefore, he is not dependent on the favor of men—therefore, he may be right.

Rhetorical questions are powerful tools with which to choose the battleground, to identify the issues (that is, to select some and repress others, thereby narrowing the focus down to preselected targets), to anticipate and neutralize objections (cf. 2:17 and 3:21) and to frame the issue in such a way that only one response is possible—as illustrated vividly by the politician and seasoned interviewer.

When rhetorical questions are combined in a sequence, they can become a most effective tool to demolish all resistance from the side of the reader. A powerful example is the series of six questions which Paul fires in quick succession in Gal. 3:1-5:

> Are you people in Galatia mad? Has someone put a spell on you, in spite of the plain explanation you have had of the crucifixion of Jesus Christ? Let me ask you one question: was it because you practiced the Law that you received the Spirit, or because you believed what was preached to you? Are you foolish enough to end in outward observances what you began in the Spirit? Have all the favors you received been wasted? And if this were so, they would most certainly have been wasted. Does God give you the Spirit so freely and work miracles among you, because you practice the Law, or because you believed what was preached to you?

The answer in every case is emphatically No! It is almost impossible to escape the force of the argument once Paul's initial premise is accepted. Here we have an example where the reader is not so much given a clue as overwhelmed by the discourse. However, in due course we shall see that the author does not always have the upper hand and that the reader can also have a strong influence on the shaping of the argument.

2.3 The double reader

A last example of a syntacto-rhetorical device that will be mentioned here is a phenomenon which may be called the double reader. This refers to instances where Paul is talking to two different sets of readers at the same time. In the case of Gal. 2:6–7, he is dependent on the opinion of people whose authority he does not necessarily accept. Although he emphasizes that his commission as apostle does not derive from the Jerusalem group, he must take into account that, as far as his readers are concerned, they represent the final authority. He, therefore, has to keep both the Galatians and the delegation from Jerusalem in his sights. At this stage of the argument he cannot afford to antagonize the Galatians. He alters his strategy to argue from their premises—even those whom the Galatians accept as the highest authority did not question the way in which he presented the gospel. At the same time—and this is with a view to the Jerusalem delegation in Galatia—his reference to the "acknowledged leaders" should not be understood as a sign of his submission to their authority. This calls for very careful formulation of his argument. In the case of the absent reader, the situation is less complicated, because the author is talking to an absent party via a present reader. Here two different types of readers with two different sets of presuppositions must be handled simultaneously.

3. The level of cultural codes

In the examples discussed so far, the power of the author in guiding his reader was very prominent. However, in the last section it became clear that the author does not wield all the power and that his argument is also influenced by the presuppositions of his audience. In the category under consideration, the role of the reader will receive more emphasis. The author is not merely scattering clues according to his own preferences—the type of clue he chooses and the way it is employed, are greatly influenced by the presuppositions of the reader.

Recent studies have emphasized the fact that an argument is only possible on the basis of shared presuppositions or values. As Perelman puts it: "The speaker can choose as his points of departure only the theses accepted by those he addresses" (21). The effect of these presuppositions on the argument can be quite extensive.

In the letter to the Galatians the matter is complicated because different sets of presuppositions play a role. In the narrower sense, Paul shares—or at least, until recently has shared—a set of common beliefs and values with the Galatians which he labels as "the gospel." But he also shares a common cultural code with his fellow Jews, which of course includes many theological precepts. In the widest sense, he shares with his contemporaries world views and values which were typical of first-century Graeco-Roman culture. In each case, the common code which Paul shares with his audience will influence the shape of his argument— from elements characteristic of the Christian faith in the first case to very general concepts in the last case and which almost amounts to the basic propositions of common sense.

To illustrate the effect of these different sets of presuppositions, we shall concentrate on one example, namely the way in which Paul develops his argument concerning Abraham and the law. When dealing with a religious text like Galatians, it is perhaps better to talk of persuasion, rather than logical argument. The latter is usually associated with demonstrating that the facts of the matter conform to some outside, independent criterion. However, some form of demonstration can form part of a religious text. Once it is accepted that religious language "argues" from a coherent structure of assumptions or "set of beliefs," then the ensuing argument can take the form of a demonstration of how the presented "facts" conform to the commonly accepted set of beliefs. This is what happens with Paul's reference to the Abraham story.

When dealing with fellow-Jews with whom he shares both the history of Israel and some fundamental concepts of the Jewish faith, Paul finds himself in a very difficult position. According to Jewish thinking, the natural order of things plays an important role. This is especially true of the first in any chronological or hierarchical sequence. The importance of the first-born, the first fruits, and similar examples testify to this assumption and is underlined by the surprise caused by any reversal of this order. A well-known transgression of this code is the episode where Jacob manages to secure the right of the first-born from his brother Esau. The basic assumption is that the first should be dominant and decisive for what follows—in other words, a combination of priority and dominance. Jewish history abounds with examples of this principle—the position of Abraham, of the sons of Jacob, the dominant position of the law over against the prophets and the writings as (later) additions or expansions of the Torah. In Galatians Paul evokes the same concept when he reminds the believers where they began and where they are now ending (Gal. 3:3)—clearly implying that the beginning should be the norm for their subsequent behavior.

In terms of their common Jewish background, Paul's opponents are virtually in an unassailable position. Paul's insistence that the observance of the law is not a prerequisite for salvation can only be understood as a deviation from the original Jewish position. In their eyes, Paul is a Johnny-come-lately, he is not even one of the original group of Jerusalem apostles and he clearly represents an aberration of the traditional faith.

One should appreciate Paul's dilemma. How can one be prior to the first? How can he do anything to alter the chronological dominance of his opponents? Elsewhere Paul is struggling with the same problem in the famous Adam/Christ-parallels (Rom. 5 and 1 Cor. 15). How can Christ be the beginning of a new mankind if Adam was first and, therefore, the dominating representative of all mankind?

In Galatians Paul's opponents occupy the higher ground and argue from the priority of Abraham. He is the original and dominant representative of the covenant, of circumcision, of the law. All this, they argue, is denied by Paul's interpretation of the gospel.

In facing up to this formidable argument, Paul begins by accepting the premise of his opponents without reservation. In fact, he presses them to take it even more seriously: "If you are concerned about the priority of Abraham, let us take your argument to its full consequences and look at Abraham as he really was at the beginning. You depict him as the father of the covenant, of circumcision and the law. But if we look closely, we see that he started out from Ur of the Chaldees without the law, without circumcision, without the security of a country or home (Gen. 12). The law was given only much later at Sinai (Gal. 3:17). So, if you want the original Abraham, you must take him as he was—uncircumcised and without law, who put his trust in God alone."

To his opponents this must have sounded blasphemous. Nonetheless, it is an accurate description, not only of the original situation of Abraham, but also of the gentile Galatians. Thereby it becomes possible to link the latter directly to Abraham and declare them to be heirs to his promise (3:15–18). In this way Paul is able to overcome the obstacle of priority. But the fact that he has to take such drastic measures to achieve his end, shows with what force the presuppositions of his audience have on shaping his argument. He is not able to do away with the argument of priority—he can make his point only by a radical application of this principle.

4. The sociology of Paul's semantic universe

The author, so it appears from the previous section, does not always have things his own way. On certain levels of the text, the reader often wields considerable influence on the shaping of the discourse. In this section, we shall look briefly at a level where it is again the author who has more free play to guide his reader.

Insights from the sociology of knowledge have recently influenced both literary and theological studies. A clearer understanding of the "world of the text" has developed, in so far as every text creates a semantic universe of its own which can be analyzed and described in terms of its own "sociology" and internal relations. As far as biblical material is concerned, pioneering work has been done by Norman Petersen in his study of Philemon. In analyzing the social relations created by the text of this short letter, he gives the following resume of the story:

> Once upon a time there was a slave named Onesimus who became a brother to his master and a servant to his father, who was also his brother (as well as a prisoner and ambassador or old man). Onesimus's father, Paul, on the other hand, was both a free man who was nevertheless a slave to a master, Jesus, who had himself been a slave, and a father to and partner with his child Onesimus's master, Philemon, who, like Onesimus, was also Paul's brother. Now one day the father / brother / slave / prisoner / ambassador / partner decided to send Oenesimus, his child / brother / servant, back to his master / brother Philemon, who was, it will be recalled, the father's child/brother/partner. It seems, however, that the father / brother / slave / prisoner / ambassador / partner might not properly welcome the return of his slave / brother, for before becoming Paul's child and his master's brother the slave had run away from the master, and possibly with the family jewels or the like. So it was, then, that the father / brother / slave / prisoner / ambassador / partner wrote a letter to his child / brother / partner on behalf of the slave / child / brother / servant in the names of their common master, the slave / son Jesus Christ, and of their common father, God, a slave / brother / son of nobody, appealing to him to receive his slave / brother as he would receive Paul himself, and asking him to prepare a room for him because he would soon be coming to visit (Petersen:2–3).

What is of interest here is the way in which the social relations suggest different roles which the reader might adopt. Philemon is in actual fact a master of the slave Onesimus, but within the context of the faith community, he could just as well understand himself as Onesimus's brother and act accordingly. Ricoeur has written extensively about the "proposed world" of the text which the reader may inhabit. By suggesting a different role to the reader, a "redescription of reality" takes place, which makes it possible for him or her to transcend the present reality (cf. Lategan and Vorster). Clues of this kind are also offered in Galatians, but an analysis of the text reveals that Paul in fact invokes images from a wide variety of "worlds." In the famous statement in 3:28, he shows that the existence in faith has direct consequences for at least three spheres of life—cultural (Jew/Greek), social (slave/free) and sexual (male/female). But the images he uses are in fact clues to a new self-understanding which he offers to his readers. In drawing from the juridical sphere (heir), the social sphere (slave), and the family sphere (sons), he gives the reader specific roles with which he or she can identify:

> Now before we came of age we were as good as slaves to the elemental principles of this world, but when the appointed time came, God sent his Son, born of a woman, born a subject of the Law, to redeem the subjects of the Law and to enable us to be adopted as sons. The proof that you are sons is that God has sent the Spirit of his Son into our hearts: the Spirit that cries, "Abba, Father," and it is this that makes you a *son*, you are not a slave any more; and if God has made you son, then he has made you *heir* (3:28–4:7).

Thinking of himself as a son in the house of the father, as a free man and as an heir, has enormous potential to transform not only the readers' self-understanding, but also the way in which they perceive reality and the way in which they will act. The focus on what they are to motivate his readers in what they should do, is typical of Pauline ethics and leads us to the last level of reader clues.

5. Ethics, gaps and the participation of the reader

In the previous sections, we looked at the various ways in which Paul guides and directs his reader. All of these presuppose a greater or lesser degree of participation on the part of the reader. On the ethical level, Paul perhaps takes his greatest risk by creating such a large "gap," to use Iser's terminology, that nothing can be actualized of the text without the fullest participation of the reader. (For an extensive treatment of "gaps" and "blanks" in biblical texts, cf. Sternberg especially 186–229 and 235–63.)

Once again Paul finds himself in a dilemma because of the Jewish background he shares with his opponents. He is convinced that the effort of gaining acceptance in the eyes of God by performing good deeds and fulfilling the prescriptions of the law is futile. In fact, being under the constant pressure of complying with the minute details of a casuistic system is nothing but a form of slavery. The gospel means liberation, also on the ethical level, but at the same time calls for ethical responsibility:

> Freedom is what we have—Christ has set us free! Stand, then, as free people, and do not allow yourselves to become slaves again (5:1). You my brothers, were called to be free. But do not use your freedom to indulge the sinful nature...(5:13).

Because of this strong stand for freedom, Paul is apparently sharply criticized by his opponents for being irresponsible to the young converts. Having convinced them to adopt a new existence, he leaves them without adequate moral guidelines to sustain them in this difficult transition—a service for which the Torah is eminently suitable. But, to Paul, such a line of thought is a denial of the real nature of faith and a return to the "weak and pitiful" state where they will again become slaves of the law (4:9). He, therefore, steadfastly refuses to fall into this trap and exhorts his readers to become what they are. They should realize that they have been liberated and that they will retain their freedom only if they exercise it by accepting full responsibility for their ethical decisions. When he describes the fruit of the Spirit in 5:22–26, he talks in very broad terms and studiously avoids the danger of replacing one set of casuistic rules with another. The implication is that the reader must accept his or her own responsibility, give content to this new-found freedom, and creatively shape the new lifestyle which characterizes an existence in faith. Whatever influence the author may have over his reader, Paul instinctively realizes that there is a cut-off point where he no longer has control and where the reader must actualize the text by his or her own actions if it should have significance at all.

6. Conclusion

The few examples drawn from the text of Galatians may give some indication of both the variety of reader instructions and the different levels on which they operate. Whether these instructions will be followed by a real reader in a specific actualization of the text is quite a different matter. To find an answer to this question would require an empirical investigation along the lines suggested in the introductory essay. What can be said at this stage is that a full reading would require an integration of the different directives on the various levels in order to realize the remarkable pragmatic potential of this letter. The history of its reception through the ages testifies that it is not a text which can be handled indifferently.

NOTES

[1] A first version of this paper appeared in the *Journal of Literary Studies*, 3 (1987), 47–59 under the title "Reader clues in the text of Galatians." Permission by the Editor of *JLS* to use this material in reworked form for the present paper is gratefully acknowledged.

WORKS CONSULTED

Betz, Hans Dieter
    1975   "The Literary Composition and Function of Paul's Letter to the Galatians." *NTS* 21:353–79.
    1979   *Galatians: A Commentary on Paul's Letter to the Churches in Galatia*. Hermeneia. Philadelphia: Fortress.
    1987   *Der Galaterbrief. Ein Kommentar zum Brief des Apostels Paulus an die Gemeinden in Galatien*. München: Kaiser.

Eco, Umberto
    1979   *The Role of the Reader: Explorations in the Semiotics of Texts*. Bloomington: Indiana University Press.

Hall, R.G.
    1987   "The Rhetorical Outline of Galatians: A Reconsideration." *JBL* 106:277–87.

Hester, J.D.
    1986   "The Use and Influence of Rhetoric in Galatians", *ThZ* 42:386–408.

Hübner, Hans
    1984   "Der Galaterbrief und das Verhaltnis von antiker Rhetorik und Epistolographie." *ThLZ* 109:241–50.

Lategan, Bernard C. and Willem S. Vorster
 1985   *Text and Reality. Aspects of Reference in Biblical Texts.* Philadelphia: Fortress.

Perelman, C.
 1982   *The Realm of Rhetoric.* Notre Dame: Notre Dame University Press.

Petersen, Norman R.
 1985   *Rediscovering Paul. Philemon and the Sociology of Paul's Narrative World.* Philadelphia: Fortress.

Schenk, Wolfgang
 1984   *Die Philipperbriefe des Paulus: Kommentar.* Stuttgart: Kohlhammer.

Smit, J.
 1986   "Redactie in de brief aan de galaten: Retoriese analyze van Gal. 4, 12–6, 18." *TTh* 26:113–44.

Sternberg, Meir
 1985   *The Poetics of Biblical Narrdtive: Ideological Literature and the Drama of Reading.* Bloomington: Indiana University Press.

Verschuren, H.
 1986   "Receptie-onderzoek en literatuursociologie." *Forum der Letteren* 27:42–55.

Wuellner, Wilhelm
 1986   "Paul as Pastor: The Function of Rhetorical Questions in First Corinthians." Pp. 49–77 in *L'Apotre Paul. Personalité, Style et Conception du Ministère.* Ed. A. Vanhoye. BETL 73. Louvain: Louvain University Press.

III

Evaluation

READING IN/TO MARK

Temma F. Berg
Gettysburg College

ABSTRACT

When investigating reading, critics often have difficulty moving beyond structuralism. The first part of this essay demonstrates *how* the various critics in this issue of *Semeia* adhere to structuralist models as they attempt to come to terms with the concept of the reader in the text. The second part of the essay suggests *why* biblical critics, even as they seek to be more open in their reading and their view of reading, remain structuralist and avoid post-structuralism. This part of the essay speculates on the relationship between religion and styles of reading, between Christianity and positivistic, objective, foundationalist models of reading. If post-structuralism means (self-) critical reading, mining the heterogeneity of the text, emphasizing the way the text differs from/defers itself, then perhaps the (Christian) reader of/in the text will never be able to embrace post-structuralism. If the reader of the New Testament text is supposed to learn of and celebrate Christ's divinity, then who other than a Christian can become the reader in/of the text?

The third part of the essay offers a post-structuralist reading of Mark, which combs the text for its gaps and discontinuities, its mysteries and contradictions, its peculiar uses of metaphor and metonymy. Ultimately, the author of this essay seeks to argue that the reader is not *in* the text and she is not *one*. The reader is legion and she can be anywhere.

When critics write about the reader in the text, they often make subtle and not so subtle shifts between structuralist and post-structuralist ways of looking at the phenomenon of reading. Often these shifts are not marked, but they should be, for paying attention to them helps us see why all our attempts thus far at formulating a model of reading have been frustrated. We have not yet even been able to answer that simplest of questions, Who is the reader? Nor, consequently, that more complex question, Is there a reader in the text and what is the relationship between that reader in the text and the actual reader (in flesh and blood)? The various critics in this issue of *Semeia* have sought to answer the above questions and to see how answers to these questions might help us better understand the Bible. In the process, they have gone far, but they have not been able to surrender their adherence to structuralist models of reading. In my response, I will concentrate not only on how they adhere to structuralist models, but also on why they avoid post-structuralism. I will end with an examination of how a move toward post-structuralism might open not only biblical criticism but the Bible as well.

Although the critics have not been arranged that way, I would like to discuss them as a spectrum running the gamut from structuralism to post-structuralism. This might better enable us to see just how strongly most critics, even those who seem sympathetic to it, resist post-structuralism. Bernard C. Lategan, Willem S. Vorster, and Wolfgang Schenk and his critics represent the structuralist end of the spectrum, and, not surprisingly, they form the largest group of critics. B.M.F. van Iersel and Robert M. Fowler represent the move toward post-structuralism, and Wilhelm Wuellner, who explicitly calls for more deconstruction in biblical criticism, represents the post-structuralist end of the spectrum.

In his general introduction, Lategan, like Wolfgang Iser (1979, 1974), focuses on the way the text creates its own ideal reader; according to Lategan, the "sophisticated" reader must use the text to ascertain "the anticipated role a potential reader is expected to play in order to actualize the text" (5). Like Iser's implied reader, Lategan's critic is able to "master" any text. Moreover, like Iser, Lategan sees mastery as the goal of reading and reading as a transcendental process. However, Lategan goes even farther than Iser when he suggests that it is difficult to analyze a temporal reading experience because it is "unnatural" to interrupt it, for "in actual fact the process proceeds uninterruptedly" (12). It seems to me that unless we speak not only of an ideal reader but also of an ideal reading experience, the process of reading *never* proceeds uninterruptedly. In the real world reading is interrupted repeatedly—phones ring, babies cry, someone knocks at the door, an idea occurs to us while we read which may or may not have been provoked by the text we are reading, and we pursue it, perhaps relentlessly, perhaps desultorily. Have you read this issue of *Semeia* uninterruptedly? Have you managed to read even one of the essays in it uninterruptedly? Perhaps you have been lucky enough to read one or two essays uninterruptedly, but who among you would suggest that this is always—naturally—the case? In his essay on Galatians, Lategan tries to complicate the notion of the reader, but he still separates the reader from the text in order to demonstrate how the text creates its reader. In his discussion of Galatians, Lategan tells us he will focus on "the reading instructions themselves and how they are designed to steer and influence a potential reader" (172). Lategan's reader, like Iser's, is always the product of the text. She is constructed by, not constructing the text.

Vorster, like Lategan, sees the reader as a construct of the text. However, he goes one (a few) step(s) farther when he suggests that reading is the process whereby we trace the outlines of the reader we should be in order to acquire the meaning we should have. The reader in the text and the meaning in the text become mirrors of each other and we are able to look into them clearly (see from one into the other?) when we enter the appropriate hermeneutic circle: "The purpose of constructing the reader in the text is not to move from the text to the context of communication outside the text, that is, to the actual reader or even the actual author, but to establish a meaning of a narrative" (27). Clearly, the reader in the text is the meaning of it. Not only does Vorster, like Lategan, see the reader and meaning as constructs of the text, but he also sees the reading process as a totalizing process—everything counts. "Granted that the reader in the text is the total equipment an actual reader needs to actualize an appropriate reading of a text, every word, every group of words, every sentence or cluster of sentences becomes important" (32). Although in a different way than Lategan, Vorster also postulates an "uninterrupted" reading process, a process where every part of the experience is available to consciousness. Nothing remains repressed when we read; nothing can be forgotten. Again, I ask you, when you read, do you pay equal attention to everything? Do you remember everything? I think not, and I think necessarily not. To read is to forget much that one has read. Many reader-response critics have remarked on the importance of forgetting to the process of reading. For example, I.A. Richards once wrote, "But in all reading whatsoever much must be left out. Otherwise we could arrive at no meaning. The omission is essential in the twofold sense: without omission no meaning would form for us; and through the omission what we are trying to grasp becomes what it is..." (93).[1] According to Barthes, "...it is precisely because I forget that I read" (11).

When Vorster goes on to apply his theory to a reading of Mark, he predictably suggests that the careful reader will comprehend what she needs to know: "Incomprehension is a trait of the disciples, but not of the reader in the text" (33). As I will try to demonstrate later, incomprehension remains a trait of this particular reader (that is, me) when reading in/to Mark, perhaps as a result of my not belonging to the religious community which forms the hermeneutic circle within which the truth of the New Testament is always already evident. According to Vorster, when the "interpreter" becomes the reader in the text, he will be able to "control" the text: "It is here [in the construction of the role of the reader in the text] that the interpreter comes into the picture and the role of the reader becomes a matter of either the reader controlling the text or the reader being controlled by the text" (36). I suppose that what Vorster means here by "interpreter" is the actual reader, the flesh-and-blood reader. At this point, "the actual reader," "the interpreter," and "the role of the reader in the text" converge to face the alternative of either mastering or submitting to the text. Of course, the implication is that any reader worth his or her salt would choose mastery. Interestingly, when critics write about mastering the text of Mark, they mean submitting to it, that is, accepting its secret that Jesus is the Son of man/God.

Lategan and Vorster remain locked into a concept of the reader that is constructed (and therefore directed, inhibited) by the text; Schenk would seem to want to move beyond this position. He insists, and I think rightfully so, that there are many roles of the reader (60), and argues, and again I think rightfully so, against the wholeness or uniformity of the text even on a physical level (66). What, he asks, constitutes the New Testament text? However, there seems to be a gap between his theoretical speculations and his practical criticism, and, as a result, his critics see his practice as very traditional. H.J. Bernard Combrink suggests that in his reading of Philippians, Schenk does not open up the role of the reader or pay enough attention to "the polyvalence of a text" (137), while James W. Voelz faults Schenk for not emphasizing enough how the reader makes meaning or how the community helps the reader determine meaning (164). In sum, his critics find Schenk more structuralist than reader-response.

The question of why biblical critics remain structuralist even as they attempt to use reader-response and theorize more openly about reading became particularly pertinent for me while reading Schenk and his three critics. Schenk's third critic, Detlev Dormeyer, began to provide some answers. Dormeyer, by focussing on the questions of who is the real reader and does the real reader have to be a Christian, raises, I believe, issues that too often remain repressed in New Testament criticism. Who is the reader in the New Testament and who can become it or who can it become?

The question I now found myself asking was, Can a Jew who lacks Christian faith become the (implied, model, ideal) reader in a New Testament text and master what the book tells her? Likewise, can a Christian who has faith *not* be the ideal reader and fail to master what the Bible tells her? What is the relationship between one's religion and one's reading in general, and does this relationship become more pertinent when one is reading a sacred text? The question of the link between Judaism and post-structuralism has already been raised and partly answered (Handelman; Hartman) and rebutted (Green). I do not want to argue that question here, but I do want to raise the possibility that the kind of radical questioning necessitated by post-structuralism cannot happen when reading New Testament texts if the object of reading such texts is to accept the word of Jesus Christ, in other words, to affirm one's Christian faith.

In a recent and extremely moving essay on Paul de Man, Jacques Derrida emphasizes the necessity of radical questioning in post-structuralism. The essay was written in response to the discovery of early writings by Paul de Man and what many people have been suggesting these early writings have to tell us about de Man's relationship with Nazi Germany. To summarize Derrida's complex argument is impossible, but I would like to point out that he wrote this essay not only to understand de Man but to understand (stand under/support) post-structuralism/ deconstruction by responding to those who attacked both man and movement as fascist. In his essay, Derrida writes that deconstruction must include "respect for the other, that is, for his right to difference, in his relation to others but also in his relation to himself....not only respect for the right to a history, a transformation of oneself and one's thought that can never be totalized or reduced to something homogeneous...; it is also respect of that which, in any text, remains heterogeneous.... We are also the heirs and guardians of this heterogeneous text even if, precisely for this reason, we ought to maintain a differentiated, vigilant, and sometimes critical relation to it" (1988:644–45). Derrida suggests here that deconstruction means guarding the heterogeneity of the text, remaining vigilant against closure, adhering to a critical stance which respects complexity, difficulty, obscurity; deconstructive readings do not seek to transcend the text and achieve a totalizing operation on it; deconstructive readings must always be critical, above all self-critical. In other words, at the same time that a deconstructive reading creates a heterogeneous text, it must guard itself against its own operations. Whether or not this anti-transcendental self-questioning is Jewish is not the question I want to ask now; the question now is, can it be Christian? Dormeyer suggests that it cannot. To be Christian is to be confident in one's knowledge. To be Christian is to be the implied reader of the New Testament; to be the implied reader of the New Testament is to be Christian. To be the implied Christian reader is to accept and celebrate what the text has to tell you:

> Through Paul the Philippians have learned the whole Old Testament and evolved from the status of uneducated lower class to the educated Christian community. This Christian religion has to be connected to the levels of the act of reading. Paul's friendship-letter C presupposes advancement from the naive to the critical reader. Through a reading-process of this kind, all the Christians of Philippi are able to become explicit, critical readers. (147)

Here Dormeyer firmly underscores the link between Christian faith and a particular kind of reading, a process of totalizing and unquestioning transcendence, something that, as my selection from Derrida was designed to demonstrate, is not possible from a post-structuralist or deconstructive position.[2]

New Testament scholars seem to want to remain within the domain of structuralism because they do not want to risk a radical deconstruction of the texts they read. When Edgar McKnight sent me early drafts of the essays in this volume of *Semeia*, he gave me the following cautionary overview of their theoretical framework, an overview which (revised) forms part of this issue's preface: "The movement into a reader oriented emphasis does not mean that we have abandoned the goal of empirical and logically consistent analysis and interpretation. At the present time, some members of the seminar are inclined toward a more 'hermeneutic' perspective as the beginning point and others are inclined toward the more 'objective' and 'positivistic' perspective as the beginning point. The interesting thing is how these perspectives meet." When I read these words, I was not sure who Professor McKnight wanted to reassure, himself or me. If he wanted to reassure me, it was too late, for I had already given up the objective, positivistic perspective. However, as I read Dormeyer, I began to understand why McKnight and his seminar were resisting perspectives that might abandon the goal of empirical and logically consistent analysis and interpretation. I began to understand why it might not be possible to open New Testament criticism to post-structural reader-response, and why it was getting so difficult for me to decide who was the real reader and who could become the implied reader of a New Testament text.

Doesn't the reader in a New Testament text always have to come to rest on the firm ground of Christ's divinity? Doesn't this need for a firm foundation inhibit any move toward a post-structuralist position in New Testament criticism? It would seem so. If we look at the essays of van Iersel and Fowler, who seem to want to move toward a post-structuralist position, we can see how adherence to a transcendental signified keeps them in the structuralist camp.

Van Iersel uses Barthes to examine the importance of connotative systems in understanding Mark. Though he uses Barthes and *S/Z*, which I believe is a post-structuralist text, he makes both Barthes and his text seem more structuralist than post-structuralist. Van Iersel uses a Barthes who limits (rather than liberates) the reader at every point. For example, van Iersel makes a distinction between connotation and association; this allows him to insist that connotation has a greater degree of objectivity than association which is simply arbitrary. He makes this distinction because he wants to keep meaning constrained to what can legitimately be found in the text. Meaning for van Iersel, despite his use of Barthes, is found in the text; the reader of Mark reads to "solve the riddle of the book and unlock the secret of the parable of the seed" (101). Reading, according to van Iersel, leads to understanding. But this is not what reading leads to in S/Z. Reading leads everywhere but there:

> To interpret a text is not to give it a (more or less justified, more or less free) meaning, but on the contrary to appreciate what *plural* constitutes it. Let us first posit the image of a triumphant plural, unimpoverished by any constraint of representation (of imitation). In this ideal text, the networks are many and interact, without any one of them being able to surpass the rest; this text is a galaxy of signifiers, not a structure of signifieds; it has no beginning; it is reversible; we gain access to it by several entrances, none of which can be authoritatively declared to be the main one; the codes it mobilizes extend *as far as the eye can reach*, they are indeterminable (meaning is never subject to a principle of determination, unless by throwing dice); the systems of meaning can take over this absolutely plural text, but their number is never closed, based as it is on the infinity of language. (5–6)

Reading, according to Barthes, is more closely connected to arbitrary chance (throwing dice) than to objective connotative systems which can reveal textual secrets. Also, as Barthes demonstrates elsewhere in *S/Z*, the secret of the text can be its emptiness, not its fullness. The text in *S/Z* is like the castrato in *Sarrasine*, the Balzac novella about which Barthes and his seminar revolve. Like the castrato, the text is inoperable and impotent, except in so far as readers are able to infuse it with the power of meaning.

S/Z marks Barthes' turn from structuralism to post-structuralism. Van Iersel chooses to concentrate on those aspects of Barthes which represent a need for structure, meaning, system. But I prefer to use *S/Z* to demonstrate Barthes' break with structure—"this text is a galaxy of signifiers, not a structure of signifieds." In *S/Z*, Barthes seeks to disrupt the connection between the signifier and the signified—"Thus it would be wrong to say that if we undertake to reread the text we do so for some intellectual advantage (to understand better, to analyze on good grounds): it is actually and invariably for a ludic advantage: to multiply the signifiers, not to reach some ultimate signified" (165). While van Iersel wants to use Barthes to describe how meaning *must* happen in Mark—"Making the connections between *signifiers* and *signifieds* is precisely the specifically semiotic, and sometimes very complex, operation which the reader must perform if the connotative meanings of a text are to come to light" (110), I want to use Barthes to demonstrate how meaning is contingent rather than determinate. Christ is the Transcendental Signified which all the text's signifiers *must* reveal/conceal only if the actual reader is Christian and thereby qualified to become the reader van Iersel finds in the text. Non-Christian readers might end up with very different readings.

Reading enlightens, according to van Iersel, and the Barthes he uses underscores how reading is a process of enlightenment. Like van Iersel, Fowler also sees reading as a process of enlightenment. He picks a different point of entry into the text of Mark than van Iersel, but he ends with the same emphasis on reading as a process of inclusion—"But as often as it [Mark] might cast us out into the dark, it more often casts us into the inner circle of privileged insight and understanding. The overall tendency of this narrative is gradually to make the narratee, by direct and indirect means alike, an inveterate insider" (131). Fowler's attempts to monitor his reading experience incorporate post-structuralist strategies —that is, he presents reading as a self-reflexive, discontinuous, temporal process—but his optimism about his ability to capture his reading experience is more structuralist than post-structuralist—"My goal is to learn to attend as closely as possible to the experience of reading. I want to understand better what is or is not happening in Mark's story as I read it, and especially what is or is not happening in me at the same time, thanks to the narrator's discourse. I want to observe and understand the workings of the gamut of rhetorical moves made by the narrator, as I encounter them in the act of reading, ranging from the most overt and direct turns, to the most covert and indirect turns. For me, this is the proper goal of a reader-response criticism of the experience of reading Mark's Gospel" (132). I admire Fowler's manifesto and I certainly share his fascination with the experience of reading, but I do not share his belief in its recuperability. For example, I would want to question Fowler on the accuracy of his description of his reading of Mark 4:11–12. When he reaches, 4:12, he finds his understanding of 4:11 confounded—"What we are to do then with this insight [that some who think they 'see' really do not perceive anything at all, and some who think they 'hear' really understand nothing] remains far from clear, but one thing it may do is to encourage us to begin to re-consider the understanding we developed back in 4:11 that the disciples are insiders and we are outsiders" (127). The phrase that stuck out for me in the above passage was "back in 4:11." While his discussion of what happened to him when he read 4:11 may indeed go back several pages in his final written analysis of the reading experience, when he actually read Mark did he read that slowly that when he read 4:12, 4:11 seemed "back"? In other words, how slowly can we go through the temporal process of reading? Well, we can go as slowly as we want (Barthes and his seminar students spent two years reading *Sarrasine*), but is it legitimate to describe this interminably slow reading as what happens when we read the text? Well, yes, but only if we enlarge the phrase "read the text" to include those intense. laborious rereadings that occur after our initial encounter with the text. Reading then becomes like Freudian dream-analysis, and the process of reading becomes the dream we can never recapture in its entirety:

> It is only with the greatest difficulty that the beginner in the business of interpreting dreams can be persuaded that his task is not at an end when he has a complete interpretation in his hands—an interpretation which makes sense, is coherent and throws light upon every element of the dream's content. For the same dream may perhaps have another interpretation as well, an "over-interpretation," which has escaped him. It is, indeed, not easy to form any conception of the abundance of the unconscious trains of thought, all striving to find expression, which are active in our minds. Nor is it easy to credit the skill shown by the dream-work in always hitting upon forms of expression that can bear several meanings—like the Little Tailor in the fairy story who hit seven flies at a blow. My readers will always be inclined to accuse me of introducing an unnecessary amount of ingenuity into my interpretations; but actual experience would teach them better. (523)

Understanding our experience of reading is a slow, laborious process, perhaps even slower, and more laborious than Fowler realizes, and observing ourselves reading is a very elusive process indeed. Observing ourselves reading is like looking in a mirror that faces another mirror; we see a series of endlessly receding images of ourselves.[3] And just as we cannot see to the bottom of the reflecting mirrors, we cannot reach the bottom of our dream/reading experience:

> There is often a passage in even the most thoroughly interpreted dream which has to be left obscure; this is because we become aware during the work of interpretation that at that point there is a tangle of dream-thoughts which cannot be unravelled and which moreover adds nothing to our knowledge of the content of the dream. This is the dream's navel, the spot where it reaches down into the unknown. The dream-thoughts to which we are led by interpretation cannot, from the nature of things, have any definite endings; they are bound to branch out in every direction into the intricate network of our world of thought. It is at some point where this meshwork is particularly close that the dream-wish grows up, like a mushroom out of its mycelium. (525)

In his introductory essay, Lategan cites a quote from N.R. Petersen which links the process of reading with the dream (11–12). Obviously, I think this connection, the ramifications of which we have only begun to explore, is an essential one.

Fowler is the most reader-oriented of the critics in this issue of *Semeia*, but he falls into the same trap that Fish and Iser often fall into (and that, in fact, Fish faults Iser for falling into [see the exchange between Fish and Iser in *Diacritics*, 1981]), though he still seems unable to catch himself falling. Like Fish and Iser, Fowler relies heavily on the rhetorical "we"; and just as Ohmann once cited Tonto's "What do you mean 'we,' white man" against Fish, I would like to cite it against Fowler.[4] It seems to me that with his use of "we" Fowler becomes guilty of perpetuating that "cultural and sexual imperialism" (49) which Wuellner warns us against in his essay. Wuellner begins his essay by warning us against "the fallacy of the encoded reader" (41). One obvious way to avoid that fallacy is to avoid the imperialism of the (royal?) we. Fish has tried to avoid the imperialism of "we" by enlarging that concept so it can include the entire interpretive community (Fish, 1980), and while I would have to agree that people usually are members of interpretive communities and these interpretive communities have an effect on the way people respond to texts, I do not think they exert the great force Fish believes they do, because people are not always either inside or outside a particular community. They are sometimes, like Jesus' disciples, both inside and outside at the same time. Like Fowler, who feels like an insider and outsider at various points as he reads through Mark, we all can become confused about where we are with regard to any particular text and its community of readers.

As I already suggested, I feel very outside of Mark; I am not a Christian and, if to be the reader *in* Mark is to be Christian, I can never be inside Mark. But, as I read Mark's Gospel, I did feel as though I entered

Mark, although I entered it at very different points than the other readers of Mark in this issue of *Semeia*. While it may seem at best impossible, at worst inadmissible, I would like to preface my post-structuralist reader-response analysis of Mark with the astounding claim that I never previously read Mark. I have, of course, read about it and read others' experiences of it (including van Iersel's, Vorster's, and Fowler's), and I thought I knew what it was about, but I had never actually read it through. I will not try to recapture my moment-to-moment experience of the text. I do not believe I could (my quibble with Fowler) and trying to do so would make this essay a book; however, I would like to point out what I found strange about the text. Fowler writes, "The workings of story and discourse in Mark's Gospel remain largely a mystery to us" (123); I would like to enlarge on that statement and suggest that much in Mark's Gospel remains a mystery to me. Maybe because all the other readers (Vorster, Fowler, van Iersel) were intent on showing how if you read Mark carefully you would be led to certain (Christian) convictions, I felt compelled to linger over the text's obscurities, to see how the text, as Derrida puts it, differs from itself, defers itself, forces us to cling to its heterogeneity. When I read Mark, I read as a post-structuralist, for I believe that structuralist models of reading invariably disempower the reader. They circumscribe and limit. They lead to variations on the idea of the implied, ideal, model reader. They lead to the idea that *the* reader is *in* the text, that there is an inside and outside the text and that we can always know which side we are on. When I read Mark, I did not feel safely inside or outside. I felt implicated in many ways, but I never felt like an "inveterate insider" and I did not find Mark enlightening.

The first strange thing....

Because of Fowler's reading I found myself stopping every time I came to the word "son" to see who was naming Jesus (S)on and what significance this naming could be made to have. He is named Son in 1:1, 9–11; 2:10, 27–28; 3:11–12; 8:31; 9:7, 9, 31; and 15:39 (and I have probably missed a few instances) . I noted that despite Fowler's supposition that there was no "uptake" in the text on this issue of Christ's Sonhood (123: "*no Son of man statement in Mark's Gospel ever receives clear and unmistakable uptake at the level of story*"), I found several "uptakes," or clear indications that someone in the text was hearing (and listening) to the word "son" at various points. Unclean spirits seemed to know right away that Jesus was the Son: "And whenever the unclean spirits beheld him, they fell down before him and cried out, 'You are the Son of God.' And he strictly ordered them not to make him known" (3:11–12). I found this recognition on the part of unclean spirits very interesting, because, I suddenly realized, I had no idea what an unclean spirit was. Was it a diseased person? Did diseased people know Jesus was the Son because they *wanted* to know him and, in the process, be healed? Or, were the "unclean" demonic spirits, and did they know him because he had the power to exorcise and destroy them? Just who were the unclean? While in the preceding case, the unclean would seem to be the diseased (3:10 tells us "for he had healed many, so that all who had diseases pressed upon him to touch him"), at other points, the unclean seem to be demonic spirits: "And immediately there was in their synagogue a man with an unclean spirit; and he cried out, 'What have you to do with us, Jesus of Nazareth? Have you come to destroy us? I know who you are, the Holy One of God.' But Jesus rebuked him, saying, 'Be silent, and come out of him!' And the unclean spirit, convulsing him and crying with a loud voice, came out of him" (1:23–26). In this second scene, it almost seems as if Jesus' appearance creates the unclean spirit. To recognize Jesus is to become unclean. To be unclean is to recognize Jesus. The connection between being unclean and recognizing Jesus becomes very perplexing indeed.

The second strange thing....

While I found Fowler's reading of 4:10–14 fascinating, I read the passage very differently. According to Fowler, when "Jesus says to his disciples that they have been given 'the secret of the kingdom of God,'" the critical reader tries to discover when and where this secret was given. "We have found it," Fowler suggests, "most difficult to accept that in 4:11 the discourse alludes to something that apparently occurred in the story, but the narrator chose not to narrate it to us" (125). However, when I read 4:11, I had a very different reaction (perhaps partly as a result of wanting to differ from Fowler, but I had already questioned his interpretation of the verse the first time I read his essay). When Jesus says, "To you have been given the secret of the kingdom of God," my reaction is not to ask, Did I miss something? but to assent that yes, faith in Jesus brings one to the kingdom of God. If you have faith, you believe; if you believe, you have faith. If you want to have faith, you have to enter the hermeneutic circle, and once you have entered the hermeneutic circle you will have faith. It would never occur to me that the kingdom of God is other than a metaphor, or a parable. Why else would Jesus ask in 4:13, "Do you not understand this parable?" Fowler identifies the "this parable" in verse 4:13 as the "sower riddle," but I would suggest that the "this parable" in verse 4:13 could also point to "the kingdom of God." Jesus does, of course, go on to explain the "sower riddle," but he also goes on to explain a series of parables, all of which can be used to help identify and clarify the concept "the kingdom of God": "The kingdom of God is as if a man should scatter seed upon the ground"; "It is like a grain of mustard seed." If one of the questions the reader in the text is supposed to ask (and be able to answer after following the instructions in the text) is, What is the kingdom of God?, then the text gives more than one answer.

The third strange thing....

Who is inside, who is outside? Who is "them," who are the disciples? Who understands, who does not? While Fowler wants to separate insiders from outsiders, Jesus' words seem to confound the two groups: "With many such parables he spoke the word to them, as they were able to hear it; he did not speak to them without a parable, but privately to his own disciples he explained everything." On the one hand, "them" seems to be a separate category from "disciples"; on the other hand, the disciples seem to slip into the larger group of "them" without our noticing it. There does not seem to be a clear inside and outside the secret; being on one side or the other is a very slippery matter indeed. There is much the disciples do not understand—"'The Son of man will be delivered into the hands of men, and they will kill him; and when he is killed, after three days he will rise.' But, they did not understand the saying, and they were afraid to ask him" (9:31-32)—and their incomprehension is contagious. Verses 4:11-12 strike me as vertiginously confusing, and I am wont to suggest that it is to them that "this parable" in line 4:13 (perhaps) refers, and if you could understand verses 4:11-12, you could understand all, but since I don't understand those two lines, I despair that I will ever understand all or even very much.

The fourth strange thing....

At one point the text takes, for me, a peculiarly metonymic turn. Jesus has just been asked to lay hands on a little girl who is at the point of death (5:22-24), when the narrative suddenly and inexplicably deviates to narrate a different miracle: "And there was a woman who had a flow of blood for twelve years...." The text goes on to tell us that the blood stops when she touches Christ, although he tells her, "Your faith has made you well; go in peace, and be healed of your disease." The narrative then returns to the dying girl, whom Jesus also heals: "And immediately the girl got up and walked; for she was twelve years old." What an odd placement for the statement "for she was twelve years old"! It almost seems to be brought forward as the reason for her walking. She walks because she is twelve years old. That's what twelve year olds do. But of course, she walks because she has been healed by Jesus. But, then, why bring in the detail of twelve years old? Well, I believe it has a metonymic relation to the story of the woman that interrupted the story of the girl. While the girl was twelve years old, the woman bled for twelve years. The narrative, at this point, begins to take on the qualities of a Freudian dream landscape where linguistic logic rather than narrative logic causes things to happen.[5]

The fifth strange thing....

In 11:13–14, Jesus blasts a fig tree for not bearing fruit even though it is not the season for fig trees to bear fruit: "And seeing in the distance a fig tree in leaf, he went to see if he could find anything on it. When he came to it, he found nothing but leaves, for it was not the season for figs. And he said to it, 'May no one ever eat fruit from you again.' And his disciples heard it." I found this arrogant action bewildering. Why blast a fig tree for not bearing fruit out of its season? And, why, the next morning, use that same blasted fig tree as a paradoxical lesson in the force of prayer? Pointing to the withered fig tree, Jesus urges his disciples to have faith that what we doubt not will come to pass. At this point, I could understand the disciples' and the people's fear of him. Why blast a fig tree for not bearing fruit out of season, when one might just as well pray for that tree to bear fruit? If, as Jesus asserts, faith empowers us to take up a mountain and cast it into the sea, surely faith might bring a fruit tree to bear out of season. Why kill the tree? Why such an arbitrary display of power? Perhaps I was particularly struck by this event because I am a Jew. What will happen to those who do not believe (who cannot—naturally—bear the fruit that Jesus wants them to bear)? If the fig tree is meant to supply an answer, it is a very frightening one indeed.

As I came to the end of the Gospel of Mark, I found myself increasingly perturbed and confused and amazed that others could find enlightenment and comfort in this Gospel. Verses 13:14–31 not only present a frightening vision of apocalypse, but they urge its imminence: "Truly, I say to you, this generation will not pass away before all these things take place." But, then, as if to offer some comfort, Jesus adds, "Heaven and earth will pass away, but my words will not pass away." From my poststructuralist view, these words of comfort are indeed words of comfort and the only words of comfort possible, for, in the end, it seems to me that words are all we have in Mark's Gospel; we have signifiers, not signifieds. And these signifiers, including the important "kingdom of God" continue to hover loosely above the narrative as it moves toward its open-ended conclusion: "And when evening had come, since it was the day of Preparation, that is, the day before the Sabbath, Joseph of Arimathea, who was also himself looking for the kingdom of God, took courage and went to Pilate, and asked for the body of Jesus." At this point, the kingdom of God and the body of Jesus become both metaphorically and metonymically linked; in fact, the distinction between the two concepts (and, possibly, between the two mental processes) collapses. The kingdom of God—the body of Jesus—the words of Jesus—the seeds he sows—the bread and fish he multiplies—the faith that heals—the faith that moves mountains—what cannot die in this generation or any generation. The series of metaphoric/metonymic condensations stretched before me, like any signifier or series of signifiers, capable of endless supplementarity.

Appropriately, the Gospel of Mark ends in an empty tomb and with the word "afraid": "And entering the tomb, they saw a young man sitting on the right side, dressed in a white robe, and they were amazed. And he said to them, 'Do not be amazed; you seek Jesus of Nazareth, who was crucified. He has risen, he is not here; see the place where they laid him. [Does the young man in white here gesture toward the now empty place?] But go, tell his disciples and Peter that he is going before you to Galilee; there you will see him, as he told you.' And they went out and fled from the tomb; for trembling and astonishment had come upon them; they said nothing to anyone, for they were afraid." This final scene left me with many questions that I doubt can ever be answered. Who is this young man in white? Why is he not afraid? How did he enter the tomb? What was he doing there? Why does he not now leave it?

Admittedly, I have, to use Fowler's term, read Mark for its "opacity." But I would assert that it is not hard to find in this text much darkness, mystery, and foreboding. I understand and empathize with the confusion and fear and hardness of heart of the disciples. I do not comprehend the secret Jesus brings. The inside/outsideness of the disciples confirms my own. However, while I do not understand the secret, I understand that the secret is open to those who are open to it. It is not hidden except to those who do not see(k) it. While I may not see the secret, and cannot embrace it, I can enter the now empty tomb and admit my amazement that a man in white calmly sits there, hand extended, pointing to the now empty place.

In "Freud and the Scene of Writing," Derrida uses an obscure text of Freud's to explore the process of reading/writing/perceiving. What he suggests in that essay wonderfully elaborates on the insufficiency of our ordinary understanding of the inside/outside opposition. For Derrida, reading/writing/ perceiving is not a process of moving from outside (a text) to inside (a text), but rather a dramatic and dynamic process of discovery and recovery:

> If there were only perception, pure permeability to breaching, there would be no breaches. We would be written, but nothing would be recorded; no writing would be produced, retained, repeated as legibility. But pure perception does not exist: we are written only as we write, by the agency within us which always already keeps watch over perception, be it internal or external. The "subject" of writing does not exist if we mean by that some sovereign solitude of the author. The subject of writing is a *system* of relations between strata: the Mystic Pad, the psyche, society, the world. Within that scene, on that stage, the punctual simplicity of the classical subject is not to be found. In order to describe the structure, it is not enough to recall that one always writes for someone; and the oppositions sender-receiver, code-message, etc., remain extremely coarse instruments. We would search the "public" in vain for the first reader: i.e., the first author of a work. And the "sociology of literature" is blind to the war and the ruses perpetrated by the author who reads and by the first reader who dictates, for at stake here is the origin of the work itself. The *sociality* of writing as *drama* requires an entirely different discipline. (1978:226–27)

Inside and outside cannot be simply opposed to one another. As we read we become what we read if we are prepared ("breached") to receive it. Perception is not a transparent process. The classic subject is a fiction that may once have empowered us, but now inhibits us. The reader in the text, the reader of the text, the writer, the listener, them, us—we can continue to try to separate out what is inextricably entwined, but we do so at the risk of alienating ourselves from the very complex process that is called reading.

Using reader-response criticism, the various critics in this issue of *Semeia* have done much to open the Bible and biblical criticism, but the process cannot stop with "the reader in the text." We need to keep looking at the words "reader" and "text" and "in" and re-examine what they mean. Reading will always escape our efforts to contain it, but that need not mean that we should stop making the effort. The effort allows us to interrogate ourselves and keeps us from cutting off too soon an infinitely ramifying experience.

The reader is in and not in the text. The reader can never be separated from the texts that surround him, partly because "reader" and "text" are interchangeable signs, but also because the reader is an active producer of what she reads. The text exists so that the reader may fill it. The reader exists so that the text may fill her. Neither the reader not the text has a single, stable center; both the reader and the text may be endlessly exchanged. For post-structuralist critics, reading is not what it is for most other critics—that is, discovering meaning or significance, looking over, scanning, decoding a text to arrive at an objective interpretation. Rather, readers read to expose themselves to the flickering significances of the text and, in the process, organize texts according to patterns preinscribed in their (un)conscious. Post-structuralism asserts that we may never attain mastery of a text, we may never come to the end of our reading experience, we may never find the reader in the text unless (like Wordsworth who found sermons in stones) we have already put her there. Post-structuralism seeks to replace the desire for mastery with a desire for desire.

At the risk of closing myself off too soon, I would like to end by insisting once again that the reader is not in the text and she is not *one*. The reader is legion. We can either exorcise or exercise (both exorcise and exercise?) this reader in the text who is legion. The choice is ours.

NOTES

[1] I have argued elsewhere (as have others) for including I.A. Richards within the reader-response fold, or at least, for seeing him as a strong precursor. See Berg; Freund; Russo; Tompkins.

[2] At this point, the reader of/in my text might be asking herself, since I use the terms almost interchangeably, what is the distinction between post-structuralism and deconstruction? I suspect there is very little difference between them. If post-structuralism is "the vigilant critique of prior delusions of mastery" (Culler 25), then I do not see how it can be seen as distinct from deconstruction as defined by Derrida above. Interestingly, Culler goes on not only to conflate post-structuralism and deconstruction but structuralism and post-structuralism. Although at first he sets up a clear distinction between the two—"Structuralists are convinced that systematic knowledge is possible; post-structuralists claim to know only the impossibility of this knowledge" (22)—he ends by collapsing this neat distinction, for, he contends, deconstructive readings often lead to feelings of mastery. Ultimately, Culler's goal in *On Deconstruction* is to establish continuity between structuralism and post-structuralism, perhaps because in his own work he exemplifies and practices such a continuity. However, it seems to me that while deconstruction and post-structuralism are alike, post-structuralism and structuralism are quite different operations (whether in literary criticism or in science or in any other endeavor) and that adherence to structuralist modes of thinking inhibit one from making post-structuralist moves.

[3] Elizabeth Freund, in *The Return of the Reader: Reader-Response Criticism*, also points out how difficult it is to capture the reading process. See, for example, p. 11: "...my main contention, if any, is that a perusal of critical theory leads to an en-

hanced awareness of the limits of its usefulness, and of the perishability of its prescriptive authority.... It is an awareness of the insufficiency of theoretical and methodological borders, the infinitizing or receding movement of their horizons or, better yet, the moment of recoil from any totalizing act of the mind, that I hope to accentuate in my discussion."

4 Richard Ohmann suggests that with rhetorical conventions like "we," Fish turns his particular reading experience into a universal one. The "we," Ohmann insists, and I would agree, is not earned, or, ultimately, truthful. "As Tonto replied to the Lone Ranger when beset by hostile Indians, 'What do you mean "we," white man?' Fish's use of 'we' and 'our,' and of phrases like 'the total and self-annihilating union with the Divine' and 'the experience of the poem' which strip the experience of particularity and imply that union with the Divine is a proper response for any reader—critical usages like these are perhaps conveniences, but they unnaturally suppress truths about real readers" (106).

5 Throughout *The Interpretation of Dreams*, Freud discusses how in dreams association works arbitrarily, but yet according to linguistic usage. Ultimately, he concludes that there is no such thing as a truly arbitrary association; it is just that the connection is repressed: "*Whenever one psychical element is linked with another by an objectionable or superficial association, there is also a legitimate and deeper link between them which is subjected to the resistance of the censorship*" (530, Freud's emphasis).

WORKS CONSULTED

Barthes, Roland
    1974   *S/Z*. Trans. Richard Miller. New York: Hill and Wang.

Berg, Temma
    1987   "Psychologies of Reading." *Tracing Literary Theory*. Ed. Joseph Natoli. Urbana: University of Illinois Press.

Culler, Jonathan
    1982   *On Deconstruction: Theory and Criticism after Structuralism*. Ithaca: Cornell University Press.

Derrida, Jacques
    1988   "Like the Sound of the Sea Deep Within a Shell: Paul de Man's War." *Critical Inquiry* 14:590–652.
    1978   "Freud and the Scene of Writing." *Writing and Difference*. Trans. Alan Bass. Chicago: The University of Chicago Press.

Fish, Stanley
    1980   *Is There a Text in This Class?: The Authority of Interpretive Communities.* Cambridge and London: Harvard University Press.
    1981   "Why No One's Afraid of Wolfgang Iser." *Diacritics* 11:2–13

Freud, Sigmund
    1953   *Standard Edition.* Vols. IV and V. Trans. James Strachey. London: The Hogarth Press and the Institute of Psycho-Analysis.

Freund, Elizabeth
    1987   *The Return of the Reader: Reader-Response Criticism.* London and New York: Methuen.

Green, William Scott
    1987   "Romancing the Tome: Rabbinic Hermeneutics and the Theory of Literature." *Semeia* 40:147–68.

Handelman, Susan
    1982   *The Slayers of Moses: The Emergence of Rabbinic Interpretation in Modern Literary Theory.* Albany: State University of New York Press.

Hartman, Geoffrey and Sanford Budick, eds.
    1986   *Midrash and Literature.* New Haven and London: Yale University Press.

Iser, Wolfgang
    1978   *The Act of Reading: A Theory of Aesthetic Response.* Baltimore: Johns Hopkins University Press.
    1974   *The Implied Reader: Patterns of Communication in Prose Fiction from Bunyan to Beckett.* Baltimore: Johns Hopkins University Press.
    1981   "Talking like Whales." *Diacritics* 11:82–87.

Ohmann, Richard
    1973   "Literature as Act." *Approaches to Poetics: Selected Papers from the English Institute.* Ed. Seymour Chatman. New York: Columbia University Press.

Richards, I.A.
    1942   *How to Read a Page: a course in effective reading, with an introduction to a hundred great works.* New York: Norton.

Russo, John Paul
    1982   "I.A. Richards in Retrospect." *Critical Inquiry* 8: 743–60.

Tompkins, Jane P.
    1980   "An Introduction to Reader-Response Criticism." Pp. ix–xxvi in *Reader-Response Criticism: From Formalism to Post-Structuralism*. Ed. Jane P. Tompkins. Baltimore: Johns Hopkins University Press.

www.ingramcontent.com/pod-product-compliance
Lightning Source LLC
Chambersburg PA
CBHW031143160426
43193CB00008B/230